CW01023883

"*No Home Like Place* is a walk poetically, guiding the reader in a thin place, offering a spaciou[...] To find someone rebuilding [...] deconstruction is beautiful. This book offers itself as a worthy companion for miles to come." **Brad Jersak, DMin. Author of *Her Gates Will Never Be Shut.***

"Too much ink has been spilled recently on the meaning of the cross, atonement, etc. The strength and unique contribution of this book is the emphasis on God's incarnation in Jesus Christ as the foundation and inspiration for the church's incarnation into the various spaces and places of our post-everything culture.

"In *No Home Like Place* Hjalmarson offers something unique: a theology of place that is biblical, holistic, incarnational, and creative, steering clear of both the universalization and relativization of place, in favor of particularization ... increasingly relevant in our fragmented, transient, globalized, and urbanized culture." **Gareth Brandt, PhD. Professor of Practical Theology, Columbia Bible College.**

"In a world of long commutes, affordable travel, global internet connections, and a host of cultural practices tending to distance us from the truth of our locatedness, *No Home Like Place* invites us to take root again. It dares us to embrace the gift of a human-scaled life. Hjalmarson integrates fresh theological reflection with thoughtful practices for inhabiting place; a magnificent and liberating practical theology of place." **Dwight J. Friesen, DMin. Associate Professor of Practical Theology, The Seattle School of Theology & Psychology. Author of *Thy Kingdom Connected* and *The New Parish.***

"I started *No Home Like Place* while travelling—it helped me be attentive to the places we were visiting and the people who belonged there. I finished reading soon after arriving home—it helped me be attentive to this place that I call home—its rhythms, beauty and gifts. Hjalmarson reminds me I am not the first to rediscover sacredness in both pilgrimage abroad and returning home. With biblical engagement and poetic allusions, he invites readers to embrace 'place' as a thing to be noticed, a gift to be treasured, a locale to be attentive to. This is a timely book. Its appeal for a wholesome embodiment helps make the missional conversation practical and local." **Darren Cronshaw, Associate Professor of Missiology, Australian College of Ministries and Editor-in-Chief, UNOH Publications. Author of** *Sentness.*

"Some books offer solace, some answers, some direction, and some mess with our minds. Hjalmarson does the latter with his No Home like Place. With stories, scripture, and poetry he takes us on a pilgrimage to discover the forgotten role of concrete "place" for drawing us into God's imago and *missio Dei.*" **MaryKate Morse, PhD. Professor of Leadership & Spiritual Formation, George Fox Evangelical Seminary. Author of** *Making Room for Leadership*

"*No Home Like Place* unfolds a message we earnestly need in the West: 'God calls us to a people and a place.' Winsomely written, deeply researched, this book will genuinely help you see where you live differently, as a 'place,' a story, a sacramental tapestry where God is steadfastly, concretely at work for the salvation of the world." **David Fitch, PhD. B.R Lindner Chair of Theology, Northern Seminary. Author of** *Prodigal Christianity: 10 Signposts into the Missional Frontier.*

"Illustrated with stories, enriched with poetry, rooted in the great themes of Scripture, attuned to both historic philosophy and contemporary urbanology, Len Hjalmarson's book presents a winsome and compelling call to recover the significance of place in our understanding of the purposes of God. *No Home Like Place* offers post-modern, post-Christendom Christians an embodied vision of mission and ministry in the city and the neighbourhood." **Stuart Murray Williams, PhD. Chair of the Anabaptist Network and the founder of Urban Expression, UK. Author of** *Church After Christendom* **and** *The Naked Anabaptist.*

"Every once in awhile a book comes along that establishes a new imaginative field for reflection and mindful living. *No Home Like Place* was, for me, such a book; offering also a framework for compassionately understanding and engaging enduring traumas associated with current conflicts over place." **Steve Bell, Singer/songwriter. Founder of Signpost Music.**

"With all the attention paid to issues of church and mission in recent years, surprisingly little has been written to reframe the biblical themes of creation and human identity in light of the *missio Dei*. Hjalmarson addresses this lacunae by pursuing an ambitious missiological agenda, arguing that even though God's mission draws his people into an often surprising journey or pilgrimage, the particularities and textures of the places along the way shape our formation and participation in the gospel of the Kingdom of God. This book provides an important contribution to a vital conversation." **Scott Hagley, PhD. Director of Education, FORGE Canada.**

"*No Home Like Place* is the rich theological and philosophical support that the movement toward place and parish has needed. The more global and mobile the world becomes, the greater the need for an artistic vision of the church that is local, grounded, and tangible in everyday life. Len's book will give both the seasoned practitioner, and the new explorer, a sound basis for what the Spirit has been drawing so many of us toward in the 21st century." **Paul Sparks, Co-Founder and Director of The Parish Collective. Author of *The New Parish*.**

"In *No Home Like Place*, Hjalmarson articulates vividly and beautifully something that is crucial to missional theology, though previously undeveloped: a theology and spirituality of place. Len's writing provokes thinking, stirs the imagination, and nurtures our inner longings for roots, investment in home, neighbourhood, workplace, and city, and joining with others in bearing witness to God's presence and kingdom in our midst. A valuable contribution!" **Patrick Franklin, Ph.D. Assistant Professor of Theology and Ethics, Providence Theological Seminary.**

"Leonard Hjalmarson skillfully weaves the threads of insight from a wide of array of disciplines and traditions into a masterful and delightful tapestry of wisdom that … reminds us that place-making is our vocation. He raises necessary warnings about the perils of allowing a disconnect to exist between people and place, and reconnects place to the *missio Dei*. Pivotal to that recovery is a sacramental embrace and thoughtful practice of the Eucharist, a recurring theme throughout the book. Superbly researched, and expressed with lucid precision and passion, this is a necessary gift to a culture and a church in danger of losing a sense of place. I am grateful for this work and enthusiastically commend the book!" **William (Bill) R. McAlpine, PhD. Professor of Pastoral Theology, Ambrose University College. Author of *Sacred Space for the Missional Church*.**

"In a society in which families are spread out across the continent, and suburban shopping malls from Vancouver to Halifax to Phoenix all seek to sell us the same goods from the same chain stores, Len Hjalmarson invites us to think deeply about 'place:' about being located and rooted. Hjalmarson draws an extraordinary range of sources into conversation, which in turn provides the reader with a marvelous array of writers and poets to explore. His closing chapter, 'Re–placing the World through the Arts,' does not so much end as invite us into the terrain of imagination and possibility." **Jamie Howison, Priest and pastor, St. Benedict's Table. Author of *God's Mind in That Music*.**

"This book is about place, rootedness, belonging, yet it reads like a travelogue. Compelling, the book weaves together theological reflection, lessons learned in life, disappointments and dreams. It draws on thinkers as diverse as Ancient Bishops, Medieval Mystics, theologians of all ages and bible interpreters of modern and post-modern worlds. Through this book I felt I journeyed with Len, experiencing sacred and human places along the way that remind us our ultimate home is just around the corner." **Tim Geddert, Ph.D. Professor of NT, MB Biblical Seminary, Fresno.**

"*No Home Like Place* makes me dream again. It makes me dream of a world in which Christians live hopefully yet scandalously as a people of radical love, risky grace, and rebellious hope. This is a call to being human while being present. Every lover of God's world must be required to read this book." **A.J. Swoboda, PhD. Adjunct Professor at George Fox Evangelical Seminary. Author of** *Messy: God Likes it that Way.*

"My own interest and admiration for the Celtic concepts of pilgrimage and place and their rejection of the dichotomy between secular and sacred in their lives has been revived by Hjalmarson's scholarly, readable and important book. *No Home Like Place* shows us in clear Biblical, theological and historical terms, that place is important to God and creation as well as to both his Old and New Covenant people in the history and plan of redemption ... From this vantage we are better able to live incarnationally in our own neighbourhoods." **Robert L Roxburgh, Church Consultant and Mentor. Author of** *Renewal Down to Earth.*

"Deep down, all humans are homesick for a place they have never been. It's the post-Eden trauma: Man searching for the one place that God hangs out. But that particular search can only be found where heaven colonizes Earth. That's the big idea of Jesus: the Kingdom as God's uncontested rule comes to a place near you. I call these places Kingdom Colonies, Gardens of God that will increasingly emerge as people stop 'doing the church thing' and start to model what the whole world has been waiting for far too long ..." **Wolfgang Simson, Coach and Innovator. Author of** *The Starfish Manifesto* **and** *Houses That Change the World.*

"There is no doubt that God is speaking to the Church in relation to our sentness in the various places we inhabit. Place is a vital aspect to both incarnational forms of mission as well as missional forms of discipleship. There is an excellent, significant, theological poetic in this book." **Alan Hirsch, FORGE USA. Author of** *The Forgotten Ways* **and** *The Permanent Revolution.*

"Most Christians do not intuitively connect 'place' and 'mission.' Len Hjalmarson argues persuasively that they are intrinsically connected.

He engages in conversation with a wide range of authors, from Duns Scotus to Walter Brueggemann, from T. S. Eliot to Bruce Cockburn, and from Wendell Berry to N. T. Wright, and takes us deep into scripture, theology and history. The book is comprehensive, thoughtful and imaginative, and I for one have been helped by it to love home, place, neighbourhood—and the Gospel—more deeply." **John P. Bowen, Professor of Evangelism, Wycliffe College, Toronto. Author of** *The Missionary Letters of Vincent Donovan.*

"Hjalmarson takes us on a pilgrimage where he opens our eyes through poetry and deep theological reflection, moving us from the abstract to the concrete in discipleship and mission by recovering a theology of place. He reminds us that deep mission is embodied, relational, particular, intimate and involves place-making." **JR Woodward, V3 Tribe Coordinator. Co-founder of the Ecclesia Network and the Missio Alliance. Author of** *Creating a Missional Culture.*

"At a time when so many people seem to be 'passing through.' longing to be somewhere else that is better than where they are, Len reminds us why we really are not at home. Expertly marshaling insights from history, culture, the bible and theology Len helps us understand our 'displacement.' before showing us how might be 're-placed' deeply and richly into the locations we already inhabit." **Jason Clark, Lead Mentor, Leadership and Global Perspectives, George Fox Evangelical Seminary.**

"There are many of us in places far and wide, practitioners seeking to live God's call to the neighbourhood. We are committed to the most local expressions of discipleship because we have a gut sense that place matters to God and to the nature of Christian mission. What Len provides in this book a wonderful resource to those of us committed to the neighbourhood, a cogent, carefully researched and sensitively written theology of place that will sustain and strengthen our commitments." **Simon Carey Holt, Author of** *God Next Door: Spirituality and Mission in the Neighbourhood.*

"Theologically sophisticated and grounded in lived (or biked) experience. This work represents a fresh and highly stimulating take on a deeply important subject." **Eric O. Jacobsen, PhD. Author of** *The Space Between: A Christian Engagement with the Built Environment.*

"Pilgrimage is an important part of the Christian life, but it was not what we were made for. We were made to make a particular corner of creation our home: we were made for place. And no better defense of the importance of place in the life of a Christian has been written than this wise and far-reaching book by Len Hjalmarson.

Even the exiles in the Babylon are told through Jeremiah to '... build house and settle down; plant gardens and eat what they produce' [Jeremiah 29:5]. Settle down. The Gospel is ultimately about making us at home here, and that is going to be a hard lesson for the church to learn. But in this increasingly place-less time, it has never been more important. *No Home Like Place* is an essential primer for that lesson." **Loren Wilkinson, PhD. Associate Professor of Interdisciplinary Studies, Regent College, Vancouver**

"*No Home Like Place* is a meaningful Trinitarian recovery of a theology of place for the postmodern Christian pilgrim. Noting the modern propensity for 'space.' Hjalmarson recovers the concept of 'place' that prevailed in early Christian thought for a new generation of believers. Hjalmarson has constructed an intriguing narrative of biography, spirituality and theology, all with academic rigor. A book for theologians, artists and ministry practitioners, it is laced with anecdotes, poetry and practical liturgical applications. I highly recommend this work!" **Jay Smith, Ph.D. President, Yellowstone Theological Institute.**

"As an architect and artist, I find place-making a creative act of joy. In *No Home Like Place*, Len Hjalmarson takes us on a journey, a re-discovery of place rooted in history, culture, and geography that brings us to that joy-filled remembrance of place in our lives. He encourages us to prefer the particular over the universal in the created world and realize that our path in life is walked in and though creation. This reminds us that the created world is a window opening toward God.

Hjalmarson also explores the paradox of being a pilgrim in the places we dwell, in our home, in our neighbourhood, while prodding us to move beyond the dualism of sacred and secular to recover a sacramental way of living. In the end, the author shows us a way of seeing our world that helps us recover our home in it." **Randall Shier, FCA.**

"In a world of increasing mobility, *No Home Like Place* makes a compelling case for Christians to be more attentive to the places that they inhabit. Hjalmarson calls us to consider how cultivating connection to place is integral to the incarnational mission of the church. Moreover, this book prompts a re-imagining of how the recovery of place might foreshadow the coming Kingdom." **Mark Mulder, Ph.D. Associate Professor, Sociology and Social Work, Calvin College, Grand Rapids.**

"In this thoughtful and interesting work, Leonard explores the importance of place, locality and presence to the Christian faith. In an age when we see the rise of the network to the demise of geographic location contemporary expressions of the neighborhood can feel like co-habilitating strangers. This book creatively explores the place of Christianity to be counter-cultural, to recover the importance of the sacred in the local." **Ian Mobsby, Anglican Minister and leader of the Moot Community, London, UK.**

No Home Like Place

A Christian Theology of Place
2nd Edition

Leonard Hjalmarson

Urban Loft Publishers | Portland, Oregon

No Home Like Place
A Christian Theology of Place

First Published 2014
Second Edition 2015

Urban Loft Publishers
2034 NE 40th Avenue #414
Portland, OR 97212
www.theurbanloft.org

ISBN-13: 978-0692393611
ISBN-10: 0692393617

Made in the U.S.A.

To be an American is to move on, as if we could
outrun change. To attach oneself to place is to
surrender to it, and suffer with it.

Kathleen Norris, Dakota

///

Geography is simply a visible form of theology.

Jon D. Levenson

CONTENTS

List of Illustrations

Acknowledgements

The irony of writing a book on place is that one is immersed in concepts and words, the world of abstractions, attempting to parse something concrete and tangible. Add to this our own sense of displacement: in 2010 we left our home and moved across the country. Yet somehow in the journey comes fresh perspective, so that we "arrive where we started" and "know the place for the first time."

A book like this is really about pilgrimage, and the formative influence of people and places. My father, and his love of all things that live and grow, and his endless curiosity about the world, deserve the greatest credit. I love you dad, and I'm forever grateful for your lightness of heart and clearness of eye.

Loren Wilkinson, in my years of exploration at Regent College, inspired me with his love of literature, love of life, and love for creation. I remember in particular the snowy ridge of Mount Thurston and Mount Mercer, above the Chilliwack valley, with fellow pilgrim Dan Coulter. It was cold that afternoon, with views to distant peaks, and the air was crisp and clear.

Arnold August, indigenous elder and friend, man of God, man of the land and man of your people. Your deep convictions and sacrificial life in view of something greater have offered me courage.

Music and poetry are "the language of what it is not possible to say." The music of Bruce Cockburn is provocative and rooted, inspiring me since 1978. A few choice samples are included here from Canada's celebrated musician.

Some friends offered feedback and encouragement with early drafts: Patrick Franklin of Providence College and Seminary, Paul Fromont of Prodigal Kiwis, and Brad Jersak. Malcolm Guite offered the inclusion of his beautiful sonnets, and I'm glad to expose them to a wider audience.

Finally, thanks to my wife, Betty. She believed in this project from the start, even when it sounded like another abstract exploration of virtual space!

Thank you Lord, for these friends, sacred companions on the journey. May this work be a blessing to your people as we seek to engage missionally, on the ground, in the neighborhoods and parishes where you have placed us.

Veni, Sancte Spiritus, reple tuorum corda fidelium,
et tui amoris in eis ignem accende.

Foreword

Loren Wilkinson, PhD
Associate Professor, Interdisciplinary Studies, Regent College, Vancouver.

In his book *This Place on Earth* Alan Durning, a globe-trotting researcher for the World-Watch Institute, describes the seed that led him to return from the good work of trying to fix the world to put down roots in his home town of Seattle. He was, he says, in the Philippines "interviewing members of remote hill tribes about their land and livelihood:"

> ... a gap-toothed chief showed me the trees, streams and farm plots that his tribe had tended for centuries. It was territory, he insisted, they would defend with their lives. As the sun finally slid lower in the sky, he introduced me to a frail old woman who was revered by the others as a traditional priestess. We sat under a sacred tree near her farm and looked out over the Ma'asam River. She asked through an interpreter, "What is your homeland like?"[1]

Durning found her question embarrassing. His base was Washington DC, where he lived with his wife and two children. But he

---

[1] Durning, *This Place on Earth*, 3.

17

was mainly (as he writes) "jet-setting on behalf of future generations," and had no roots there.

She repeated the question, thinking I had not heard. "Tell me about your place." Again, I could not answer ... The truth was, I lacked any connection to my base in Washington.

"In America," I finally admitted, "we have careers, not places." Looking up, I recognized pity in her eyes.[2]

For a long time Christians have suffered from a similar sickness. We would use different words: "In Christianity," we might say, "we have *callings*, not places." And usually in those callings, or "vocations," we regard place as irrelevant. By definition, callings "call" us somewhere else. So rootedness is not a widely-practiced Christian virtue. In fact it is often not considered a virtue at all, but a spiritual impediment. Consider one of the classics of Christian Spirituality, John Bunyan's *Pilgrim's Progress*. It begins with a man leaving his home, wife and children behind and setting out for the heavenly city. He leaves those roots for the good of his soul.

Pilgrimage is an important part of the Christian life, but it was not what we were made for. We were made to make a particular corner of creation our home: we were made for place. And no better defense of the importance of place in the life of a Christian has been written than this wise and far-reaching book by Len Hjalmarson.

The little story with which Durning begins his own secular defense of being rooted in a place reflects one of the main problems Christians have with the idea: it sounds vaguely pagan. After all, the woman who asks the question is a priestess sitting under her sacred tree. In Biblical faith, we have no sacred groves, no sacred places. The Biblical narrative begins (like Bunyan's story) with a man (Abraham) uprooting from his homeland. Jesus tells his disciples, "I go to prepare a place for you," with the promise that he will return so "that you also may be where I am" (John 14:3 TNIV). And we have assumed that means taking us away to heaven, our eternal home: another place, which by contrast makes all our places here temporary and unimportant. So our tradition is filled with images of pilgrimage, and songs like, "This World is Not my Home," and "I'll Fly Away."

---

[2] Ibid., 4.

Those images and songs express a partial truth about our Christian calling. But like so many partial truths, they can be deadly when detached from the whole. And "the whole" in this case requires us to recall that the Biblical story is *not* about going to heaven when we die: it's about heaven and earth becoming one: God's purposes in creation being fulfilled. The final great image in the Bible is of that planet-sized garden city descending to (and merging with) earth, accompanied by the words, "God's dwelling place is now among the people, and he will dwell with them" (Rev. 21:3 TNIV). So when Jesus told us, through his disciples, that he will come again, it wasn't to take us away. It was to abide with us in a renewed place. Our pilgrimage through this barren land is ultimately about becoming (in the words of the great text from Isaiah) a "well-watered garden" ... "Repairer of Broken Walls, Restorer of Streets with Dwellings" (Isaiah 58: 11-12 TNIV).

As Len points out in this book—even the exiles in Babylon are told through Jeremiah to "... build house and *settle down*; plant gardens and eat what they produce" (Jeremiah 29:5). Settle down. The Gospel is ultimately about making us at home here, and that is going to be a hard lesson for the church to learn. But in this increasingly place-less time, it has never been more important. *No Home Like Place* is an essential primer for that lesson.

It is a lesson I have spent my whole life learning. I had the privilege of growing up deeply rooted in one place—a collection of fields, which my family was slowly carving out of an old forest, that bordered a bend in the South Santiam River in Oregon's Willamette Valley. Both that river-front farm and Christian teachings—from the little country church, and various Bible camps—were two main influences on me. I knew they *both* were good and in some way true—but I had no way of seeing them as part of one truth, one story, so I assumed that the goodness of Oregon's fields, rivers, forests and mountains were ultimately unimportant in my Christian life.

The last big old-growth trees on our family's farm became logs, and then money, to send me to college, and when I boarded the Greyhound bus for the three-day trip to Chicago, I was sad to be leaving the place that had shaped me—but thought that leaving place behind was what one did as a Christian. The highest Christian calling, I had learned, was (following the words of Jesus) to "Go into all the world and preach the

Gospel." I thought I was preparing to do that: perhaps to go to people like that old Philippine woman looking over her fields that Durning refers to. But: What might that gospel mean for her and her place? I hadn't thought about that yet.

To take the Gospel "into all the world" is a high calling: we are, as an old Gospel chorus puts it, "saved to tell others." But I never thought much back then about what would happen if everyone were "told" and everyone were "saved." What would those "others" do then? What, from the beginning, and in the end, are we earthlings here on the earth for? The obvious Biblical answer is that we are to dwell: to make our home in a place. For (again in Jeremiah's words to the exiles in Babylon) "... if it prospers, you will prosper."

At college, a long way from the place that had nourished me, I began the slow process of learning the bigger story of the Gospel: that it is not about saving us out of creation, but of restoring us to creation, giving back our original job, to be gardener of a place. When I met Mary Ruth, the young woman who was to be my wife, she pointed out an oddity of my conversation: when I talked about home, I always referred to it as "The Place." I had absorbed in my bones a deep truth about being human: that we were made for place. It took a lot longer— and a lot of moving from place to place—to begin to realize that taking corners of creation and coming to know them, love them, and make them home, is part of the Good News. And for me, it was essential to be married to a woman with a great gift for putting down roots, an ability for making every stop on our Pilgrimage, "The Place." Mary Ruth has that ability to a rare degree but it's an essential calling of our humanity.

"Home-making" has long been somewhat trivialized as a woman's thing, as has attachment to place. Thus the wisdom in Wendell Berry's "Manifesto: The Mad Farmer Liberation Front."

> So long as women do not go cheap
> for power, please women more than men.
> Ask yourself: will this satisfy
> a woman satisfied to bear a child?[3]

---

3 Berry, *The Mad Farmer Poems*, 12.

Wallace Stegner, one of the most perceptive writers about the complicated relationship between North Americans and place, said that there are two kinds of people: "boomers," who want to move on to the next place their career takes them, and "nesters," people who want to settle down, build a home. He describes a conversation between his (fictionalized) parents, as they hopefully await a good wheat crop on the southern Canadian prairies:

> "If we get a good wheat crop will you fix the house up a little?" she said, "rig some kind of water system so I could plant flowers and things."

> "I tell you one thing," he said, "if we don't make it this year we won't even be camping in it. We'll be going someplace where we can make a living."

> "We've made a living. Even with the drought last year and the rust the year before we made a living."

> He stooped to lay a spoonful of poison at a gopher hole. "When we came up here," he said, "we didn't come up just to make a living. We came up to make a pile."[4]

Jesus said "I am the Way, the Truth and the Life"—and often in our attempts to follow the Way we have forgotten the Truth that part of our Life in Christ is "Making a Living." And even if it is only one stop on the Way, that living involves putting down roots in a place.

So welcome to this splendid invitation to join with our Creator in the blessing of places. *No Home Like Place* may well change the way you think about your life.

The book ranges widely: from the complicated history of our *placelessness*; to the strong Biblical affirmation of place in both Old and New Testaments; to the hallowing that the Incarnation gives to all places in their particularity; to the need to recover a more Trinitarian Christianity in which we recognize that all things hold together in the Word, and are brought to life by the Spirit; to the need to make our cities dwelling-places of delight; to how art makes visible and hallows

---

[4] Stegner, *The Big Rock Candy Mountain*, 215-216.

the particulars of place; to the way Christian worship, and the Eucharist in particular, brings heaven and our place together; to the place-making disciplines of gardening, baking, and hospitality … and much more.

Through all of these insights (as should be the case in a book like this) we catch engaging glimpses of a particular life, a particular family, lived in particular places. You will enjoy coasting down the hill in Kelowna, BC with Len on his bike!

One of the strong themes of this book is the value of Sabbath: the recognition that this hallowing of time is ultimately for the purpose of bringing people to an awareness that their place is a gift from God. So Wendell Berry's short poem—from a collection of poems written over years of Sabbath walks around his place in Kentucky—is a perfect introduction—and invitation—into *No Home Like Place*:

> *There is a day*
> *when the road neither*
> *comes nor goes and the way*
> *is not a way but a place.*[5]

---

[5] Berry, *A Timbered Choir*, 216.

Whether I kneel or stand or sit in prayer
I am not caught in time nor held in space,
But, thrust beyond this posture, I am where
Time and eternity are face to face;
Infinity and space meet in this place
Where crossbar and upright hold the One
In agony and in all Loves embrace.

Madeleine L'Engle[6]

---

[6] Mel'Engle, "Communion."

No Home Like Place

Introduction

It was 1981, and I was reading in Thomas Merton, "New Seeds of Contemplation." Merton was both a mystic, and rooted, embodying in his life and in his work a paradox that expressed a gospel journey. I was drawn to his work, and in my own life recognized the threads of a common pilgrimage: a search for a place to belong.

As the son of an Air force Sergeant, I grew familiar with home by its absence. The postings came every two or three years, and when I left home for college my travels continued in the same pattern: my first year in Vancouver, three years in Winnipeg, back to Vancouver again, and then not long afterward two years in Fresno, California. Never enough time to set down roots, but in that wandering my sensitivity to roots increased.

That isn't the whole story. My father bought his first piece of land in 1968: 4.5 acres on the border of CFB Chilliwack. A few years later he bought 6 acres on a hillside in Yarrow, BC. He cleared land, and his children helped. He planted trees and harvested fruit. He taught me the rudiments of pruning. His own roots in central Manitoba on a small farm found new expression. And his love of all animals and trees, and especially fruit trees, was passed on to another generation. My father retired from the Air Force around 1980, but he is a gardener still, and everywhere I have lived I have planted trees.

Michel de Certeau, writing in the dying days of Modernity, tells that in modern Athens the vehicles of transportation are called *metaphorai*. To go to work or come home, one takes a "metaphor"—a bus or a train. But a metaphor is a story compressed. Stories help us to organize our memories, and memories root us in place. They select and link places together, and relate them to our lives and the lives of others. They express our pilgrimage and create spatial trajectories. To de Certeau, "Every story is a travel story—a spatial practice."[1]

To return home is to return to a *place*; through experience human hearts become rooted in place. The paradox of place is that it is both given, and socially constructed. Place is storied, and so contested, because stories themselves are placed—conditioned by history and culture. Open the lens wider, and place has its own story dating back to Plato and Aristotle. But place has become transparent to us. Like air, we are immersed in it and can't live without it, but don't *see* it. Yet to exist at all is to be some-*where*.[2] Edward Casey writes, "Nothing we do is unplaced: how could we fail to recognize this primal fact?"[3]

For one thing, place, like love, makes a poor abstraction, and the Modern world was infatuated with abstractions. In Modernity we sought for that which is universal, for both philosophical and practical reasons, but primarily because the needs of science (and through knowledge, power) demanded abstractions. Only now are we taking the measure of the cost.

Our loss of ability to see place as a category in its own right, preferring the universal over the particular, daily impacts our ability to partner with God on mission. God, it seems, is infatuated with place: with the particular and the concrete. The Incarnation demonstrates the extent of this commitment. The loss of place dates back to certain Fathers of the church and the influence of the neoplatonic movement, and more recently to the great physicist and intellectual Isaac Newton. More recent advances in communication technology, the ability to

---

[1] De Certeau, *The Practice of Everyday Life*, 115.

[2] Heidegger insisted that place is the house of being. A person is Dasein, or "being-there." *The Question of Being*, 26.

[3] Casey, *The Fate of Place*, 93.

compress time and space through networks of optical cables, only compound our danger.[4]

The movement from place to space that occurred with Galileo and Newton, and the justification that accompanied it, highlights the social construction of place, and therefore its politics.[5] There are forces that resist the recovery of place, because a love and appreciation for the local may threaten larger commercial interests. The universalizing of place and the free movement of goods is the goal of multinational corporations. Utopia, says the president of Nabisco Corporation, is "One world of homogeneous consumption ..."[6]

Of course, achieving that vision of the good life requires a lot of power. But it also requires a moral imperative: we distance ourselves from the creation in order to do it violence. Place separated from the people who inhabit it becomes a mere fact, a calculation in a formula, subject to the application of power in the interest of profit. We pursue abstractions: removing what is personal and unique from the equation. What we fail to see is that when we franchise fast-food, we abstract humanity itself.[7]

Even now we walk a tightrope between the particular and the universal. We aren't quite sure what it means to be Holy, created in the image of God. Should our sanctity lead to greater uniformity? Does spirituality tend toward the impersonal, as Eastern religions tend to maintain? Or is there something Holy in the particular, in the unique, the warp and woof of a person or a place? Does God love diversity, or does he prefer a universal sameness? Can we truly embrace diversity while loving the familiarity of a place?

The lives of saints often answer exactly these questions. Thomas Merton recognized that what was most universal was most personal. Rather than escape the world, he perceived the path to life was in and

---

[4] Resulting in the curious phenomenon, as Heidegger expressed it, of a paradoxical presence: "the nearness of things remains absent." *Poetry, Language, Thought*, 165-6.

[5] Various writers note that even the discipline of geography resisted the exploration of place as a category in its own right. See Inge, *A Christian Theology of Place*, 14-15.

[6] Quoted in Jerry Mander, "The Rules of Corporate Behavior," 321.

[7] We create our tools, then our tools create us. See Jacques Ellul on the dehumanizing tendencies of technology, *The Technological Society*, 1967.

through creation. Life became sacramental: the created world a window opening toward God. All around him creation was continuing—the dance of the Lord in emptiness. He saw perfection not as conformity to an ideal, but as agreement with God in being. He would have heartily approved of the words of Bruce Cockburn:

> *Light pours from a million radiant lives*
> *Off of kids and dogs and the hard-shelled husbands and wives*
> *All that glory shining around and we're all caught taking a dive*
> *And all the beasts of the hills around shout, "such a waste!"*
> *Don't you know that from the first to the last*
> *We're all one in the gift of grace.*[8]

This sacramental sensibility has been preserved in some parts of the church, and may offer promise for the recovery of place, a way of seeing our world that can help us recover our home in it.

There is another side to the loss of place, relating to the perennial human desire for something more from this world. When that *moreness* loses its moorings in the actual people and places of this world, it takes on escapist overtones, and we dream of space more than the places we have known. The incredible ubiquity and power of the world-wide-web in the last ten years has opened up the arena of virtual space, and further enabled our ability to escape the world of the real. Our loneliness and hunger to belong have increased as space tears away from place "by fostering relations between 'absent others.'"[9]

The question that many will be asking, even as they intuit the recovery of place in their own lives and neighbourhoods, is this: why now? What is it about the conditions of our time, particularly for those of us in the West, that allow us to see through new eyes, and re-enter the textures and rhythms, colors and tones, beauty, severity, and complexity of the places we dwell? This is a question worth considering, and a story I want to tell. It's a story that engages us in a wider conversation between the gospel and culture, and its telling may help us to see more clearly what the Spirit is doing in our time.

---

[8] Cockburn, "In the Falling Dark."

[9] *A Christian Theology of Place*, 12.

I am excited about this book for a few reasons. First, it represents a pilgrimage of sorts in my own life: I love places, and the longer I live the more I appreciate the peculiar textures and rhythms of place. Second, because I observe in many of the missional conversations an implicit theology of place begging for articulation, which asks for a fresh encounter with the Word. As T.S. Eliot expressed it, "the Word within The world and for the world."[10] We'll consider this phrase more closely under a Johannine Christology in chapter four.

It's always difficult and costly to articulate those things that are so familiar as to be transparent: but it's a sacred task, which leads me to my third point. I am excited because the more we "see our seeing" the more intentional we can become in loving the places where we dwell, entering the neighbourhoods in which we live, where God is already at work, and learning to partner with Him.

Learning, participation, seeing, place: these are the elements of pilgrimage. Pilgrimage was one of the first things lost when place was subsumed under the infinite category of space; it is also one of the first things we recover when we discover that God loves places in all their mess, diversity, and color. It's no accident that the Camino de Santiago is again figuring in the stories of ordinary people. Similarly, it's no accident that thousands are rediscovering a sense of the sacred in real places, walking labyrinths, and talking about their own lives as a journey. When the first disciples were forced out of Jerusalem they discovered that following Jesus meant they would always be on pilgrimage. The experience of being in transit became a metaphor for encounter with God, and the Holy city of Jerusalem again became both a physical location, and a symbol for something more.

Allow me to summarize the flow of this book: to lay out the itinerary for this journey.

In chapter one we will consider the social location that is helping us to see our seeing, as well as generating the need to renew foundations. This particular location, largely the collapse of the Enlightenment project, is allowing us to recover an appreciation for the particular, for those places that have formed us, root us, and yet also beckon us on. We'll begin to think about belonging and the tensions

---

[10] Eliot, "Ash Wednesday."

between place, and space, the universal and the particular. And we'll introduce in more detail the metaphor of pilgrimage.

In chapter two we will hear the story of place, largely through the lenses of history: the early philosophers and the church Fathers. We'll consider how we arrived in this cultural location where place has been largely transparent. Then we will consider the biblical data, and work at theological foundations, starting with Genesis: the imago Dei and God in his temple. We'll look at the importance of land in relation to covenant in the Old Testament, and outline the basics of a theology of creation.

In chapter three we will consider land and covenant in the New Testament, categories which linger just below the surface of the text. Then we'll look at the final destiny that God intends for humankind, and examine kingdom and incarnation as setting the reign of God in place. We'll consider a kingdom eschatology, and look at both Jerusalem and the Temple in relation to a recovery of place. Do Jesus words on worship in John 4 mean the end of sacred space? We'll close chapter 3 with a look at place-making in relation to the *missio Dei*.

In chapter four we'll continue to work with the biblical data, beginning with the motifs of ascent and ecology as alternate frames for the imagination supporting a theology of place. We'll consider the relationship of sacred and secular, and hearken back to thoughts on thingness from Duns Scotus in the Middle Ages. Then we will examine the concept of sacrament as a metaphor for bridging the universal and particular, heaven and earth. We'll consider the recovery of place occurring in neighbourhood and parish, then close with some thoughts on the importance of local culture.

In chapter five we'll shift our focus to the cultural realities of place as expressed primarily in Western urban contexts. We'll consider the politics of place. Who tells the stories of a particular place? What about master-narratives like that of globalization? What might the old idea of "the commons" offer for the future of place? We'll consider pace and fragmentation and virtual reality as challenges to our ability to richly inhabit the places we dwell.

In chapter six we will attend to urban place and the call to place-making in the city, and the need to balance private and public expressions of place. We'll consider the purpose of transitional places and the hope of hospitality, and close with some thoughts on the power of social capital in place-making.

In chapter seven we'll take what we have learned and ask some specific questions about sacred space: are there holy places? How do places of transition become ritual space, and how do these relate to the recovery and possibility of pilgrimage? How can displacement help us to engage in fresh ways in the places to which we are called? How does the Incarnation, the ultimate affirmation of matter, become an unstable space that opens the complex possibility of catholic place?

In chapter eight we'll consider the missional implications of the recovery of place, and reflect on the role of the arts in re-placing our life in this world. The artist lifts the veil on ordinary things to reveal hidden glory, assists in our reconnecting the world to the life of God, and helps us to see our seeing. Moreover the arts re-enchant the world and invite us to bow before mystery.

Finally in chapter nine we'll consider biking, baking, gardens and hospitality. These subversive practices re-place us in the world, slow us down, and invite us to an embodied faith in community, lived at the intersection of heaven and earth.

Today in the Okanagan Valley the sun refracts brilliantly from the uncut grass beneath my window. The world is aglow with light. As we move beyond the dualism of sacred and secular to recover a sacramental way of seeing, we will find that holiness is much larger than heaven, because "the earth is the Lord's, and the fullness thereof."

"The fleeting intimacies of direct experience and the true
quality of a place often escape notice because the head is packed
with shopworn ideas. The data of the senses are pushed under in favor
of what one is taught to see and admire."

Yi-Fu Tuan[11]

///

Never in history has distance meant less. Figuratively,
we "use up" places and dispose of them in much the same way we
dispose of Kleenex or beer cans. We are witnessing a historic decline in
the significance of place to human life. We are breeding a new race of
nomads, and few suspect quite how massive, wide-spread and
significant their migrations are.

Alvin Toffler[12]

---

[11] Tuan, *Space and Place*, 146.

[12] Toffler, *Future Shock*, 75.

CHAPTER 1

An Exploration of "Place"

Part I

> *We shall not cease from exploration*
> *And the end of all our exploring*
> *Will be to arrive where we started*
> *And know the place for the first time.*[1]

I was living in the west end of Vancouver while attending Regent College and it was spring. The trees were alive with light, and the rhododendrons were opening their buds. I was driving a 1976 Honda Civic, a snappy little car about the size of a VW Beetle. It was aging and starting to smoke a bit, and the front shocks were frozen. I had patched the tail pipe a half dozen times but the patches never held. It was time for a new buggy!

A friend was selling a 1973 Renault. I had never seen one before, and when I drove it I was impressed by the handling as well as the shifter. The car felt tight, especially when compared to my dying

---

[1] Eliot, *Four Quartets.*

Honda. I bought it for about a thousand dollars, and a whole new world opened up.

When I first saw the Renault I assumed it was a rare car. I had never seen one before. After my first few days of driving I saw them everywhere. Why had I not noticed them before? Renault seemed nearly as common as my little red Civic. What changed?

My seeing had changed. Richard Rohr writes, "The mind only takes pictures using the film with which it's loaded."[2] Humans develop mental maps as aids in orienting in a complex world. It isn't only our attention "span" which is limited, it's also our attention bandwidth. Mental maps are like lenses with which we see the world, and they vary in breadth and detail. With time and engagement and work, our lenses gradually expand and the scope increases.

Most of our maps are updated in small increments, like my experience with a new car. We get a bit more information, and it requires only a small adjustment. Sometimes our maps are upgraded wholesale, and we experience something like a conversion. "The lights go on," and we see in new ways.

In 2003 my wife began work which required her to make appointments all over our city. As a one car family, that meant that my appointments had to be local or required public transport. I began using my bicycle, and quickly discovered that the speed and openness of a bicycle changed my way of seeing the world. The vulnerability of bike travel requires much greater attention, and the relaxed pace allows for it. It requires effort: it is embodied travel that connects the traveler to the physical reality of the environment. Every hill is felt, every change in the air experienced. In riding I discovered a richer texture to my neighbourhood than I had ever seen in a car, and the boundaries of my neighbourhood expanded. I began to notice rhythms and people and qualities I had not seen before.[3]

---

[2] Rohr, *Everything Belongs*, 66.

[3] See also "How Walking and Biking Add Value to Your Community and Change the System."

Why had I not seen our neighbourhood before? What is it about "place" that is transparent?[4]

In his primer on theology, Karl Barth tells the story of a series of lectures he gave in the post-war ruins of the Kurfürsten castle in Bonn, Germany. A rebuilding project was underway. In the summer of 1946 Barth began his lectures. Every morning at seven they met to sing a psalm or a hymn to cheer each other up. By eight o'clock, "the rebuilding of the quadrangle began to advertise itself in the rattle of an engine as the engineers went to work to restore the ruins."[5] Barth notes that this is where we accomplish vigorous theological work—in the ruins of an old world in hope of the new. Unlearning—deconstruction—opens the way for new work, and new learning. It takes effort, and sometimes it's messy.

The deconstruction project that is post-modernity is well underway. A few days ago the media was buzzing with the 11th anniversary of 9/11, a date that has become a metaphor for terror, but also a metaphor for "wake up!" The world as we know it is passing away.

Paradigms and Cultural Shift

My own life has been marked by change. I was third of three children, and the only son to an RCAF Corporal stationed in Germany in 1957. Not long after my birth my family returned to Canada, and began a fifteen year game of shuffleboard in Western Canada. We moved on average every two years until we finally settled on the west coast in 1973. I drove myself east again in 1975, and then back to the west coast in 1977. Then I moved east to attend college in 1978, and back west to attend graduate school in 1981. After two years in one graduate school and a few years working, I moved south to attend a second graduate school in the USA.

By the time that my father had settled on the west coast in 1973 the turbulent sixties had come and gone. It was in the early sixties that

---

[4] James K.A. Smith, commenting on the work of Charles Taylor, notes that particular configurations of the social imaginary become so dominant that we fail to recognize them as a particular, contingent construal. *Desiring the Kingdom*, 28.

[5] Barth, *Dogmatics in Outline*, 7.

Carl Jung observed what he described as the disintegration of the western psyche. In 1962 he gave the West fifty years before its inner structures collapse. He felt that we were abandoning the images and beliefs that held our lives together in coherence and health.

Also in 1962, Thomas Kuhn published his historic work, "The Structure of Scientific Revolutions." Kuhn tracked several of the greatest breakthroughs of the Twentieth century, and discovered that great breakthroughs do not occur based strictly on factual evidence. Instead there are two different phases of scientific progress. In the first phase, scientists work within a paradigm (a set of accepted beliefs that are a framework and a lens for their study). When the foundation of the paradigm weakens and new theories and scientific methods begin to replace it, the next phase of scientific discovery occurs. Kuhn argues that progress from one paradigm to another has no logical method, but instead is based on intuitive and supra-rational factors, something akin to faith. Kuhn coined the phrase "paradigm shift" to describe this process. Leonard Sweet comments on Thomas Kuhn's "paradigm shift" that,

> When Thomas Kuhn introduced the language of "paradigm change" ... I wish he had used another phrase for "paradigm shift:" metaphor change.
>
> They mean the same thing. Paradigm is another word for "root metaphors." When the root metaphors change, so does everything else. The imaginative architecture of the modern world has collapsed, is in ruins, and a new imaginative architecture is emerging.[6]

Newton's imaginative frame changed the world, but when "place" became mere "space," the consequences were more serious than anyone could have suspected. Could it be that "space," the dominant image of our era, an abstraction that dominates our imagination, could again become "place?"

---

[6] Sweet. "Seven Questions."

Seeing Our Seeing

"We don't know who invented water—
but we know it wasn't fish!" - Santayana

The ordinary is transparent to us; we tune it out. In the Greek mind the *idea* of a thing was more real than the thing itself. The Western church is heavily influenced by this dualistic spirituality.[7] My maps were formed in a hectic and isolated church culture that knew a lot about heaven (the real) and not much about earth (the temporal). We tended to think of salvation FROM history rather than salvation IN history. But this *dis*-placed, disembodied salvation has little resonance with biblical faith. OT scholar Walter Brueggemann writes of the biblical view of land:

> Land is always fully historical but always bearer of over-pluses of meaning known only to those who lose and yearn for it. The current loss of and hunger for place participate in those plus dimensions—at once a concern for actual historical placement, but at the same time a hunger for an over-plus of place meaning.

> Land is a central, if not THE central theme of biblical faith. Biblical faith is a pursuit of historical belonging that includes a sense of destiny derived from such belonging ...[8]

What does it mean to belong? Peter Block writes that, "to belong is to be related to and a part of something. It is membership, the experience of being at home in the broadest sense of the phrase."[9] At the Q gathering in 2010, urbanologist Richard Florida observed that young adults meeting one another no longer ask, "What do you do?" They ask, "Where do you live?" Today more people will change careers in order to stay in a place—stay connected—than will change place to stay in a career. "The 20th-century American dream was to move out

---

[7] A detailed history of place is offered by Craig Bartholomew in *Where Mortals Dwell.*

[8] Brueggemann, *The Land,* 3-4.

[9] Block, *Community,* 2.

and move up; the 21st-century dream seems to be to put down deeper roots."[10] Block continues,

> The social fabric of community is formed from an expanding shared sense of belonging. It is shaped by the idea that only when we are connected and care for the well-being of the whole that a civil and democratic society is created ...

> What makes community building so complex is that it occurs in an infinite number of small steps, sometimes in quiet moments that we notice out of the corner of our eye. It calls for us to treat as important many things that we thought were incidental. An after-thought becomes the point; a comment made in passing defines who we are more than all that came before. If the artist is one who captures the nuance of experience, then this is whom each of us must become.[11]

The structures of belonging in our culture are shifting, as are the patterns of belonging. But what I want to highlight in the paragraph above are two things: the emphasis on the "whole," and the emphasis on the ordinary and incidental. Belonging—like place—is socially mediated in infinite small steps and ordinary moments. The experience of being at home is largely an affective experience: subjective, and communal. "Scholars have highlighted how the affective experience of locatedness—of being here—is iteratively created and recreated through social and political processes, which work to define and make specific places."[12] In *Daniel Deronda*, George Eliot writes,

> A human life, I think, should be well rooted in some spot of a native land, where it may get the love of tender kinship for the face of earth, for the labours men [sic] go forth to, for the sounds and accents that haunt it, for whatever will give that early home a familiar unmistakable difference amidst the future widening of knowledge: a spot where the definiteness of early memories may be

---

[10] Crouch, "Ten Most Significant Cultural Trends of the Last Decade."

[11] *Community*, 2.

[12] Merrifield, "Place and space," 516–531.

inwrought with affection, and kindly acquaintance with all neighbours, even to the dogs and donkeys, may spread not by sentimental effort and reflection, but as a sweet habit of the blood ... The best introduction to astronomy is to think of the nightly heavens as a little lot of stars belonging to one's own homestead.[13]

"Kindly acquaintance with neighbours," and "sweet [habits] of the blood" require embodiment, and casual repetition. These interactions create what Robert Putnam has described as "social capital."[14] But they also indicate that place is something more than given: it is socially mediated. In other words, place is also political. Place is both given, in the physical surroundings we encounter, and contested as a social construct.[15] It is both real and concrete, subject to our senses, and a symbol for something more.[16] As Brueggemann notes above, Israel's destiny was bound up with the land, and all experience is mediated by place.

Place as Contested Space

I wear corrective lenses, and I have never really liked contacts. But that means I have to look for clip-on sunglasses from time to time. Clip-ons wear out, are damaged by abrasive surfaces, and they are easily left behind. Last summer I left a pair somewhere, and then picked up a new pair at a local drugstore. But these were more brown than green, and suddenly all my familiar places looked different. Where before I had seen green, I saw more yellows and browns. My wife noticed the change in the way I described my world. The places I described look different to her, with her 20/20 vision and unfiltered view.

"Unfiltered view?" Actually, we all use filters, without exception. Some are internal, and others external, but there is no "pure" place; even

---

[13] Eliot, *Daniel Deronda*, Book I, 50.

[14] Putnam, *Bowling Alone*. See further discussion in chapter 6.

[15] "As competing discourses about places are contested ... they become constitutive of new, shared place identities." Pierce, et al., "Relational Place-Making," 55.

[16] *The Land*, 3-4.

the surface of the moon is socially mediated. Likely you have not been there, but you've heard the stories. Who told them, and why? Were they stories related to the moon-landings, or related to astronomy in general? Or were they future oriented stories, science-fiction built around an apocalyptic future and the need for more mineral resources, or more room for human habitation?

As Michel de Certeau expressed it, every story is a spatial practice.[17] Stories are *placed*. Moreover, in the real world of profits, scarcity and need, place is a political reality.[18] In my Canadian context large corporations are investing huge financial and physical resources in developing the oil-sands. The environmental impact of extraction and processing is debated, but it will be substantial. And who tells the story of the land itself: the history, occupancy, and future? It certainly isn't our First Nations people, who were once the sole tenants of these large tracts of land. Various groups are contesting the right of Canada's government to determine the future of these lands and resources. The stories of Exxon and Shell have a corporate goal in mind, relating to profits and control. What role might the church play? Michael Northcott connects the renewal of the parish church to the hope for community-based ecological politics as a corrective to statist, corporatist, and globalizing frames for environmental policy, those forces of free-market capitalism that threaten to remove control of natural resources from local inhabitants. Not only from local inhabitants, but even from local law, with control passed to impersonal, multi-national corporations whose bottom line is profit.[19]

It can seem attractive to abstract place to "space." Global mapping, "globalization," appears beneficial at first glance because it gives the appearance of overcoming the limits of both place and time. The universalizing of place and the free movement of goods is the goal of

---

[17] de Certeau, *The Practice of Everyday Life*, 108.

[18] A particularly poignant example is offered by Michael Northcott in the use of the first blue-planet photos of the earth from space. These images were later used by certain multi-national corporations to justify a unitary management of the earth's "commons" that would benefit powerful Northern interests at the expense of the South. Michael Northcott, "From Environmental U-topianism to Parochial Ecology," 71-85.

[19] Ibid.

corporate and statist interests. Utopia, says the president of Nabisco Corporation, is "One world of homogeneous consumption ..."[20] This goal is presented as good news, one which will "produce peace through the overcoming of division."[21] (Though what is really intended is the overcoming of "difference.") Zygmunt Bauman notes that there is a new stratification of the world population into the globalized rich, who overcome space and never have enough time, and the localized poor, who are chained to the spot and can only "kill" time.[22] The disconnect between people and place erodes human community by eroding humanity itself: we are reduced to "consumers" and our behavior is reduced to self-interest.[23]   Singer-songwriter Bruce Cockburn remembers an older way of seeing:

In this cold commodity culture
Where you lay your money down
It's hard to even notice
That all this earth is hallowed ground?[24]

McDonaldization was first coined by George Ritzer (1993), and it is motivated by the interests of global capitalism. Globalization has been compared to a "secular catholicity" by several authors.[25] McDonaldization is in part an attempt to overcome difference, and distance, in the name of profits, and so amounts to a secular catholicity. The word "catholic" at root simply means "universal." The Body of Christ is thus catholic in this rich sense, transcending time and culture,

---

[20] Mander, "The Rules of Corporate Behavior," 321.

[21] Cavanaugh, "The World in a Wafer," 183.

[22] Bauman, *Globalization: the Human Consequences*, 89.

[23] Post development and human security theorists advocate relocalization in response to the colonializing forces of globalization. Moreover, they recognize that the separate self of liberal theory has served corporate interests while eroding human community. Escobar, *Encountering Development*, xxii–xxiv.

[24] Cockburn, "The Gift."

[25] Sheldrake, *Spaces for the Sacred*, 74-77, 169. A Christian catholicity offers a different hope: William Cavanaugh offers that "the Eucharist refracts space in such a way that one becomes more united to the whole the more tied one becomes to the local."

so that the living reality of the Church in any particular place is always partial. But like the hologram, in the part is hidden the whole. By the Spirit, in the gathering of any particular body, Christ is present, and so sacramentally the entire Church is present, one new people in Christ.[26]

But this summing up of "all things in Christ," is vastly different from the goals of the World Bank or the IMF. Christ does not erase difference, but hallows it. We don't escape the limits of place, but embrace and enter them. A sacramental way of seeing the world offers a way of holding a creative tension between place and space, between the particulars and the universal. The infinite God enters place, so that matter is hallowed, and ordinary things like bread and wine become sacred. As Carrie Newcomer sings, *"Holy is the dish and drain/The soap and sink, the cup and plate ..."*[27] Because the Word became flesh in Jesus, all the world reveals his glory.

It is not accidental that this discussion of sacrament occurs under the rubric of place as contested space. Real sacramentality does not merely emphasize that we live in a graced world; but also reminds us that Christ died to redeem all places, all cultures, all nations. To hold to a view of the world where God becomes flesh is to acknowledge that God loves places, loves the particular. As Philip Sheldrake puts it, the Church is called to be an ethical space: "a practice for making place for the fullness of all things and all people."[28] The Eucharist calls us to embodiment: to become our words of faith and promise and act them out in the world.[29]

---

[26] Ephesians 2:14-18.

[27] Newcomer. "As Holy as a Day is Spent."

[28] *Spaces for the Sacred*, 74

[29] Rodney Clapp comments, "The Eucharist for its enactment requires [us to] gather and the physical bodies of the members of Christ must go through certain motions and assume particular positions ... bodily gestures communicating and reinforcing a wealth of tacit knowledge. To kneel ... to stretch out empty and receptive hands for the bread of life ... So the Eucharist leads us to say that corporality is the very mediation where faith takes on flesh and makes real the truth that inhabits it." *Border Crossings*, 74.

Place and Secularization

In Modernity we sought for that which is universal, for both philosophical and practical reasons, but primarily because the needs of science (knowledge—and through knowledge, power) demanded abstractions. More recent advances in communication technology, the ability to compress time and space through optical cables and networks, only compound our danger.[30]

In *The Secular Age*, Charles Taylor asks one question: What occurred between 1500–2000—during the modern age of western society—where before 1500 it was virtually impossible not to believe in God while in 2000 it became possible? His answer: *disenchantment*, which led to secularism.[31]

Christians today tend to see the prevailing culture as the *secular* world—a dark and unholy place. In the world we hold secular jobs, attend secular schools, listen to secular music, and watch secular movies. Even though all cultures express religion and spirituality in one form or another, the so-called "secular" world is often wrongly perceived as *disenchanted* from the "sacred" realm: the realm where God and Christian faith reside. Accordingly, Christians must keep society at a distance. Some Christians perceive the world and culture as together in one realm and perceive the institutional church, Christian faith, and spiritual practices together in another realm.[32] This dualism is *secularization*.

Peter Berger argues that the seeds of *secularization* go back to the Enlightenment and Western Protestantism, whose theology generally separated reality into the natural and supernatural, reason and revelation, science and faith, immanence (God is near) and transcendence (God is beyond).[33] The result "western religion sponsors

---

[30] Resulting in the curious phenomenon, as Heidegger expressed it, "of a paradoxical presence: the nearness of things remains absent." *Poetry, Language, Thought*, 165-6.

[31] Taylor, *A Secular Age*.

[32] Material in this section is dependent on our arguments in *Missional Spirituality*.

[33] For a detailed documentation of this view, see Conrad Oswalt, *Secular Steeples*; Berger, *The Sacred Canopy*, 105-171; Schaeffer, *Escape From Reason*.

the divided worldview that allows reality to be divided into secular and sacred realms in the first place."[34]

What's left is a perceived natural (secular) world devoid of the sacred. This process of de-godding the world allowed inquirers to see the world as "objective," something neutral, and subject to empirical investigation. In this world separated from God, Reason was Queen. Transcendence and immanence grew further apart. Creation became mere nature—the realm where we work and play, not the realm of God's caring and immanent providence.[35] We lost the ability to perceive God at work in culture. We lost the ability to see and hear God at work in ordinary ways around us.

It isn't only the ubiquity and transparency of place that are problems; our seeing is conditioned by cultural and historical factors. In Plato's account of creation (Timaeus) space is pre-existent, but "place" is created.[36] The notion of place as "container," with a dynamic role in enabling a thing to be somewhere, arises with Aristotle. Later both Galileo and then Newton needed to assert the concept of infinite space, where "places were just portions of infinite space and have no value in their own right."[37] A similar process occurred among the church Fathers. In Modernity the dominant discourse has been Time and Space, and in the twentieth century the amalgam "space-time," with place a neglected cousin.

Kathleen Norris has noticed these trends, and she writes, "To be an American is to move on, as if we could outrun change. To attach oneself to place is to surrender to it, and suffer with it."[38] In a culture of expressive individualism, we aren't comfortable with this idea that our freedom is not absolute. We have to ask ourselves if our lives are better, living under the homogenization of place. Walter Brueggemann reminds us that a sense of place is to be sharply distinguished from a

---

[34] *Secular Steeples*, 15. Summarizing *The Sacred Canopy*, 110-118, 123.

[35] Hooykaas, *Religion and the Rise of Modern Science.*

[36] Ibid., 3.

[37] Ibid., 7.

[38] Norris, *The Cloister Walk*, 244.

sense of space. "Space" means an arena of freedom, without accountability, and void of authority. But "place" is space which has historical meanings. Place is space,

> where some things have happened which are now remembered and which provide continuity and identity across generations. Place is space in which important words have been spoken which have established identity, defined vocation, and envisioned destiny. Place is space in which vows have been made, and demands have been issued. Place is indeed a protest against the unpromising pursuit of space. It is a declaration that our humanness cannot be found in escape, detachment, absence of commitment and undefined freedom.[39]

Tourists or Pilgrims?

There is a certain approach to life, a particular posture, that dominates in our culture: it's the posture of the tourist. The challenge we face as followers of the Incarnate One is to move from the posture of tourist, to the posture of pilgrims.

Tourists are escaping life; pilgrims are embracing it. Tourists are trying to forget; pilgrims are trying to remember.

Tourists are looking for bargains, and aren't really SEEING at all. They are like technicians, cataloging reality as if it can be accrued in a bank balance. And they hate to be surprised.

Pilgrims love to be surprised, and are looking to *see*, to connect with something larger, something other than themselves. Charles Foster comments that, "What sets the pilgrim apart [from the tourist] is that he hopes, and at some level believes, that someone will hear his footsteps coming from afar ... and that from inside will come music that he has heard somewhere before."[40]

Sean Benesh writes of the need for churches to be developed with walkability as a key value, because we have a stake in the places we

---

[39] *The Land*, 5-6.

[40] Foster, *The Sacred Journey*, 109.

live.[41] We are less likely to be tourists where we are personally invested. Walkability "elevates the chance for investment in the local neighborhood that otherwise might be missing if the church is built and grows based upon the auto-based commuter mentality."[42] The commuter is the consumer and tourist, viewing the world through a pane of glass, and not entering into the lived story of the neighbourhoods they visit. In contrast Phil Coniseau writes, "Pilgrimage is the kind of journey ... that moves from mindless to mindful, soulless to soulful travel."[43] We can't locate ourselves, much less find ourselves, apart from the places we inhabit.

We can speak of a "geography" of the Eucharist, in that the table of the Lord incarnate invites us to inhabit the concrete particularities of this world. The pilgrim moves from place to place, and each place is unique. There is no desire to experience homogenized space. The universal place is literally U-topos, "no-place." William Cavanaugh comments on the universalizing tendencies of Modernity, where "place" was abstracted and we were lifted out of the world into the realm of ideals.

> Pre-modern representations of space marked out itineraries which told "spatial stories," for example, the illustration of the route of a pilgrimage which gave instructions on where to pray, where to spend the night, and so on. Rather than surveying them as a whole, the pilgrim moves through particular spaces, tracing a narrative through space and time by his or her movements and practices ...[44]

In contrast the tourist uses a map, and the point of view of the map user is detached and universal, with space itself rationalized and homogeneous. Place becomes space, and the pilgrim herself is detached from the world.

---

[41] Portland, Oregon, a city with 1000 neighbourhoods, uses PDX20 as a development standard. "A 20-minute community is defined as everything you need for life within a 20-minute walk." Portland Church Planting, "20- Minute Communities (PDX20)."

[42] Benesh, *Metrospiritual*, 156-157.

[43] Coniseau, *The Art of Pilgrimage*, 16.

[44] Cavanaugh. "The Church as God's Body Language," 186.

Immersed in Modernity, the church in the last generation absorbed the abstracting tendencies of the age.[45] Our knowing was disembodied, displaced knowledge, and our soteriology became inward and private, rooted outside of this world, a spiritual exchange in favor of a disembodied afterlife.[46] Why go on pilgrimage if the bushes of this world cannot burst forth in flame? Contrast Jacob's words in Genesis 28:16, "Surely the Lord is in this place, and I was not aware of it!"

The Gospel of the Kingdom

Similarly, contrast an other-worldly pietism with the rich ecclesiology of John Howard Yoder, viewing the church as the embodiment of the gospel, where the new community is not only a vehicle of the gospel but IS the good news.[47]

The good news, by definition, is "the gospel of the kingdom."[48] In the last generation, leading out from about 1950 to 2000, we recovered an understanding that the gospel Jesus preached was the good news of God's kingdom.[49] That in itself has been revolutionary, opening up trails and perspective that were largely obscured. But that gospel revolution was still set firmly within Modernity. It is only now, in this post-whatever location, with kingdom theology taking root in a new soil, that we are seeing further implications of that biblical vision.

In the last phase of that recovery, we conceived of kingdom as *reign* or rule, and understood that reign to be spiritual and universal: over all humankind, all creation, everywhere. That is a valid application of the

---

[45] Teri Merrick argues that this is a huge issue in post-colonial conversation. "Until evangelical institutions re-examine and modify the concept of objectivity permeating their speech and practice, they will continue to perpetuate the system of epistemic injustice inherited from their predecessors." In *Evangelical Postcolonial Conversations*, 108

[46] Anabaptist scholar Delbert Wiens argues that "The modern congregation is not a coherent context which can teach us how the abstracted aspects of our lives fit together to create a unified reality. It is itself an abstraction, that institution which has the function of servicing the 'spiritual' aspect of life." "Mennonite Brethren," 38-63.

[47] Yoder, "A People in the World," 91.

[48] Mark 1:14, 15.

[49] See in particular the work of George Eldon Ladd, *The Gospel of the Kingdom.*

meaning of "kingdom of God," but it overlooks the New Testament anchor: the Incarnation. The Incarnation is universal in scope—no doubt. But it was not universal as an EVENT.[50] Jesus did not appear to Caesar in Rome, or to any Romans in that day so far as we know. He was not born a Roman. His story, and his life, were placed: kingdom is both reign and realm.

The tension between the universal and particular cues us to the rich application of Trinitarian theology. Our faith has a unique capacity to hold plurality and unity together. God's self-revelation offers a dialectical movement between the universal and the particular. Particularity is not merely a tension, but a location in which to discover our rich capacity for communion. Personal space is simultaneously space for "the other," with obvious implications for politics and for human flourishing. In *Descent*, Malcolm Guite contrasts the distant and passionless Greek gods with the God who walked the dusty places of our world in Jesus:

> *You dropped down from the mountains sheer*
> *Forsook the eagle for the dove*
> *The other Gods demanded fear*
> *But you gave love*
> *Where chiseled marble seemed to freeze*
> *Their abstract and perfected form*
> *Compassion brought you to your knees*
> *Your blood was warm.*[51]

A Saturday in September

On a Saturday morning in September I bike to the Starbucks a half-mile away to meet a friend for coffee. Since our house is built into a hill there are two living levels, each opening out to gently sloping turf.

---

[50] Fitch and Holsclaw write that one of the signposts of post-Christendom is that it is post-universal. They write that "the Sent One shows us what being post-universal looks like ... not an abstraction living above the daily grind [but rather] the Word become flesh." *Prodigal Christianity*, 14.

[51] Guite, "Descent."

Access to the roadway is on the higher level, so I push my bike up the stairs ... BUMP ... BUMP ... BUMP.[52]

I reach the top of the stairs where the car is parked, and check my brakes and shifter mechanism. Then I strap on my helmet and push the bike up the driveway to the road. The change I face now is a simple one, moving downhill from the precarious perch of our home on the hillside.

The first part of the descent is fairly mild. It's a beautiful day; the sun is shining and the birds are singing. It must be around 18 C.

From the top of the hill I can see most of Kelowna and the hills across the valley, the orchards and vineyards green on the slopes. Looking to the south I can see the blue blaze of Lake Okanagan, just catching some rays. The air is clear: not much dust or haze at this time in the mid-morning.

My bike quickly picks up speed as the elevation drops. I can barely keep up with the pedals, and then I just let the bike coast. What was method becomes surrender. Change is sometimes like that; it begins slowly and then the pace increases. We can feel fear and respond with excessive control, or relax and learn to enjoy the ride. Change does involve risk, and the greater the pace the more likely we are to react in anxiety. It is our disciplines that will keep us grounded when all things about us are being shaken. Gordon Cosby comments that,

> God's dream for radical newness will require discipline... discipline that roots us in Christ, deepening our connection to God and one another. This rootedness will come from having consistent, ordered ways in which we remain open to Grace, and they will be unique to each one of us ...[53]

Our culture promotes a constant filling up, but our disciplines will draw us toward a greater emptiness, so that we can be better

---

[52] Readers who are interested in simpler modes of transportation and their impact on knowledge of place could check out Andy Crouch post here: http://www.culture-making.com/five_questions/.

[53] Bailey, "Church of the Savior," 10

prepared for obedience and, ultimately, for finding our place in God's plan—finding true relevance.[54]

In the next chapter we will hear the story of place, largely through the lens of history: the early philosophers and the church Fathers. We'll consider more deeply why "place" became mere space, and how we arrived in this cultural location where place has become largely transparent.

Then we'll consider the biblical data and work at theological foundations, starting at the beginning: Genesis. We'll look at the importance of land in relation to covenant in the Old Testament, and sketch the basics of a theology of creation. We'll consider a kingdom eschatology: the final destiny that God intends for humankind, and use kingdom as a category for weaving OT and NT together in the promise of Jesus the Messiah. Then we'll finish by considering the Incarnation and the Trinity as rooting a relational theology of place.

---

[54] Ibid.

"We were driving that morning in 1982 from the city of Xi'an. We drove through a gate in the city's rammed-earth walls and followed a paved road into the countryside. A Chinese writer drove the big car. The soil there in central China was a golden loess so fine it was clay.

"We were talking and paying scant attention to the country. What was it we were going to see today? Some emperor's tomb, the one with the clay soldiers. We parked… we made our way up some wide stairs into a low, modern museum building's entrance… and took a side door to what proved to be the whole thing.

"There, at the top of the stairs, was the world: acres and miles of open land, an arc of the planet, curving off and lighted in the distance under the morning sky.

"At my feet, and stretching off into the middle distance, I saw nothing resembling an archeological dig. I saw what looked like human bodies coming out of the earth. From the trench walls emerged an elbow here, a leg and foot there, a head and neck. Everything was the same color, the terra-cotta earth and the people: the color of plant pots.

"The earth was yielding these bodies, these clay people: it erupted them forth, it pressed them out. The same tan soil that embedded these people also made them; it grew and bore them …"

Annie Dillard[55]

---

[55] Dillard, *For the Time Being*, 14-15.

No Home Like Place

CHAPTER II

Foundations I: Culture, Creation and Covenant

Geography is simply a visible form of theology.[1]

Place has its own history, its own story, and our ability to perceive and to talk about "place" is conditioned by culture. Culture is a complex matrix of ideas and practices and beliefs. Some of these are framed in root metaphors; others are expressed and shaped by philosophical and theological systems.[2]   Matthew Crawford tells us that even when rebuilding a motorcycle, we bring our ways of seeing with us as pre-conditions that limit us. The process involves many measurements and judgments. The wear of each part must be determined by visual inspection and with special instruments. Crawford had looked again and again at a worn part and not seen the problem. Attentiveness has a certain direction to it, and "without the pertinent framework of meaning, the features in question are invisible." Once pointed out, it seemed impossible that he had not seen it before.[3]

---

[1] Levenson, *Sinai and Zion*, 116.

[2] "Culture" has been described as one of the two or three most complex words in our language.

[3] Crawford, *Shop Class as Soul Craft*, 90-91.

Our ability to perceive, to see what is there, is conditioned by previous experience and by culture, a history of seeing passed on to us in our families and via education and experience. Place is no different: it has a history, and our approach to place is conditioned both by what we bring, and by the stories attached to it.

I begin this chapter by rehearsing the story of place in broad terms in philosophy and in theology, relating the triumph of the abstract and universal "space" over place. Together we attempt to "see our seeing." Then we go to the biblical text to hear the story of creation, and consider the meaning of the *imago Dei* in relation to the mandates of God. Then we'll situate the purposes of God in land and covenant before moving to the New Testament.

The Triumph of Space

Yi-Fu Tuan writes from the point of view of human geography, and at a time (1977) when "place" was absent from the discussion. His intention is corrective, and the correction was necessary because even within this discipline, "space" was a vital and current category, while place was nearly absent. "Place" was absent in human geography? How did "space" triumph over place?

Writers like Paul Santmire and John Inge have detailed the cultural history that led to the eclipse of place in favor of "space."[4] In Plato's account of creation (Timaeus) space is pre-existent until the Demiurge converts it into defined "places."[5] Place is everlasting, and so very significant in Plato's influential cosmology.

The notion of place as "container," with a dynamic role in enabling a thing to be somewhere, arises with Aristotle. The consequence of this idea, however, was to mitigate and relativize the value of place. As a merely inert environment where things happen, things might as well happen in one container as another.[6] Later in neoplatonic thought there grew the idea of "spaceless spirit," which was later connected to the

---

[4] Inge, *A Christian Theology of Place*.

[5] Ibid., 3.

[6] Ibid., 4-5.

concept of soul. This in turn bred the conviction that our embodied relations are to be transcended and left behind, further eroding the value of place.[7]

A similar process occurred among the church Fathers. Justin Martyr and Irenaeus were well rooted in a biblical theology of creation, affirming the goodness of creation against Gnostic heresies. Moreover, both placed the Incarnation firmly at the center of God's redemptive purpose. Origen, however, took a more philosophical stance, viewing space and time as temporary, with the ultimate end of humankind a non-corporeal existence as pure spirit. Craig Bartholomew notes that, "It is hard to overemphasize the negative effect of Neoplatonism ... in terms of a positive theology of placemaking."[8]

While Augustine was influenced by Neoplatonism, like Irenaeus he retained a strong biblical anchor. Like Origen he was a philosophical theologian, but the later Augustine "was able to sense the textures and resonances of biblical faith, above all the biblical concern for history, far more adequately than Origen."[9] Augustine affirmed a new creation at the close of the age: he "historicized goodness," with the Incarnation standing decisively as the mid-point of human history.[10] Moreover, for Augustine immutability was not an abstract sameness, but a relational constancy toward all things.

Both Origen and Augustine remained influential through the Middle Ages, but the triumph of "space" over place was cemented after the death of Thomas Aquinas when the Bishop of Paris, in 1277, issued a series of condemnations seeking to suppress any teaching that limited the power of God. If God is limitless in power, then the universe at large must also be unlimited. The universal presence of God therefore required spatial infinity, and the idea of space triumphed. This created room for scientific exploration, and both Galileo and then Newton needed to assert the concept of infinite space, where "places were just

---

[7] Ibid., 5.

[8] Bartholomew, *Where Mortals Dwell*, 200.

[9] Santmire, *The Travail of Nature*, 55.

[10] Ibid., 58.

portions of infinite space and have no value in their own right."[11] Casey comments,

> In the past three centuries in the West—the period of "modernity"—place has come to be not only neglected but actively suppressed ... A discourse has emerged whose exclusive cosmological foci are Time and Space. When the two were combined by twentieth century physicists into the amalgam 'space-time,' the overlooking of place was only continued by another means. For an entire epoch, place has been regarded as an impoverished second cousin of Time and Space ...[12]

However, there remains a paradox of presence in Christian faith, expressed in the reality of the Incarnation, and followed by the empty tomb. Jesus ascends, and the particular man is gone from our world, replaced by the universal Spirit. God cannot be pinned down to a particular place, but is particular in places as God chooses to make Godself known. These are hints toward the now and not yet of the kingdom, a kingdom eschatology, with which we shall deal in the next chapter.

Creation and Imago Dei

The Genesis account grounds us in place, with Genesis 1 and 2 offering complementary accounts of God's work in creation. The sixth day, Genesis 1:26-27 has dominated our vision. On this day God makes human beings, and we discover we are made in God's image, created for a purpose.

> Then God said, "Let Us make man in Our image, according to Our likeness; and let them rule over the fish of the sea and over the birds of the sky and over the cattle and over all the earth, and over every creeping thing that creeps on the earth." God created man in His own image, in the image of God He created him; male and female He created them.

---

[11] Ibid., 7.

[12] Casey, *Getting Back Into Place*, xiv.

God blessed them; and God said to them, "Be fruitful and multiply, and fill the earth, and subdue it; and rule over the fish of the sea and over the birds of the sky and over every living thing that moves on the earth."

We are told to "subdue" and to "rule over." We'll say more about this directly. In the second account (Gen. 2:7-9, 15) we discover the manner of our making, more about our purpose, and what we share with other creatures.

Then the LORD God formed man of dust from the ground, and breathed into his nostrils the breath of life; and man became a living being. The LORD God planted a garden toward the east, in Eden; and there He placed the man whom He had formed.

Out of the ground the LORD God caused to grow every tree that is pleasing to the sight and good for food; the tree of life also in the midst of the garden, and the tree of the knowledge of good and evil.

Then the LORD God took the man and put him into the Garden of Eden to cultivate it and keep it.

Humankind, the Genesis account of creation asserts, is a species among species, fully embedded in the natural world, created not just from the same matter, but coming out of the creation itself, "dust from dust."

The text is humbling. We are made from the *adama*, the ground; we are given the same spirit of life as the other animals, and we are given the same blessing as the other animals. As Jürgen Moltmann argues, we are created both *imago Dei*, in the image of God, and *imago mundi*, in the image of the earth. We share a kinship with the rest of God's creation. We are beings in relation: first to God, and then to God's creatures. Furthermore, the other creatures are not merely dumb animals, waiting for our rule: they are blessed even before humans arrive on the scene!

This sense of participation in the larger life of creation is nearly lost to us. Our dualisms of God and world, sacred and secular, nature and super-nature, pushed God out of the world. The church separated itself from the rest of reality by locating religious activities and symbols in one sphere, and defining the rest of the world as separate and secular. What's left is a perceived natural world devoid of the sacred. Nature has become the realm where we work and play, not the realm of God's caring and immanent providence.[13]

But not every Christian tradition has taken this view. Eastern views of the Trinity are more relational, so that the participation of God in the world, and of the world in God, is mediated by the Spirit. As in Col. 1:15-17 Christ, "upholds (present tense) all things by the word of his power." Eastern Orthodoxy has been better at keeping central the abundant witness of Scripture that creation is not so much a process that God began and occasionally intervenes in. Rather, creation involves a relationship in which the whole cosmos is at every point dependent on the self-giving God whose very nature is love, involving community and relatedness. This dependence and relatedness is preserved in the Trinitarian frame of St. Patrick's breastplate, attributed to Patrick during the Celtic Christian movement of the 6th to 8th centuries.

> *I arise today*
> *Through a mighty strength, the invocation of the Trinity,*
> *Through a belief in the Threeness,*
> *Through confession of the Oneness*
> *Of the Creator of creation.*
> *I arise today*
> *Through the strength of heaven;*
> *Light of the sun,*
> *Splendor of fire,*
> *Speed of lightning,*
> *Swiftness of the wind,*
> *Depth of the sea,*
> *Stability of the earth,*
> *Firmness of the rock.*[14]

---

[13] Hooykaas, *Religion and the Rise of Modern Science.*

[14] The *Lorica*. Attributed to St. Patrick and penned circa 600 AD. Gayle Salmond penned a beautiful version of the Breastplate for the Steve Bell album, *Devotion* (Signpost Music, 2007).

This accent on God's immanence[15] mirrors the Hebrew vision we find in the Psalms, as Psalm 65: "You care for the land and water it; you enrich it abundantly. ... [T]he valleys are mantled with grain; they shout for joy and sing." Similarly in Paul's sermons to pagan peoples in Acts 14 (God "provides you with plenty of food and fills your hearts with joy") and Acts 17 (God "is not far from each of us. For in him we live and move and have our being"). This sense of God's loving, active presence pervaded all of life. All of life was sacred, and to participate in the ordinary things of life was to grow closer to God.

Much of our self-understanding in relation to creation hinges on a word and a phrase. The word is *dominion* (KJV; NASB "rule"), and the phrase is *imago Dei*. Both come loaded with the baggage of history and interpretation, therefore we need to spend a moment on each.

This word for dominion is a strong word. Ellen Davis translates *radah* as, "skilled mastery." She notes that the word suggests something like a craft or an art in our mastery.[16] Then at the end of Genesis 1, immediately after this command to exercise skilled mastery, the Lord talks about food, and His provision for food for all the creatures. Davis wonders: perhaps this is the best clue in the context to the meaning of the exercise of "skilled mastery." We are the one creature among all the creatures that is conscious that everyone has to eat.

Yet human beings are not, in the Genesis account, just a species among species because we alone among all of the creatures are made *imago Dei*, in the image of God. At times this idea has been distorted and secularized to support domination more than dominion. The current environmental problems we face, what St. Paul describes as the groaning of creation in Romans 8, demonstrate the dangers of *domination*.

A recovery of a sense of our relatedness to creation helps us move away from the detachment that leads to abuse. The Trinitarian renaissance that is under way has reinforced the turn to relationality, while also helping us to escape some of the interpretive dualism of the

---

[15] Wilkinson, "Saving Celtic Spirituality."

[16] Tippett. "Land, Life and the Poetry of Creatures."

Enlightenment, which led to secularization.[17] Part of this secularization was to conceive of the imago as an inward reality, expressed outwardly not through embodiment but through rationality.[18] Salvation, in turn, became an inward and private experience. We should note, however, that if we let *imago* rest in the text and not tradition and culture, embodiment and relationality are the horizon. God's fiat is itself relational ("let US make man") and its outcome is plural and implicitly relational ("in the image of God he created THEM").[19]

The Eastern tradition begins "with the relationality of the three divine persons, whose unity is found in the source or origin of the Father, as well as in their *perichoresis*, or mutual indwelling."[20] In John Zizioulas, relational personhood is constitutive of being: a component of essence. There is no personal identity without relationality. Van Gelder notes that the Orthodox tradition has stressed the generative, outward-reaching love (*ekstasis*) and communion of the three persons. "The Trinity is seen as a community whose orientation is outward, and whose shared love spills over beyond Godself. Moreover, the concept of *perichoresis* ... [a] dynamic, circulating movement, has offered rich analogies for human interdependence ..."[21]

The work of Zizioulas[22] reaches back to the Cappadocian fathers, who understood God's being (substance or *ousia*) as an essentially relational achievement among the three persons (*hypostasis*) of the Trinity: Father, Son, and Holy Spirit. Therefore, the unified being of the One God is only to be found in the relational communion of the three persons. Lesslie Newbigin notes that "Interpersonal relatedness belongs to the very being of God. Therefore there can be no salvation for human beings except in relatedness. No one can be made whole except by

---

[17] See the note on Charles Taylor, *The Secular Age*, in chapter one. We will return to this in later chapters.

[18] Shults, *Reforming Theological Anthropology.*

[19] Similarly, Richard Middleton in *The Liberating Image*, 55-60.

[20] Van Gelder and Zscheile, *The Missional Church in Perspective*, 103.

[21] Ibid., 105.

[22] Zizioulas, *Being as Communion.*

being restored to the wholeness of that being-in-relatedness for which God made us and the world ...."[23]

What does this mean for the *imago Dei*? It means that personhood is a relational quality. Put another way, to speak of persons we must speak of relations, and not merely being. "The Christian concept of a human person is not that of an autonomous individual, and especially that of the Western Cartesian notion of the self ... [but] the notion of a human as person-in-community."[24]

This specifically Christian ontology of the person stands in contrast to the individualistic and dualistic anthropology of the Greek philosophers. The soul was thought to be a refabricated and Godlike or spirit-like substance that was merely added to our material bodies as if it were an afterthought. In contrast, in the Incarnation the distant and invisible God comes near and is embodied, taking humankind and creation into Godself. Malcolm Guite writes in his sonnet for Epiphany:

> *Here's an epiphany to have and hold,*
> *A truth that you can taste upon the tongue,*
> *No distant shrines and canopies of gold*
> *Or ladders to be clambered rung by rung,*
> *But here and now, amidst your daily living,*
> *Where you can taste and touch and feel and see,*
> *The spring of love, the fount of all forgiving,*
> *Flows when you need it, rich, abundant, free.*[25]

In a fully Trinitarian understanding of personhood, we find that it is our embodied relationality which constitutes our being. We are, in fact, *nothing if not* for the relationships in which we exist: relationships to a people and a place. We must "reinterpret the image, not as an individually held static quality of the mind, but as a relational

---

[23] Newbigin, *The Open Secret*, 70.

[24] Hastings, *Missional Church, Missional God*, 98. A Trinitarian view of human personhood is distinct from divine personhood in that in God persons are mutually internal to one another, where humans can only know mutual interdependence and limited intimacy.

[25] Malcolm Guite, "Epiphany: The Miracle at Cana."

achievement which is constituted between others-in-relation."[26] The church is not a collection of individuals "who choose to associate in order to have their spiritual needs met," but rather "a community of mutual participation in God's own life and the life of the world."[27]

There is, then, simultaneously a recovery of a fuller view of *imago Dei* to the image of the Trinity (*imago Trinitatis*). "God's character is defined more by the quality of relational life within community than by certain abstract attributes."[28] A relational view provides a richer basis for engaging relationally in mission than the focus on imitating Jesus that tends to grow out of a focus on abstract qualities.[29]

We should also note that this relationality is mediated by the Spirit.[30] The Spirit not only hovers *over* creation, and is the breath *of* creation, but has an ongoing role in sustaining all things. Renewed arguments for a Spirit-Christology carry weight and may help us avoid the limitations of social Trinitarianism.[31]

Some interpreters argue for a functional reading of the *imago* over a substantive reading. In this approach, the text is not so much a description of the being (ontology) of humanity, as our purpose and function in the creation. Thus *imago Dei* indicates that God created humanity to represent him in ruling the world.[32] This argument has been strongly reinforced by the work of John Walton in *The Lost World*

---

[26] Stephenson, "Nature, Technology and Imago Dei," 6–12.

[27] Guder, *Missional Church*, 107. They reference John 17:21b-23.

[28] Ibid., 108.

[29] Though we may also note that a rejection of monarchical, hierarchical qualities attributed to God the Father may be premature, and rooted primarily in our current radical pluralism and egalitarianism.

[30] Pinnock, "Divine Relationality," 3-26.

[31] Karen Kilby argues that social Trinitarians turn to the concept of divine perichoresis "to name what is not understood, to name whatever it is that makes the three Persons one." The concept of perichoresis "is filled out rather suggestively with notions borrowed from our own experience of relationships and relatedness," projected onto the inner-life of the Trinity and offered back as a model for human society. "Perichoresis and Projection: Problems with Social Doctrines of the Trinity" *New Blackfriars* 81 (2000): 441-442.

[32] Middleton, *The Liberating Image*, 25-26.

of Genesis One. Walton demonstrates, through comparative ancient literature, that the Genesis creation account does not describe material origins but rather a functional *ontology*. In this account something exists only when it has a role and a purpose in an ordered system. In the first six days, God sets up a cosmos to function for human beings. The seventh day then becomes the climax of the story.

In traditional readings of Genesis, the seventh day is often treated as a theological appendix tacked on after the important details are out of the way. We devalue the seventh day because it feels to us like a footnote in a story of material creation. But a reader in the ancient East would read the Genesis account and immediately see what modern readers miss: *Deity rests in a temple, and only in a temple*. The temple was the control room from which the god exercised control of the cosmos.

Of course this is substantively different from the way we use the word "rest." The Hebrew word *sabat*, from which our word Sabbath is derived, has the sense of "ceasing." Walton uses the analogy of a presidential election, with the new president now "at rest" in the White House. In the ancient world, "rest involves engagement in the normal activities that can be carried out when stability has been achieved."[33]

Deity rests in a temple. "When Genesis indicates that God rested on the seventh day, it tells us that ... the cosmos is being portrayed as a temple."[34] Ancient temples were made functional in a seven day ceremony. On the seventh day the deity was brought in and the temple then *existed:* could function as it was designed to do. Walton writes,

> Genesis 1 is composed along the lines of a temple dedication ceremony ... The functions center on the royal and priestly roles of people, but the imagery is defined by the presence of God who has taken up his rest in the center of the cosmic temple. Through him, order is maintained, and nonfunctional disorder is held at bay—through him all things cohere.[35]

---

[33] Walton, "Creation in Genesis 1:1-2:3 and the Ancient Near East," 73. Walton references other biblical uses of the word, as in Deut. 12:10 and Josh. 21:44.

[34] Ibid., 60.

[35] Ibid., 61.

Walton's work brings out the broader *telos*, or direction, of the biblical narrative: our destiny is both kingly and concrete—to rule an earthly kingdom with Christ. More than this, however, we serve as priests in God's *earthly temple*, which is at the center of God's work in the cosmos. This sense of the world as God's temple comes out clearly in the Psalms and in Isaiah:

> Heaven is my throne,
> And the earth is my footstool.
> Where is the house you will build for me?
> Where will my resting place be?
> Has not my hand made all these things,
> and so they came into being?
> declares the Lord. (Isa. 66:1-2)

The cosmos is seen as a temple, with God resting at the center. How does this connect to place and place-making? Following the Hebrew priority on function, we are priests at work in God's temple. Place-making is more than the creation of a temporary culture: it begins here and now in the common and ordinary places of this world and extends into the kingdom of God. Moreover, if God sits at the center of his creation, then all the earth is sacred space. Walton notes, "Without God taking up his dwelling in the midst, the (cosmic) temple does not exist. The most central truth to the creation account is that this world is a place for God's presence."[36]

Imago, Land and Sabbath

From the beginning, in the first accounts of God and humankind in creation, purpose and function is at the fore. What did God create humans *to do*? The Genesis account addresses this question beginning in Genesis 1:28, "Be fruitful and multiply, and fill the earth, and subdue it; and rule over the fish of the sea and over the birds of the sky and over every living thing that moves on the earth." We noted Ellen Davis translation of dominion (*radah*) as, "skilled mastery," suggesting

---

[36] Walton, *The Lost World of Genesis One*, 83-84. Walton also notes the connection of gardens to temples in the ancient world, and particularly the imagery of Ezekiel 47.

something like a craft or an art in our work and our place-making. Now we need to notice the narrative that connects the two accounts of the creation of humankind. We read Genesis 2:2-3,

> By the seventh day God completed His work which He had done, and He rested on the seventh day from all His work which He had done.

> Then God blessed the seventh day and sanctified it, because in it He rested from all His work which God had created and made.

What's going on here? This text offers a picture of God's enthronement over the whole creation. It is the event in which the whole creation, including humans and human dominion, finds its meaning and purpose. We noted above that in the ancient world rest did not have our modern connotation but that rest represented stability achieved, and that normal activity can be resumed. Semantically, *sabat* as "ceasing," describes a transition into stability. Psalm 132 offers us a helpful picture:

> Let us go to his dwelling place;
> Let us worship at his footstool—
> "arise, O Lord, and come to your resting place,
> You and the ark of your might."

> For the Lord has chosen Zion,
> He has desired it for his dwelling:
> "This is my resting place for ever and ever;
> Here I will sit enthroned, for I have desired it." (Ps. 132:7-8, 13-14)

The Psalm pulls together the idea of divine rest, the temple, and enthronement. After creation, God takes up his rest and rules from his place of residence in the cosmos. From this place he assumes control of all things.

Therefore human dominion, the six days work to which we are called, find its pattern in God's activity, and its beginning and end in God's rest. The earth not only belongs *to* God, it is inhabited *by* God, and is a gift *from* God.[37] Our more destructive patterns reveal that we easily treat the earth as our possession rather than as the place where God rules. Walter Brueggemann notes this as Israel's perennial temptation: "Time after time … the land of promise became the land of problem,"[38] as Israel's rulers became agents of death. The issue, of course, was this: whose land is it anyway? "When the Creator God is eliminated from the question of land-creation, then the land question is characteristically resolved … on the basis of *power*, without any question about legitimacy."[39]

This role of mastery under God is revealed in two other powerful ways. First, by another mandate given in Genesis 2:15, *"Then the Lord God took the man and put him into the garden of Eden to cultivate (shamar) it and keep it."* The word *shamar* means to keep, protect, preserve, watch, and guard. Often, the word is used to talk about how God cares for humankind, as in Psalm 121. The psalm contains a beautiful expression of this idea in verses 5-8:

> The LORD is your keeper [shamar];
> The LORD is your shade on your right hand.
> The sun will not smite you by day,
> Nor the moon by night.
> The LORD will protect [shamar] you from all evil;
> He will keep [shamar] your soul.
> The LORD will guard [shamar] your going out
> and your coming in from this time forth and forever.

In Genesis 2:15, the Lord tells humanity to *shamar* the land – to watch over it, protect it, guard it, and keep it, as stewards given a trust. And then secondly, as if this were not enough, Psalm 8 clearly identifies God's role as caretaker of the earth, and humankind as his regents.

> What is man that You take thought of him,

---

[37] Thus Brueggemann, "land is a gift from Yahweh and binds Israel in new ways to the giver … Israel had land because God keeps his words." *The Land*, 47.

[38] Ibid., 11

[39] "To Whom Does the Land Belong? 2 Samuel 3:12," 29. Brueggemann notes that questions related to land are always settled with reference to power. Italics original.

And the son of man that You care for him?
Yet You have made him a little lower than God,
And You crown him with glory and majesty!
You make him to rule over the works of Your hands;
You have put all things under his feet,
All sheep and oxen,
And also the beasts of the field,
The birds of the heavens and the fish of the sea,
Whatever passes through the paths of the sea. (Ps. 8:4-8)

The exegesis of this Psalm in Hebrews 2 makes Christ the archetype for human dominion over nature. Christ is identified as the Word of God through whom all things were created. In Col.1:15-17 he "upholds (present tense) all things." We are called to participate in Christ's role as sustainer of creation. Walton notes that these roles— creator and sustainer—are less distinct than once we thought. Because Genesis 1 is not a material account of origins so much as a functional account of God's enthronement, the focus is on God's continuing work in creation.[40] God "is not only the Creator of the original state of affairs but of all present and future realities."[41] He is intimately involved in our world.

Secondly, the role of mastery is relativized by Sabbath. Sabbath requires the humility of knowing that we obtain nothing by our anxious striving. Sabbath reminds us of this by offering a full six days of labor and a seventh day to confess our failings, to seek God's wisdom, and to rest in dependence on God who rules. The accent is not on inactivity, but acknowledging that God *remains active*. Even while we sleep, God is at work. In *Living the Sabbath*, Norman Wirzba writes, "Our role as stewards or servants of creation is to actively seek to promote creation's ability to enjoy the [rest] of God, and to enable creatures to attain their potential ... [We must] give habitats and organisms the freedom and the space to be healed and restored. As we do this we will approach the

---

[40] A participatory understanding of our relationship to God opens up a much stronger view of the God-world-church relationship. See Hagley, et al., "Toward a Missional Theology of Participation," 75-87.

[41] Walton, *Lost World*, 121.

Sabbath command to 'provide for the redemption of the land' (Lev. 25:24)."[42]

In other words, as Brueggemann expresses it, "The gifted land is covenanted land. It is not only nourishing space, it is covenanted space."[43] Land comes to God's people because of God's promise, and God's promise is the entry point into covenant relationship. Brueggemann contrasts space with place in making this point: "'Space' means an arena of freedom, without coercion or accountability ... But 'place' is a very different matter. Place is space [with memory], in which important words have been spoken which ... vows have been exchanged, promises have been made, and demands have been issued."[44]

Exercising skilled mastery falls broadly under what we know as the cultural mandate: to participate with God in his work of creating. This is both a result of our sending, and a fruit of our participation in the life of God (We are "in Christ;" he dwells in us by the Spirit and by the Spirit we live in him—John 17:20-23). As we participate in the life of the Trinity God's work in caring for the world is expressed through us. Paul Stevens notes the importance of coinherence of the Trinity for every member ministry of the whole people of God:

> The Father creates, providentially sustains, and forms a covenantal framework for all existence. The Son incarnates, mediates, transfigures and redeems. The Spirit empowers and fills with God's own presence. But each shares in the other—coinheres, interpenetrates, cooperates—so that it is theologically inappropriate to stereotype the ministry of any one.[45]

Life in the covenant is a life that respects not only the words of God, but the rhythms he has set down. Our faith has always been more than belief and commitment, it has always been a way. Yet in spite of our labor saving technologies, we seem more pressed for time than

---

[42] Wirzba, *Living the Sabbath*, 151.

[43] *The Land*, 52. Italics mine.

[44] Ibid., 5

[45] Stevens, *The Other Six Days*, 57.

other more simple cultures. At issue is our attempt to commodify time.[46] We have forgotten how to live graciously in time and to receive it as a gift.[47] Eugene Peterson comments from Genesis on the invitation to enter the sacred rhythms of life in the covenant.

> The Hebrew evening/morning sequence conditions us to the rhythms of grace. We go to sleep, and God begins his work. As we sleep he develops his covenant. We wake and are called out to participate in God's creative action. We respond in faith, in work. But always grace is previous. Grace is primary ... Our work settles into the context of God's work. Human effort is honored and respected not as a thing in itself but by its integration into the rhythms of grace and blessing. We experience this grace with our bodies before we appreciate it with our minds ...[48]

Peterson's appeal is to a *practice* that embodies knowledge. We hardly know what to do with a phrase like "embodied knowledge," because in Modernity it's an oxymoron: knowing has devolved to rationality, something abstract and divorced from the world of hands and feet and work and clay. Although we are embodied creatures, *imago mundi*, and although there is no salvation apart from the body (the Incarnation and resurrection), we still tend to conceive of salvation through the lens of Greek wisdom more than the biblical and Hebraic worldview.

So the word of God comes to us in surprising ways, to remind us that salvation is offered only to embodied creatures, and only as a gift. As embodied creatures, we are invited into a living rhythm, a rhythm in place, with body and soul. The Biblical doctrine of creation provides a cadence of daily life that is formative for human community. The rhythm of ecclesial life—in, and out, gathering, and being sent, community and mission, work and rest—is one of the primary means by which these rhythms are counted out and help to shape the community. This can also be true of the yearly rhythms of celebration

---

[46] Jacobsen, "Redeeming Civic Life in the Commons," 41.

[47] See also the rich description of gift in Gregory Walter's book, *Being Promised.*

[48] Peterson, *Working the Angles*, 69-70.

and remembrance, from Advent to Christmas and lent to Easter, followed by a stretch of ordinary time.

One of the most important aspects of creational place making, then, is respecting rhythms of work and rest. Sabbath rest illumines the reality that God creates and sustains, is actively enthroned above, and all life, both human and nonhuman, is a gift. Our vocation is that of stewards. This sense of vocation is a fundamentally different way of remembering our landscapes and our places, and it encourages a very different imagination for their future. We are reminded that place has *telos*. Richard Lowery puts it this way: "Creation climaxes and finally coheres in Sabbath rest. It is the glue that holds the world together."[49]

Land and Covenant

Kingdom, land and covenant are intimately connected. God's purpose in making and renewing creation begins with his work in making covenant. Craig Bartholomew offers that the covenant frame is so critical to biblical thought that it is a means of escaping Christian dualism.[50] In Genesis we read:

> Now the Lord said to Abram,
> "Go forth from your country, and from your relatives
> and from your father's house, to the land which I will show you ...
> (Gen. 12:1)

> The Lord appeared to Abram and said,
> "To your descendants I will give this land."
> So he built an altar there
> to the Lord who had appeared to him. (Gen. 12:7)

In making covenant, God promises a place and creates a people. Covenant sets the foundation for God's formative work in creating a people to show his glory, and it sets the foundation within the church

---

[49] Lowery, *Sabbath and Jubilee*, 82. He writes, "Sabbath is the final piece of the creative process by which the world comes into being. It is the crowning touch, the cosmic sign that God's universal and benevolent dominion is fully extended and secure."

[50] Bartholomew. "Covenant and Creation," 32.

for our relationships one to another. We are a people because of what God has done in history and in place. Walter Brueggemann writes, "Land is always fully historical but always bearer of over-pluses of meaning known only to those who lose and yearn for it."[51]

A rich connection to place is part of our creational identity: we are embodied beings and we yearn for roots. In our hectic and mobile and fragmented culture, and in a time when our cultural ideals of freedom disavow our need for roots and encourage rootlessness, our hunger and sense of dis-placement is only more acute. Add to this the universalizing and abstracting tendencies of Modernity, and "the yearning to belong somewhere ... is a deep and moving pursuit. Loss of place and yearning for place are dominant images."[52] Brueggemann notes that,

> Land is a central, if not THE central theme of biblical faith. Biblical faith is a pursuit of historical belonging that includes a sense of destiny derived from such belonging... [and yet] the dominant categories of biblical theology have been either existentialist or 'mighty deeds of God in history' formulations. [But] it is *rootlessness* not *meaninglessness* which characterizes the current crisis. There are no meanings apart from roots. And such rootage is a primary concern of Israel and a central promise of God to his people.[53]

God's promises come to Israel, and then to us, through a series of covenants. Covenant is one of the most prominent themes in the Old Testament. From Genesis through the prophets, God is displayed as one who is wedded in covenant love to all that he created. One of the most prominent covenants is the Deuteronomic covenant with Israel:

> Now this is the commandment, the statutes and the judgments which the LORD your God has commanded me to teach you, that you might do them **in the land** where you are going over to possess it, so that you and your son and your grandson might fear the

---

[51] *The Land*, 3-4.

[52] Pohl, *Living Into Community*.

[53] *The Land*, 3-4.

LORD your God, to keep all His statutes and His commandments which I command you, all the days of your life, and that your days may be prolonged. O Israel, you should listen and be careful to do it, that it may be well with you and that you may multiply greatly, just as the LORD, the God of your fathers, has promised you, **in a land** flowing with milk and honey. "Hear, O Israel! The LORD is our God, the LORD is one. You shall love the LORD your God with all your heart and with all your soul and with all your might." (Deut. 6:1-5)

The latter words, what we call the "Great Commandment," occur prominently in three of the four gospels. What is often missed is the context: the command is rooted in place—*in the land*. "Land" occurs twice before the great commandment, and five times after it in Deuteronomy 6. The promise to Israel specifically takes shape around the land, and the blessing grows out of the land: milk and honey—a promise of fruitfulness and prosperity—of *shalom*. Brueggemann helps us make sense of the context, in words that evoke richness of placement and practice.

> Love of God correlates with occupation of land; consequently, *love of God* means to *order the land* in ways that are congruent with YHWH's character; this character, we know everywhere in Scripture, is marked by mercy, graciousness, steadfast love, compassion, fidelity, generosity, and forgiveness.
>
> And of course if we characterize the proper ordering of land in such covenantal ways, it follows that the way we may "love God" in land-as-creation is to love neighbor, for finally we have no other way to love God (1 John 4:20-21). Thus our love of God is to order the land for the sake of the common good.[54]

We don't readily connect loving God to such concrete practices, and certainly not to place, and these are legacies of dualism, our tendency to spiritualization, as well as to the romanticized notion of love. We'll explore this notion of the "common good" in chapter five.

---

[54] Brueggemann, "To Whom ... Belong?" 30. Italics original.

Meanwhile, we note that the ancient word for covenant is *berîth*, and in place of our romantic notions of love the biblical practice is *hesed*.

The Hebrew word for covenant is *berîth*. While not certain in its etymology, *berîth* may derive from *bârâ*, meaning "to eat." This makes sense, because the phrase for "making a covenant" is *kârat berîth*; literally "cutting a covenant." The ancient Semitic ritual involved cutting a sacrificial animal in two halves and the covenant parties then pass between the halves. The common meal which usually followed made use of the sacrificed meat. A covenant was a physical and spiritual life-bond, the bringing together of two separate bodies and all that they represented into a new unified whole.[55] (This becomes the background of the Eucharistic meal, an important element of our discussion that we will approach in chapter 4.) Shalom and *berîth* are practically synonymous. "Shalom refers to the state of those who participate in the harmonious society. *Berîth* refers to the community and all the privileges and obligations that community implies. Covenant and shalom go hand in hand; God's community must have one to experience the other."[56]

A second critical word is *hesed*. Mounce's *Expository Dictionary* describes the meaning: "*hesed*" is one of the richest, most theologically insightful terms in the OT. It denotes "kindness, love, loyalty, mercy ... *Hesed* describes the special relationship God has with his covenantal people ..."[57] Mounce describes *hesed* as defining God's rule: "Righteousness and justice are the foundation of your throne; steadfast love (*hesed*) and faithfulness go before you" (Ps. 89:14).[58]

Why covenant with humankind, who demonstrated our rebellious nature in the garden? God longs to restore the broken relationship. He created us, male and female, in his image, and sin has distorted that image and placed our future in jeopardy. In redemption God reveals to the world his love and faithfulness as we are restored to wholeness. God

---

[55] In Genesis 15:7-21 the animals are cut in two and a smoking fire pot and torch pass between them.

[56] Stock, et al., *Inhabiting the Church*, 112.

[57] Mounce, *Mounce's Expository Dictionary of Old and New Testament Words*, 426.

[58] Ibid.

is on a mission to rebuild what was lost, and his method of choice is covenant. Through the agency of a people, God then reaches out to all humanity and every place.[59]

"For in the gospel the righteousness of God is revealed—a righteousness that is by faith" (Ro. 1:17). We filter these concepts through our cultural context, and justice becomes something we find in a court of law. But the prophets intended something different, and justice referred to the fulfillment of responsibilities that rose out of particular relationships within the covenant community.[60] Anderson writes, "Each relationship has its specific obligation, and all relationships ultimately are bound by relationship to God ... When the demands of various relationships are fulfilled, justice or righteousness prevails and there is shalom, 'peace' or 'welfare.'"[61]

Yahweh's covenant love, or *hesed*, was expressed through steadfast love and loyalty. Similarly, our response is to be faithfulness, obedience, and justice. Our obligations to Yahweh are to be manifest in every relationship: to people and to place.[62]

Sabbath and Shalom

> *The mind that comes to rest*
> *is tended in ways it cannot intend;*
> *Is borne, preserved, and comprehended*
> *by what it cannot comprehend.*
> *Your Sabbath, Lord, thus keeps us*
> *by your will, not ours. And it is fit*
> *Our only choice should be to die*
> *Into that rest, or out of it.*[63]

---

[59] This idea of a mediating priesthood to the nations is picked up in 1 Peter 2: 9-10.

[60] Anderson. *The Eighth-Century Prophets*, 43.

[61] Ibid.

[62] But doesn't this connote a loss of freedom? Every time we make a commitment, our choice of one thing excludes something else. True freedom always occurs within a particular form.

[63] Berry, "Sabbath."

The motto of the Hasidic movement was "serve God with joy," taken literally from the Psalms. In John 15:11 Jesus says to the disciples, "These things I have spoken to you that my joy might be in you, and your joy may be full."

For the Hasids, the day of greatest joy was the Sabbath. On this day God assumed the throne, and delighted in his creation. God's kingdom and shalom were established. Sabbath may be a critical practice for the church on mission, connecting God's covenant with people and place. Sabbath illumines the reality that life, both human and nonhuman, is a gift, and it encourages a new imagination for their future. Place has *telos*: "Creation climaxes and finally coheres in Sabbath rest. It is the glue that holds the world together."[64] Sabbath,

- gets the rhythm of work and rest into our very bones;
- is present-future, reminding us that the end is the Kingdom of shalom;
- is an act of memory and identity—we are more than our actions;
- embraces the paradox of the kingdom—when we rest God acts, the kingdom is a gift;
- is rooted in a theology of creation, embracing people and place.

But some will ask, why does the word "covenant" appear so rarely in the New Testament? And why is the connection to land muted into the background, or absent entirely? What has happened to the promise of land? Does the New Testament support an other-worldly spirituality after all, as so many appear to believe? How important is eschatology to the theological meaning of place? To these issues we now turn. Alan Roxburgh reminds us that God in Christ, "breaks into creation in order to call forth that which was promised from the beginning—that in this Jesus all things will be brought back together and made new."[65]

---

[64] Lowery, *Sabbath and Jubilee*, 82. "Sabbath is the final piece of the creative process by which the world comes into being. It is the crowning touch, the cosmic sign that God's universal and benevolent dominion is fully extended and secure."

[65] Roxburgh, "What is Missional Church?" 4.

For many years now my walks have taken me down an old
fencerow in a wooded hollow on what was once my grandfather's farm.
A battered galvanized bucket is hanging on a fence post near the head
of the hollow, and I never go by it without stopping to look inside.

For what is going on in that bucket is the most momentous thing I
know, the greatest miracle that I have ever heard of: it is making earth.
The old bucket has hung there through many autumns, and the leaves
have fallen around it and some have fallen into it. Rain and snow have
fallen into it, and the fallen leaves have held
the moisture and so have rotted.

Nuts have fallen into it, or been carried into it by squirrels ... This
slow work of growth and death, gravity and decay, which is the chief
work of the world, has by now produced in the bottom of the bucket
several inches of black humus. I look into that bucket with fascination
because I am a farmer of sorts and an artist of sorts, and I recognize
there an artistry and a farming far superior to mine,
or to that of any human.

It collects stories, too, as they fall through time. It is irresistibly
metaphorical. It is doing in a passive way what a human community
must do actively and thoughtfully. A human community, too, must
collect leaves and stories, and turn them to account. It must build soil,
and build that memory of itself—in lore and story and song—that will
be its culture. These two kinds of accumulation, of local soil and local
culture, are intimately related.

Wendell Berry[66]

---

[66] Berry, "On Work."

Creation waits now for the gardener to speak:
And the eager weeds await their release
From the bondage of being weeds.
Eden and Zion lie far apart
But atom and ocean, beasts and plants
Wait for the one who will grant them peace.[67]

---

[67] Wilkinson, "Imago Mundi."

No Home Like Place

CHAPTER III

Foundations II: The New Testament and Eschatology

He is not the high who stands over against the low, but is the infinite act of existence that gives high and low a place.[1]

Why is there so little mention of covenant in the New Testament? Only the book of Hebrews develops the idea at all. The rarity of occurrence of the word "covenant" in the New Testament would seem to add fuel to the fire of those who assert the irrelevance of covenant for the life of the believer. Similar questions can be raised for the issue of land. The word doesn't really appear, so we could conclude it's irrelevant. Are we indeed on a new spiritual footing in the New Testament, where the concerns of the kingdom are divorced from life in this world?

This would be a hasty conclusion, because it is clear in the gospels of Luke and John that Jesus is "the prophet like Moses," to whom all must listen or die. That matters, because Moses was the prophet of the land of Promise. It would also be hasty because it is evident in the new perspectives on Paul that "righteousness" had a different meaning than that assumed by Martin Luther. When Paul uses this word he has a

---

[1] Hart, *The Beauty of the Infinite*.

covenantal framework in mind.[2] That's significant, because the biblical idea of covenant is meaningless apart from the land.

The idea of covenant is intrinsic to the New Testament. Apart from a covenantal perspective and disconnected from the exodus event, many passages of Paul make no sense. Why does Paul talk about baptism in chapter six of Romans? Paul understood baptism in terms of a new exodus. He had already made this link in 1 Cor. 10:2, speaking of the wilderness generation being "baptized into Moses in the cloud and in the sea." Paul brings out the parallel between the experience of Israel and that of Christians, the new exodus people, and then stresses the obligations as a result.

While it is an argument from silence, could it be that covenantal language is submerged in Paul and the New Testament writers because it was so fundamental to their thought? Could it have been the very air they breathe? In the gospels, Jesus' reference to the covenant occurs in the context of the last supper. Jesus said, 'This is my blood of the covenant' (Mk. 14:24). It's interesting to reflect that Mark does not supply an interpretation. Instead, he clearly assumes that the disciples— and we later readers—would understand Jesus' meaning. Covenant language assumes a whole history of God's dealing with his people: promise and deliverance. Moreover, it assumes an understanding of the sacrificial system, with Jesus taking on the role of the sacrificial lamb who is slain in our stead.

Similar questions apply to "land." Do God's people still have a "landed" inheritance? Have we moved from a concrete and historical spirituality in the Old Testament, to a spiritualized, other-worldly goal in Christ? Is the Resurrection significant only in its demonstration of the atonement, or is the Resurrection indeed the first-fruits of all creation, intended for a new and physical life in an earthly kingdom under God's rule?[3]

---

[2] Wright, *Romans and the Theology of Paul*, 30-67.

[3] Hjalmarson, "Which Atonement?"

The New Testament and Land

A Boyd Luter argues that God's promise to Israel, his covenant with them, includes a literal return to the land. My interest here is not in any particular eschatological system, but in establishing that land and covenant remain important themes for God's people. Luter makes this argument by connecting Rev. 11:1-13 with Romans 11:25-27.

> I do not want you to be ignorant of this mystery,
> brothers and sisters, so that you may not
> think you are superior: Israel has experienced a
> hardening in part until the full number of the
> Gentiles has come in, and in this way all Israel
> will be saved. As it is written:
>
> "The deliverer will come from Zion;
> he will turn godlessness away from Jacob.
> And this is my covenant with them
> when I take away their sins." (Rom. 11:25-27)

Luter argues that the text Paul cites in verses 26b-27a is Isa 59:20-21a, and verse 27b is echoing concepts in Jer. 31:31-34.[4] For my purpose, the use of Jeremiah 31 here is the more significant. Jer. 31:31-34 is the only location in the Hebrew Bible of the phrase, "new covenant." Luter notes that most of the context of Jeremiah's prophecy of the new covenant focuses on the people of Israel. He continues,

> However, the same wording that begins that wondrous passage in verse 31 ("Look, the days are coming ...") shortly thereafter brings directly into play the land aspect of the new promise (vv. 38-40; note especially the end of v. 40). Here we begin to get the sense as to how the ongoing land promise functions in regard to the new covenant: as what I call a "covenant backdrop."[5]

---

[4] Luter, "The Land as Covenant Backdrop," 65.

[5] Ibid., 67.

He then asks, "Is there a legitimate biblical basis for Israel currently being in the land of Palestine?"[6] From here Luter will argue that Ezekiel 36-37 contain the most directly relevant passages to this issue. Ezekiel 36-37, written roughly ten years after Jeremiah 31, is the parallel passage.

One of the major ways Jeremiah 31 contrasts the new covenant with the previous one the Lord made with Israel coming out of Egypt (v. 32) is by his declaration, "I will put my teaching within them and write it on their hearts" (v. 33). But the continuity with the original covenant is equally important. The passage in question closes like this:

> "Behold, days are coming," declares the LORD, "when the city will be rebuilt for the LORD from the Tower of Hananel to the Corner Gate. The measuring line will go out farther straight ahead to the hill Gareb; then it will turn to Goah. And the whole valley of the dead bodies and of the ashes, and all the fields as far as the brook Kidron, to the corner of the Horse Gate toward the east, shall be holy to the LORD; it will not be plucked up or overthrown anymore forever."

These are astonishing words, for those of us who have been taught to consider only a spiritual implication for the New Covenant.[7] Here in Jer. 31 the promise includes being *rooted in the land*, and the city rebuilt. Luter similarly comments on the parallel passage in Ezekiel 37: "the vision in Ezekiel 37 does not allow the reader to think of this spiritual rebirth for Israel without bringing the land into play. In 36:24, the Lord promises, 'I will take you *from the nations* and gather you from all the countries, and will bring you *into your own land*.'"[8] Following this is the promise of the new heart and new spirit.

This reminder of the shape of the covenant as it applies to land, then, is not merely a historical note, but a call which should ring in our ears today. We only know ourselves rightly when we first know our

---

[6] Ibid., 70.

[7] In the next chapter we'll consider two divergent movements in creation theology under the motifs of ascent—the spiritual motif—versus fecundity—the ecological motif.

[8] Ibid., 71. Italics original.

God. And we only know Him rightly when we know Him as the sovereign Lord of all creation, and then receive the place God gives as gift. In other words, as Brueggemann expresses it, "The gifted land is covenanted land. It is not only nourishing space, it is covenanted space."[9]

To know ourselves rightly, the memory of the promise should always be before us. The shape of the covenant has not changed: God, people, place. But the promises of God are subverted by our loss of memory, and by our rootlessness. Again and again in Scripture, one of the fundamental rhythms is that of remembrance.

In our time we have lost our sense of identity because we have lost our sense of place. We have lost our sense of place because we have lost our immersion in the ongoing story of God in history. Sometimes we lose that place because we are separated from deep community, the kind of belonging, sharing, and mutual encouragement we all need. But mobility and abstraction are fragmenting forces not only to people but to *place*. Through re-telling the stories of Israel, and through remembering our own stories and how they are placed, we can reconnect with the covenanting God.

In Scripture we are constantly reminded of our identity as a *covenant people*. We find ourselves today entering a new, post-Christendom location, an experience that has been rightly compared to Israel in exile in Babylon.[10] In times of exile we face the unique danger of loss of memory and loss of community. In that void, we are apt to believe the promises of the Empire to give us a home, to bring us security, to provide meaning and to offer unlimited consumption in an eternal Now.[11] Who needs memory when life is so good today? Who needs community when we have everything we need? Yet the cost of such satiation is high, and it is recorded in scars on the face of the

---

[9] Brueggemann, "To Whom Does the Land Belong?" 52.

[10] Notably by Walter Brueggemann and Stuart Murray Williams. Murray defines Post-Christendom as "the culture that emerges as the Christian faith loses coherence within a society that has been definitively shaped by the Christian story and as the institutions that have been developed to express Christian convictions decline in influence." He also warns that this is not equivalent to secularization. "The End of Christendom," 6.

[11] See in particular the work of Walter Brueggemann in *Cadences of Home*.

earth, and in climbing cancer rates, spontaneous abortions and still births. Brazilians destroy massive tracts of Amazonia because it somehow represents for them the hope of a prosperous future. The forests of British Columbia fall for similar reasons. Overfishing, James Bay, toxic waste, ruptured pipelines and the irretrievable loss of one hundred species a day: the welfare of the entire world hinges upon the land, but somehow the more immediate concerns about jobs and profits take precedence. In Chief Seathl's words, we "kidnap the earth from our children."[12]

Elmer Martens points out that land has four theological dimensions: as promise, gift, blessing, and in relation to a specific life-style.[13] Under this latter heading follow the questions of Sabbath and Jubilee. From Mt. Sinai had come these words: "When you come into the land which I shall give you, the land shall keep a Sabbath unto the LORD" (Lv.25:2). This portion of Leviticus describes the year of Jubilee, which occurs after seven sets of seven complete years are finished. This fiftieth "liberty" year is proclaimed with the sound of a trumpet on the Day of Atonement, so that all may know that this holy period has begun.

> The LORD then spoke to Moses at Mount Sinai, saying,
> "Speak to the sons of Israel and say to them,
> 'When you come into the land which I shall give you,
> then the land shall have a sabbath to the LORD.
> 'Six years you shall sow your field,
> and six years you shall prune your vineyard and gather in its crop,
> but during the seventh year the land shall have a sabbath rest,
> a sabbath to the LORD;
> you shall not sow your field nor prune your vineyard.
> 'Your harvest's aftergrowth you shall not reap,
> and your grapes of untrimmed vines you shall not gather;
> the land shall have a sabbatical year.'" (Lev. 25:1-5)

The text which follows points up two purposes: a religious one--to witness to God's ownership; and a humanitarian one--that the poor of

---

[12] Attributed to Chief Seathl of the Duwamish people, approximately 1852.

[13] Martens, *God's Design.*

the people may eat. Some scholars argue that Deut. 15:1-3 couples a regulation about the release of all debts every seven years to the land's rest. Richard Austin in *Hope for the Land* writes that,

> those who manage land are tempted to create a sabbathless society in which land is never rested, debts are never cancelled, slaves are never released ... and all of life can be reduced to a smoothly functioning machine. The powerful must resist this temptation, stop managing, and relax in openness to their community; then concerns for equity, justice, and mercy may come to the fore.[14]

That land is real and spatially definable points to the wholeness and value of life in this world. Quality of life is all-embracing: relating to Yahweh, neighbor, and the environment. The promise of land and all that it signifies keeps God's design firmly rooted in the world, and leads us to see the wholeness of the call to discipleship in the New Testament.

Incarnation, Resurrection and the Coming Kingdom

The importance of place is seen in the New Testament, first with the centrality of Jerusalem, and then secondly in that God promises to create not only a new heaven, but a new earth. The prayer that Jesus teaches his disciples is not that they experience a heavenly kingdom, but that they will join God in his work of making heaven on earth: "May your kingdom come, may your will be done on earth as it is in heaven."[15]

John Inge begins his survey of New Testament material with reference to the monumental study by W. D. Davies, *The Gospel and the Land.* Davies' survey is exhaustive, but for our purposes we need note only a few points. Davies maintains that Paul has no interest in land in relation to God's promises. God's promise is now for all people in all places. He notes that Paul does not reject the significance of the Temple, but relativizes it in view of the dwelling of the Spirit in the

---

[14] Austin, *Hope for the Land.*

[15] See in particular Middleton, "A New Heaven and A New Earth," 73-97.

church. Similarly, Davies relativizes the place of Jerusalem. With reference to Paul, he writes that, "Theologically, he no longer had need of it [Jerusalem]; his geographical identity was subordinated to that of 'being in Christ ...' Paul had been set free from the Law, and therefore, from the land."[16] Davies does note, however, that Jerusalem is central in Luke's gospel, appearing twice more than in any other gospel. When Davies arrives at the fourth gospel, he argues that John maintains that the temple is transcended by Christ. He summarizes,

> Our discussion of the fourth gospel drives us back to the beginning of the gospel to 1:14 where the flesh of Jesus of Nazareth is said to be the seat of the Logos. That Logos, whether as Wisdom or as Torah, is no longer attached to a land, as was the Torah, but to a person who came to his own land, and was not received ...[17]

The thrust of Davies work is that land is no longer important in the New Testament. Land is only important as a backdrop, a setting: Christianity transcends land, Jerusalem and the Temple even though our history demands attention to these things.

Is this the only conclusion we can come to, or is there another way to reconcile Christ and place?

The Nicene Fathers abandoned an Aristotelian view of place, as noted in chapter one. In considering the Incarnation, they were forced to see that place is more than merely a setting in God's work in the world: place is the seat of relations, of meeting and activity between God and humanity. Torrance comments that, "the incarnation does not mean that God is limited by space and time, it asserts the reality of space and time in the actuality of His relations with us ... God can no more contract out of space and time than he can go back on the Incarnation."[18] (Torrance does not work at distinguishing "space" and place, and uses place in the sense of particular places, not in the universal sense so common post Enlightenment.)

-----

[16] Inge, *A Christian Theology of Place*, 48.

[17] Ibid., 50.

[18] Torrance, *Space, Time and Incarnation*, 67.

Even where the Incarnation is understood as an affirmation of embodiment, it has sometimes been understood as a *devaluing* of place toward the universal and spiritual. But the Incarnation is more than a radical entry into materiality, it is a radical affirmation of the *particular*. Malcolm Guite reminds us,

> *Where chiseled marble seemed to freeze*
> *Their abstract and perfected form*
> *Compassion brought you to your knees*
> *Your blood was warm*
> *They sought to soar into the skies*
> *Those classic gods of high renown*
> *For lofty pride aspires to rise*
> *But you came down.*[19]

Not an affirmation of an abstract ideal, God came down—God meets us and makes Godself known—in place. "The intelligibility [of the Word] ... communicates itself in the particular ... and yet without prejudice to his universal processes of love. The phrase, 'Universal love,' expresses the ultimate paradox ... for love is not universal but particular, intimate and selective,"[20] writes O'Donovan. As carriers of the Incarnation, we love particular people and particular places as Christ-ones. The Church, Jesus body in the world, is itself a resolution of the tension between the universal and the particular. We'll explore this affirmation in chapter four in a sacramental approach to place.

While the tension between the particular and universal remains, the Incarnation supplies continuity between the Old Testament and New Testament narratives. Walter Brueggemann reminds us of the connection:

> In the Old Testament ... place ... has meaning because of the history lodged there. There are stories which have authority because they are located in a place. This means that biblical faith cannot be presented simply as an historical movement indifferent to place which could have happened in one setting as well as another,

---

[19] Guite, "Descent."

[20] O'Donovan, "The Loss of a Sense of Place," 53.

because it is undeniably fixed in this place with this meaning. And for all its apparent "spiritualizing," the New Testament does not escape this rootage.[21]

These roots are on display from Jesus to Paul, and in particular in the expectations of a coming age that is both continuous, and discontinuous with the present age. Manson has commented on the early Christian perspective that it, "does not cut out the earth, or bypass it in process, but takes the world and history up into itself ... New Heavens and a New Earth signify not the final destruction or displacement of the cosmos, but its [renewal]."[22] Paul in Romans 8 speaks about the groaning of the creation and anticipates its emancipation, culminating in a new heavens and new earth. The frame in which Paul's anticipation is set is his understanding of the death and resurrection of Jesus. Paul is not so much interested in speculative timetables as he is determined to show the meaning of the lordship of Christ in the concrete, lived experience of the church in history.

> *Fruit will burgeon from scattered seeds*
> *And garden and town be clean as a fleece*
> *Early in the morning, on the first day of the week.*[23]

Thus when we return to the book of Ephesians, the heart of the Pauline letters, God is shown as having a plan for the whole universe, revealed and fulfilled in Christ. His plan is to "unite all things in him, things in heaven and things on earth" (1:10). There is no comparable cosmology in the ancient world, and no comparable vision of a movement uniting the two spheres of heaven and earth.

Moreover, this theme is nourished by Old Testament narratives, especially themes found in the Royal Psalms. These psalms depict the universal reign of Yahweh and envision the ascent of the divine King to the heavenly throne so that he might rule over, and fill, all things.

---

[21] Brueggemann, *The Land*, 185.

[22] Manson, in *Eschatology: Scottish Journal of Theology Occasional Papers*, 11.

[23] Wilkinson, "Imago Mundi," 10.

God has ascended with a shout,
The LORD, with the sound of a trumpet.
Sing praises to God, sing praises;
Sing praises to our King, sing praises.
For God is the King of all the earth;
Sing praises with a skillful psalm.
God reigns over the nations,
God sits on His holy throne.
The princes of the people have
assembled themselves as the people of
the God of Abraham, For the shields of
the earth belong to God; He is highly exalted. (Ps. 47:5-9)

It is Jesus ascent to the heavenly throne that Paul has in view in Ephesians 4, based on Psalm 68, another Royal psalm. The theme of divine rule connects us back to the covenant promises of the Old Testament. So much are these theological threads connected that, "Covenant and kingdom are like two sides of a single coin. Accordingly, we may say that in creation God covenanted with a view toward the coming of his kingdom ... Similarly, in the beginning God created his kingdom—'the heavens and the earth', the realm over which he rules."[24]

In contrast to the work of Teilhard de Chardin, Paul's vision is not that of a spiritual evolution, of the unity of all things in Christ spiritually, but rather the fulfillment of God's promises on earth. The final consummation is both visible and physical. The Resurrection itself tells us that there is renewal and continuity with the old world. Jacques Ellul writes, "For even in the resurrection, God does not shatter men's hopes. Rather, he fulfills them there ... And all this happens in the New Jerusalem, so as to forever link man's work with Christ's ... Man's version of the incarnation finds an eternal home."[25]

Jerusalem and the Temple

When believers consider questions of place, they tend to concentrate on Jerusalem, the Temple and the Holy Land. Both Peter

---

[24] Spykman, quoted in Craig Bartholomew, "Covenant and Creation," 15.

[25] Ellul, *The Meaning of the City*, 177.

Walker and N.T. Wright have considered these questions extensively, and both acknowledge the physical and symbolic power of Jerusalem and the Temple. The question of the meaning and destiny of the Holy Land is complex, and highly politicized. Here my interest is restricted to Jerusalem and the Temple and their meaning in relation to place.

The Temple comes to the fore in the familiar story of Jesus with the Samaritan woman, and the setting is Jacob's well in John 4. In this story Jesus not only affirms the centrality of Jerusalem, he then tells the woman that, "a time is coming and now is, when neither here nor in Jerusalem you will worship the Father." Have we therefore disposed of the temple, so that it is now irrelevant to Christian life in this world?

Walker rightly maintains that the arrival of Jesus changed the status of both Jerusalem and the Temple.[26] There is a consensus among NT scholars that Jesus is the new Temple, the new meeting place of heaven and earth.[27] By extension, this dwelling is now in the church (1 Peter 2). In Revelations we read that the New Jerusalem has no temple because, "the Lord God Almighty and the Lamb are its temple" (21:22). How then do we hear Jesus words to the woman at the well?

Jesus statements to the Samaritan woman are not denigrating the place of Samaritan worship or the Jerusalem Temple but *rather challenge the attachment of ethnic identity to those places*. Tod Swanson notes that the memory of Jacob providing this well, plus its utilization by his descendants for years to follow, rendered it a sacred place in the woman's mind.[28] By drinking water from this well, the Samaritans connected themselves to their heritage, and to Jacob in particular. Swanson argues that by asking for a drink from this well, Jesus challenged one particular allegiance; he was not making place irrelevant.

However, we must also reckon with Walton's work on Genesis 1 and the theme of cosmic temple inauguration. What is more holy than the temple? Answer: the God who occupies it. But the literature of the

---

[26] Walker, "Centre Stage," 1.

[27] Wright, *How God Became King*, 236.

[28] Swanson, "To Prepare a Place," 250.

Intertestamental period demonstrates that the Jews are grieving the loss of God's voice and of God's presence: there has been no new Scripture in four hundred years. NT Wright helps us to make the connection between OT and NT with what happened next.

> When Solomon built the Temple and dedicated it, it was filled with the cloud which veiled God's presence. The priests couldn't stand there, because God's glory filled the whole house. Ezekiel's vision of the restored Temple climaxes in the glory of the Lord returning to the house, sweeping in from the east with the sound of many waters, illuminating all the earth with its glory. Many, many first-century Jews, though continuing to worship in the Jerusalem Temple, lamented the fact that this still hadn't happened. The Temple seemed a place of memory and imagination rather than the vivid reality spoken of by the prophets.[29]

Yet the promise of Malachi 3:1 was, "The Lord, whom you seek, will suddenly come to his temple." This Jesus accomplishes literally in a dramatic visit. But Walton's work makes it clear that there is another layer. The wider frame is the cosmic temple, and the rule of God over all creation. *With Jesus coming, the Lord has occupied his temple.* This is a fundamental meaning of the Incarnation. Jesus testimony to the woman at the well, therefore, is a recognition of the relative nature of any building or location *in view of the Christ in her presence.* The temple is creation and the Deity sits before her. *She is already in the most holy place.*

This narrative, therefore, doesn't address the question we have asked of it. There may still be a role for temples, and by extension, for sacred places. The tension here is that Christ is not everywhere present until the sending of the Spirit; this narrative occurs prior to Pentecost. This conversation occurs at a specific location in the salvation story, and we will return to the relevance of the temple in chapter six.

What then of Jerusalem? N.T. Wright argues that much of Galatians is about Jerusalem. Jerusalem is the place where the Torah has kept Israel firmly anchored to her racial and national identity, and it is for this reason that God will disperse the young church and focus her vision on a Jerusalem yet to come. There is a "Jerusalem above," and

---

[29] Wright, "New Law, New Temple, New World," 3.

although there are only two references to this theme in the New Testament (Heb. 12:22 and Rev. 21:2), that Paul "casually introduces it here implies that already in the early church there was a well-established idea of an alternative city, a city 'to come.' Which God would bring to birth at its proper time."[30]

Wright notes that this is not a Platonic "idea" of Jerusalem, of some non-material reality, but rather, "heaven in both Old and New Testaments is ... the place of God's present and future reality."[31] While heaven is truly God's realm, it's not a remote dimension hopelessly removed from human reality. In the ancient Judaic worldview the two dimensions intersect and overlap so that the divine bleeds over into this world. The "heavenly" is that which God intends to bring to birth on earth, and the city "which he has prepared for them is not simply a 'mansion in the sky,' but a human community of the redeemed in the coming Kingdom. The present Jerusalem belongs to the created places that will be shaken; the new community is of the order that cannot be shaken.[32]

The final destiny of believers, therefore, is not divorced from place.[33] Our final destiny is not a disembodied state, but life in a renewed creation, a renewed earth.[34] According to Romans 8 all creation will be renewed. Likewise in the final chapters of Revelation, "there will be a marriage of heaven and earth, as God dwells with humankind."[35] The world will be flooded with the love of God as the waters cover the sea. The Jerusalem we know will pass away, and the new city will descend from above (Rev. 21:10).

---

[30] Wright, "Jerusalem in the New Testament."

[31] Ibid., 11.

[32] Ibid., 12.

[33] "The logic of biblical redemption ... requires the restoration and renewal of the full complexity of human life in our environment, yet without sin." Middleton, "A New Heaven and a New Earth," 77.

[34] Wright notes, "Our questions have been about a salvation that rescues people from the world, instead of for the world... this is simply untrue to the story the gospels are telling." *How God Became King*, 242.

[35] "Jerusalem in the New Testament," 13

It's important that we note the concrete description in Revelations. The new city is constructed of precious materials, and on each side there are three gates. The light of the city is the glory of the Lord God and the Lamb (21:23) who sit at the centre, and from the throne flows the river of the water of life (22:1). On each side of the river is the tree of life. The images are of a *real place*, and the character of the place is between a garden and a city. It is in this place that God restores all things.

Now we see God's ultimate purpose: he intends to establish his new city as the place where he will live with his people forever. "Redemption does not reverse, but rather embraces, historical development."[36] Ellul writes that in Christ, "God adopts man and his works ... He has chosen to dwell in [the city]. And just as the man living in the city is directly subject to the spirit of the city, now those who dwell in it are in communion with God, for he has truly assumed it ... and has transfigured it."[37]

---

[36] "A New Heaven and a New Earth," 76.

[37] *The Meaning of the City*, 177.

CHART from Richard J. Middleton, "A New Heaven and a New Earth"[38]

	Saving Activity of God Described	Object of God's Saving Activity
Acts 3:17-21 (esp. 21)	*Restoration*	*Everything*
Ephesians 1:7-10 (esp. 10)	*Bringing together, unifying* (under one head)	*All things in heaven and on earth*
Colossians 1:16-20 (esp. 20)	*Reconciliation* (by removing the source of enmity, through the blood of the cross)	*All things whether on earth or in heaven*
2 Peter 3:10-13 (esp. 10 & 13)	*Uncovering, laying bare* (having purified) *Re-creation, renewal, making new*	*The earth and everything in it* *Heaven and earth*
Romans 8:19-23 (esp. 21 & 23)	*Liberation, setting free* (from bondage to decay) *Redemption*	*Creation itself; humanity* *Our bodies*
Basic Characteristics of Salvation:	*Restorative* **Salvation is God repairing what went wrong with creation**	*Comprehensive and holistic* **God intends to redeem or restore "all things" in heaven and on earth, including our bodies**

If, then, we are called to anticipate what God is going to do in the future with our acts now, then our work in place-making and culture creating anticipates the nature of the renewed and healed Jerusalem. This gives meaning to our work for shalom and in place-making in all cities, but especially in Jerusalem. "We are called, while forswearing all racial, cultural or geographical imperialism, to create communities of love and justice out of which healing can flow to others. What better place to do this than in the old city of peace, Jerusalem?"[39]

Kingdom as Place: Reign and Realm

Since George Eldon Ladd's work in kingdom theology in the 1950's our perspective on the gospel in the Gospels has been reworked and expanded. Ladd, and later exegetes like N.T. Wright, have helped us move beyond the narrow sense of personal salvation to the wider

---

[38] *Journal for Christian Theological Research*, 11 (2006) 73-97.

[39] Ibid., 15.

purpose of God in redemption, his intention to restore all things in an earthly kingdom, and to unite all things in Christ.[40]

As we have seen, the *imago* does not only indicate the nature of our making, but also our *destiny*: God created humanity to represent him in ruling the world.[41] Implicit in this vision is place: and so the shape of kingdom becomes not only God's reign, but extends to a realm. Envisioning kingdom as both reign and realm may help us escape the tendency to spiritualize God's reign, making it an inward and private factor that excludes the physical and public. "As the word 'Kingdom' indicates, this is not a reign over hearts and minds only, but a visible, tangible community that continues as God's chosen people."[42] Our distancing God from the world resulted in secularization of the creation, and spiritualization of God's reign. We need to recover the sense of God's presence and involvement in His world through the Spirit, hovering over world and church in the ongoing work of creation.[43]

Craig van Gelder has noted that the missional church literature offers little attention to creation. "Creation is viewed either as lacking God's presence or as the mere object of missionary work."[44] We need to recover the sense of God's presence and involvement in His world through the Spirit. Classically, God's relation to the world has been viewed through the analogy of being (*analogia entis*); a more fruitful view will be an analogy of relation (*analogia relationis*). God makes

---

[40] For a helpful perspective on a wider view of the gospel in relation to human destiny, see Stanley Grenz, "Jesus as the Imago Dei," 617-628.

[41] Middleton, "The Liberating Image," 25-26.

[42] Cavanaugh. "The Church as God's Body Language." 10.

[43] See note 57 on the importance of a Spirit-Christology for a theology of creation. The Spirit is active in more than Jesus anointing, but in the empowerment of Jesus, and in the ongoing work of God in creation.

[44] Van Gelder and Zscheile, *The Missional Church in Perspective*, 112. The authors note that since the created world participates relationally in God's life, it is never a mere target for mission. The church must enter into a deep reciprocal engagement with the world.

space within His triune life for creation, and creation "participates relationally in that life."[45]

H. Paul Santmire notes that creation is totally dependent on God, and he rules it immediately. While his speaking it into existence gives a certain structure, this "law" is not a fixed, self-sufficient force, but rather "the faithful and powerful presence of God working within his domain, directly it toward his Final Future."[46] God's plan for the creation is concrete and dynamic and involves his pervasive work. Santmire argues that God's kingdom comprehends geographical territory, both Divine rule and a Divine realm. "The first idea points primarily to activity by the Sovereign; the second primarily to the sphere governed by the Sovereign. This double connotation expresses the fundamental biblical conviction that God both *rules majestically* throughout his creation and rules majestically throughout *his creation*. The biblical writers take seriously both the government of God and the world in which his rule holds sway."[47]

In Christ God has redeemed all places. As in the Incarnation itself, this is neither a universalization of place nor a relativization of place: rather, God in Christ is making all things new, and we meet God in particular places. Inge in his discussion restates the position of Torrance: the incarnation implies that, "places are the seat of relations or the place of meeting and activity in the interaction between God and the world."[48]

Place-Making and Christian Mission/Vocation

The first Great Commission was given in Genesis 1-2.

God blessed them; and God said to them,
"Be fruitful and multiply, and fill the earth, and subdue it;
and rule over the fish of the sea and over the birds of the sky

---

[45] Ibid., 112.

[46] Santmire, *Brother Earth*, 97.

[47] Ibid.

[48] Torrance, *Space, Time*, 67.

and over every living thing that moves on the earth."

Then the LORD God took the man and put him
into the garden of Eden to cultivate it and keep it.

The first Great Commission was a divine invitation to humankind
to co-regency, to rule the earth God created, and to cultivate it. In
Genesis 2:15, the Lord tells humanity to *shamar* the land—to watch
over it, protect it, guard it, and keep it, as stewards given a trust.

The classic way of conceiving God's mission is in two mandates:
the creation mandate, and the evangelism mandate. We have tended to
see the evangelism mandate as primary, separating the second Great
Commission from the first. But the evangelism mandate is actually the
"new creation" mandate restored. "If anyone is in Christ, a new creation
has come: the old has gone, the new is here!" (2 Cor. 5:17). God's plan
in Christ is to restore all things. "Mission is ... not the saving of
disembodied souls *out of* creation but participation with God in the
redeeming of whole persons to become fully alive *in* creation."[49]

What we have called the Great Commission is actually the second
commission, and its purpose is *to restore the first*. "Christian mission
operates within the context of the cultural mandate of Genesis 1-2, and
not in isolation from it."[50]   A Christian theology of mission is
inherently creational—is placed.

Exercising skilled mastery falls broadly under what we know as the
creation or cultural mandate: to participate with God in his work of
creating. As we participate in the life of the Trinity God's work in
caring for the world is expressed through us. We noted in chapter two
the relation of the work of the Trinity to every member ministry, to
Christian vocation:

The Father creates, providentially sustains, and forms a covenantal
framework for all existence. The Son incarnates, mediates,
transfigures and redeems. The Spirit empowers and fills with God's
own presence. But each shares in the other—coinheres,

---

[49] Hastings, "Identity in a Missional God."

[50] Hastings, *Missional God, Missional Church,* 155.

interpenetrates, cooperates—so that it is theologically inappropriate to stereotype the ministry of any one.[51]

Place-making is one component of Christian vocation, which grows out of the cultural mandate. Christian vocation is as broad as culture itself: believers serve as priests in business offices, driving buses, in medical clinics, in homes, and in churches.[52] Place-making is culture creating. Culture is what we get when humans work the raw material of creation to produce something significant.[53]

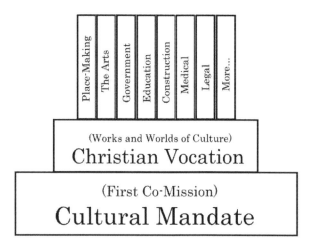

Place-making as a sub-set of vocation is part of God's redemptive mission, and something we all do, often transparently. When we build,

---

[51] Stevens, *The Other Six Days*, 57.

[52] Amy Marshall articulates four pathways for deploying congregational members in the stewardship of their vocations. *Kingdom Calling*, 2012.

[53] Yoder makes the point that "The Jubilee is on the level of productive capital; everyone should have one's own land." He also takes on the Reformed limitations of vocation conceived under "sphere sovereignty." *Body Politics*, 25-27.

or paint a building, or plant trees, or decorate a coffee-shop, we are place-making. Caring for the environment is also an expression of place-making, and working for justice can be another. When we advocate for native land rights or oppose the destruction of old growth forest, we are place-making by honoring the lived stories and connecting place to people and their commitments.

A simple illustration of the relationship of place-making to the cultural mandate looks like this (Figure 1). But what if we saw place-making as a specifically Trinitarian venture? Dorothy Sayers, in her reflections on the creative process, gives us a clue as to how this might work. In her play *The Zeal of Thy House* she puts the following speech in St. Michael's mouth:

> For every work (or act) of creation is threefold, an earthly trinity to match the heavenly. First, (not in time, but merely in order of enumeration) there is the Creative Idea, passionless, timeless, beholding the whole work complete at once, the end in the beginning: and this is the image of the Father. Second, there is the Creative Energy (or Activity) begotten of that idea, working in time from the beginning to the end, with sweat and passion, being incarnate in the bonds of matter: and this is the image of the Word. Third, there is the Creative Power, the meaning of the work and its response in the lively soul: and this is the image of the indwelling Spirit. And these three are one, each equally in itself the whole work, whereof none can exist without other: and this is the image of the Trinity.[54]

This analogical treatment of the creative process offers us a Trinitarian window into the task of place-making as culture creation. (In this framework I am departing significantly from Sayers work.)

The place-making process begins with a particular *way of seeing*. These ideas related to place comprise a social imaginary, existing as a shared understanding in a community of people before they are ever

---

[54] Sayers, *The Zeal of Thy House*. See also *The Mind of the Maker*.

expressed in the world.[55]   Place-imagination, as we have seen, is frequently ordered around faulty views of God, humankind, and creation. Our place-imagination should mirror the truth that God knows, as well as the *telos* of God's purpose in creation: shalom. This requires a contemplative stance in creation.

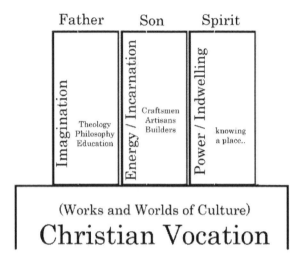

Next our place-imagination is incarnate in the world—expressed in the world in a particular form. If by an artist, it might be seen in an image that speaks of connectedness, or place-history, or a cityscape. If by an architect, it might be seen in a building design that is both functional and beautiful, and that integrates into a larger whole. If by the owner of a business, it might be seen in the arrangement of the office space, the art on the walls, and even the common space where employees meet for discussion or lunches. If by a writer, it might be the story that is told that connects a history and a place. Whatever our particular vocation, we know it more completely when it is expressed in

[55] Taylor, *Modern Social Imaginaries.* Taylor argues that "worldview" is too narrowly cognitive. A social imaginary is not a plausibility structure held by a privileged minority but rather resides in the stories and images held by common folk and incorporates an affective element.

the world in a concrete form. We know our imagination of place, or a community's imagination, when we see it expressed in art, in a building, in a landscape, neighbourhood or city, or in an initiative that connects people and place in a way than enhances beauty, justice and harmony.

Finally, the creative Power is that by which we indwell those places and know them as such, and this is also how place knows itself. Perhaps we are the priests of place, and its *spirit*, as we bring place to speech. As the Son of God was incarnate by the Spirit, the logos that was always pre-existent takes flesh in place by the breath of the Spirit.[56] As Wendell Berry expressed it, to live authentically in a place requires knowing, "what the nature of the place permits me to do here, and who and what are here with me. To know these things, I must ask the place."[57] This deep knowing, this intimacy with place, requires a loving and contemplative sensibility. Without love of a place, our place-making is likely to be skewed.[58]

Place is real, upheld and embraced by God as we participate in his ongoing work of creation. Things and places in the world respond to God's creative work by becoming what they are. Similarly, place-making is our participation with God in his ongoing creation. It is effective when a place images God's idea of it, and when we know it in its form in the world as faithfully representing itself. We'll expand on these thoughts in the next chapter when we consider "inscape."

Earlier we commented that love of God means to *order the land* in ways that are congruent with God's character. This ordering has a sacramental nature when it is done with the intention of action toward God. When done with godly intention actions are sacramental. Martin Buber contends that "something infinite flows into a (holy) deed of a man; something infinite flows from it ... the fullness of the world's

---

[56] The recovery of a Spirit-Christology and its value for a richer study of the imago as well as for the Incarnation is demonstrated by Clark Pinnock in his *Pneumatological work in Flame of Love*.

[57] Berry, *Sex, Economy, Freedom and Community*.

[58] Eric Jacobsen quotes G.K. Chesterton that, "Men did not love Rome because she was great. She was great because men loved her." *The Space Between*, 240. Elsewhere Yi-Fu Tuan coins the word *topophilia*—"love of place" (*Space and Place*).

destiny, namelessly interwoven, passes through his hands."[59]   Action with godly intention becomes a means of grace, both reveals something of God in the act, and opens a channel for grace in the doing.

This idea is actually rooted more broadly in the traditional Jewish understanding of the *Shekinah* (a word we translate in the Old Testament as 'glory' in relation to God). In the metaphorical manner of Jewish teaching, the *Shekinah* is portrayed as a part of God's person, a female part that since the fall, is in exile. The separation was part of a cosmic crash, where God's glory was splintered into myriad sparks that are now caught in matter. The role of humankind is to restore these sparks to God through holy actions. Writes Buber, "The Shekinah is banished into concealment; it lies, tied, at the bottom of every thing, and is redeemed in every thing by man, who, by his own vision or his deed, liberates the thing's soul."[60]

The story is told of Rabbi Jacob, a godly and zealous man. One day he has a vision. He meets a woman who is the exiled *Shekinah*, trying to make her way back to God. The woman is covered in a long black veil. Her feet are bare, and caked with dust and blood from long traveling on harsh roads. She says to the rabbi, "I am weary unto death, for people have hunted me down. I am sick unto death, for they have tormented me. I am ashamed, for they have denied me. You are the tyrants who keep me in exile. When you are hostile to one another, you hunt me down. When you plot evil against each other, you torment me. When you slander each other, you deny me. In doing these things you send your fellow human into exile and so you send me into exile. And for you Rabbi Jacob, do you realize that while you intend to follow me with your religious rituals you in actual fact estrange yourself from me all the more? One cannot love me [the Shekinah] and abandon people."[61] And she concludes, "Dream not that my forehead radiates heavenly beams. And has haloes all around it. My face is that of the created being."[62]

---

[59] Buber, *On Judaism*, 86.

[60] Ibid., 106.

[61] Frost and Hirsch, *The Shaping of Things to Come*, 133.

[62] Ibid.

She then raises her veil from her face, and he recognizes the face as that of a neighbor.

In Mark 12 Jesus answers the question, which is the greatest commandment? As we have understood it, the great commandment has two directions: toward God, and toward the other.

> Jesus answered, "The foremost is,
> 'Hear, O Israel! The Lord our God is one Lord.
> And you shall love the Lord your God with all your heart,
> And with all your soul, and with all your mind
> And with all your strength.'
> "The second is this,
> 'You shall love your neighbor as yourself.'"

In the passage Jesus is quoting, Deuteronomy 6, "land" is prominent, appearing seven times—twice before the great commandment, and five times afterward. God's covenant with Israel involved the land as a partner. Jesus knew the context, as did the gospel writers. We can't simply assume that "land" drops out of the picture in favor of a "spiritual" salvation, and an inward relationship to God. Rather, the Incarnation tells us that the physical world—our bodies, and land—remain the locus of God's saving work. But why the connection to neighbour here? Because both people and place remain at the center of God's purposes. Walter Brueggemann comments on Deut. 6:1-5,

> Human utilization and human enjoyment of the land—the use of its resources—comes under the rubric of "love of God." Indeed the command to love God "with all your heart and with all your soul and with all your might" (Deut. 6:5) is designed precisely for entry into the land:
>
> Hear therefore, O Israel, and observe them diligently,
> so that it may go well with you,
> and so that you may multiply greatly
> in a land flowing with milk and honey,
> as the Lord, the God of your ancestors,

has promised you. (Deut 6:1-3)[63]

Suddenly Jesus weaving together loving God and loving neighbour makes sense. Love of God correlates with the places we occupy; loving God means to order the land in ways that fit God's character: mercy, grace, compassion, generosity, faithfulness. "The land, its' potential for power, and its resources are to be devoted to the common good,"[64] that all our neighbors may enjoy the fruitfulness and well-being of the land. We must understand that we need to expand "the human vision of neighbourliness ... to include all creation, seen and unseen ... The earth is, willy-nilly, our common neighbourhood."[65]

---

[63] "To Whom Does the Land Belong?" 30.

[64] We don't have room in this discussion to pursue the thread of Jubilee. Yoder argues that Jesus quoting of Isa. 61 in Luke 4 has implications for the land and for economics. *Body Politics*, 24-25. More recently but related, and indirectly taking on the limited Reformed concept of vocation as "sphere sovereignty," see Martin Sheerin, "Why I Left World Vision for Finance."

[65] Oduyoye, *Beads and Strands*, 46–47.

"The world is charged with the grandeur of God," wrote Gerard Manley Hopkins. "It will flame out, like shining from shook foil."

Walking one day to a remote monastery at Rde-Zong, he was distracted from his self-conscious quest for spiritual attainment by the play of the sun on stones along the path. "I have no choice," he protested, "but to be alive to this landscape and this light."

Because of his delay, he never got to the monastery. The beauty of the rocks in the afternoon sun, the weathered apricot trees and the stream along which he walked refused to let him go. He concluded that, "to walk by a stream, watching the pebbles darken in the running water, is enough; to sit under the apricots is enough; to sit in a circle of great red rocks, watching them slowly begin to throb and dance as the silence of my mind deepens, is enough."[66]

---

[66] Lane, "Fierce Landscapes and the Indifference of God."

I cannot think unless I have been thought,
Nor can I speak unless I have been spoken.
I cannot teach except as I am taught,
Or break the bread except as I am broken.
O Mind behind the mind through which I seek,
O Light within the light by which I see,
O Word beneath the words with which I speak,
O founding, unfound Wisdom, finding me,
O sounding Song whose depth is sounding me,
O Memory of time, reminding me,
My Ground of Being, always grounding me,
My Maker's Bounding Line, defining me,
Come, hidden Wisdom, come with all you bring,
Come to me now, disguised as everything.[67]

---

[67] Guite, "O Sapientia."

CHAPTER IV

The Practice of Place

"Nobody ever noticed a place except at a time,
or a time except at a place."
Einstein's teacher, Hermann Minkowski[1]

In the preceding chapters we considered the story of place, through ancient philosophy to the church Fathers and then through the Enlightenment and into Modernity. We then examined the biblical data, beginning with the creation accounts and establishing humankind's relationship to the land, and our mandate as caretakers to exercise skilled mastery.

We followed this discussion with a consideration of the role of land in God's covenants, and asked whether "covenant" remains a meaningful term in the New Testament. Then by extension, we considered whether land, or place, remains a significant player in the relations of God and humankind. We brought this into specific discourse around two redemptive themes: the Temple and the New Jerusalem, the "heavenly city." In the process we challenged some of the assumptions that have been made post-Enlightenment about the nature of heaven itself, and God's plans for our final destiny. God emphatically intends a renewed physical existence, and not a disembodied future in a

---

[1] Source unknown.

spiritual and immaterial state. Both the Incarnation, and the Resurrection, affirm that God sustains and is intimately involved in the physical world.

Now in this chapter we will build on the foundations established. We'll examine the motifs of ascent and ecology as alternate frames for the imagination supporting our engagement in place. Then we'll use creation and the Incarnation as a means of approaching a logocentric reading of place within a theological frame offered by Duns Scotus and embraced by Gerard Manley Hopkins: *haaecitas*—thingness—the perfection of ordinary things.

Next we'll attempt a brief definition of place and we'll consider the human experience of place. We'll consider place through the lens of neighbourhood and parish, and consider the way we love and indwell the places where we are rooted. Then we'll talk about the practice of sacrament as a via media between our experience and our longing, between the idolatry of place on the one hand and the de-sacralization of place on the other. We'll close by considering the Eucharist as an alternative geography, a practice of resistance to any attempt to homogenize place.

Ascent and Ecology: Two Motifs in Tension

St. John of the Cross, the classic mystical writer of the 16th century, describes the longing of the soul for its Lover. He uses several metaphors in his work, but especially that of ascent.

> *One dark night,*
> *fired with love's urgent longings*
> *—ah, the sheer grace!—*
> *I went out unseen,*
> *my house being now all stilled.*
> *In darkness and secure,*
> *by the secret ladder, disguised,*
> *—ah, the sheer grace!—*
> *in darkness and concealment,*
> *my house being now all stilled.*[2]

---

[2] St. John of the Cross, *Ascent of Mt. Carmel.*

For St. John, as for many religious through the centuries, freedom *for* became freedom *from*. The world was to be transcended. To rise above the world, however, is to lose our rooting, and that loss results in a parallel loss of meaning. We are reduced to a fragmented, individualistic quest for experience. The reduction of the journey to an inward and personal one creates lonely people who are, "in short, a people without 'habit,' with no common custom, place, or dress to lend us shared meaning."[3]

Yet this is not where God's people come from. This is not our story, but rather tells of the loss of the narrative that gave meaning to our faith, which after all was a *Way* as much as a system of belief. "Christianity is not the religion of salvation *from* history, it is the religion of the salvation *of* history, of a salvation, that is, which passes through the intimately connected events and words with which divine self-communication is made."[4]

Apart from history, our faith is unintelligible, yet Gnosticism is common in our churches. In part this is because, as Malcolm Muggeridge once framed it, "we human beings have a wonderful faculty for snatching fantasy from the jaws of truth."[5] Moreover, there remains a tension between the universal and the particular at the heart of our faith. H. Paul Santmire helps us examine this tension through two dominant motifs: the spiritual motif and the ecological motif. Why these motifs, and how do they function in our experience of place?

In chapter one I related the story of moving from a car to a bicycle, and how my mode and speed of transport changed my experience of the world: a new way of seeing helped me revise my mental map of the world. We noted that mental maps are aids to orienting in a complex world. They act as a kind of shorthand, because our mental bandwidth is limited. Metaphors function in a similar way, as a kind of map, and as

---

[3] Lane, The Solace of Fierce Landscapes," 10.

[4] Forte, Quoted in Inge, *A Christian Theology of Place*, 91. Italics original.

[5] Muggeridge, *Jesus Rediscovered*, 31.

Leonard Sweet noted, "When the root metaphors change, so does everything else."[6]

H. Paul Santmire, in his dynamic work on a theology of nature, begins by examining root metaphors.[7] Santmire wants us to understand that our maps and frameworks act as an interface between the experiential moments of religious life and the secondary, more conscious levels of reflection. Root metaphors, often only implicit, function like maps and assist in our seeing. When these metaphors cluster together and shape a theological tradition, or when a single metaphor exercises a formative influence over many years, it can be labeled a "theological motif."[8] Santmire argues that there are three root metaphors that have exercised a formative influence on two dominant motifs.

Two of the root metaphors are dependent on a single, almost universal experience in human history, and are captured by the image of the overwhelming mountain. These are the metaphors of ascent, and fecundity. A third metaphor is dependent on a different kind of experience, which is less universal: the experience of the promising journey, migration to a good land.

Henry Wadsworth Longfellow in his poem, "The Ladder of St. Augustine," captures well the metaphor of ascent.

We have not wings, we cannot soar;
But we have feet to scale and climb

By slow degrees, by more and more,
The cloudy summits of our time.

The mighty pyramids of stone

---

[6] He notes, "The imaginative architecture of the world has collapsed, is in ruins, and a new imaginative architecture is emerging." "Seven Questions."

[7] Santmire references Alfred North Whitehead, who observed that, "Every philosophy is tinged with the coloring of some secret imaginative background, which never merges explicitly onto its traces of reasoning." *The Travail of Nature*, 14-15. Similarly, Langdon Gilkey maintains that we often work at pre-reflective levels of awareness that grow out of a subjective response to the world.

[8] Ibid.

That wedge-like cleave the desert airs,

When nearer seen, and better known,
Are but gigantic flights of stairs.

The distant mountains, that uprear
Their solid bastions to the skies,

Are crossed by pathways, that appear
As we to higher levels rise.[9]

Santmire argues that the metaphor of ascent became the "spiritual motif" in Western theology. The other two metaphors tend to cluster, and when they do, through time they become what he calls the "ecological motif."[10] The ecological motif is complex, because the metaphor of fecundity is rooted, like that of ascent, in the image of the overwhelming mountain. The difference is determined by vision and intention. One may climb the mountain with eyes fixed on heaven, or one may climb to gain renewed perspective of the earth. In other words, one climber seeks escape, or exaltation, while the other seeks engagement.[11]

Santmire notes that the metaphors of ascent and fecundity, like the metaphors of ascent and migration to a good land, stand in tension with one another. In developing a theology of nature he is particularly interested in the latter pair. He argues that where these two metaphors appear in the same system of thought, one or another will always emerge victorious. He cites Origen, where both metaphors appear, but the metaphor of ascent is so dominant that, "the land he has in mind is spiritualized to the point where it has lost all its tangibility ... abstracted from its concrete setting in Hebraic thought, and used to [express] a spiritualizing vision of reality."[12]

---

[9] Longfellow, *The Complete Poetical Work of Henry Wordworth Longfellow.*

[10] Ibid., 16.

[11] Shades of Scott Peck, who somewhere commented that there are two reasons people become religious: to approach mystery, and to escape mystery.

[12] Ibid., 28.

Santmire sees Moses as an exemplar of the metaphor of ascent. Likewise Dante in his Divine Comedy writes within that imaginative frame. The metaphor of fecundity dominates in Psalm 104, and in the life and myths surrounding St. Francis of Assisi. The experience of the promising journey is detailed in Deuteronomy and in the life of Moses. The narrative contains layers, of a promised inheritance in a good land as well as a distant fulfillment.

The case Santmire wants to make is echoed in the sub-title of his book, "The Ambiguous Ecological Promise of Christian Theology." Wherever the motif of migration to a good land dominates the field, theology is rooted and identity is connected to the land. Under the dominance of this metaphor, even the most intense spiritual experience will be located within nature, surrounded by earthly creatures. Noah is a prime case, who although he was rescued from the chaos on earth, *took the animals with him*, and anticipated a new beginning on the land.

Thus the land and place must exist both as physical location, a partner in redemption, and as a symbol of something more. Santmire affirms the import of the plus-dimension of land noted by Brueggemann: "Land is always fully historical but always bearer of over-pluses of meaning known only to those who lose and yearn for it. The current loss of and hunger for place participate in those plus dimensions—at once a concern for actual historical placement, but at the same time a hunger for an over-plus of place meaning."[13] The hunger for roots becomes first an earthed experience, and then a hope for something more, the kingdom yet to come.

Our physical journey in place roots us, and then acts as a symbol and foretaste of the coming age, a restored world under the reign of God. A contemporary poet expresses it like this: *"Moon over junkyard where the snow lies bright / Can set my heart to burn."*[14]

It is precisely because we are rooted that the world can speak to us of something more. Nina Beth Cardin comments, "Jewish tradition, especially in its biblical stories, intimately combines event and place. Indivisible from the telling of our sacred history is the story of land itself. For the Jewish people, land is not just a backdrop, not a prop, but

[13] Brueggemann, *The Land*, 3-4.

[14] Cockburn, "Mystery."

a partner, a covenantal character in our long unfolding sacred saga."[15] It is revealing that the often quoted promise of healing in 2 Chr. 7:14 is not a promise of deliverance *out of* the world, but of a salvation *into* it. The promise is explicitly that God will "hear from heaven and *heal their land*."

A Logocentric Reading

Abstracting place to "space" was one means of escaping the bonds of the world. The results of that apparent "freedom" have now become evident in increasing fragmentation and loss of meaning, so that our experience is one of rootlessness and anxiety. We no longer feel at home in the world. We need a way to connect with place so that we can engage in place-making, enter the stories and rich potential of the places we live, and receive the world as a gift.

In the last chapter we considered some aspects of a theology of creation, but did not examine the Johannine theology of the logos. Both John and the book of Colossians help us here, with a Christocentric view of creation. John tells us that,

> In the beginning was the logos, and the logos was with God,
> And the logos was God. He was with God in the beginning.
> Through him all things were made;
> Without him nothing was made that has been made.

The *logos* pervades all creation. The word is borrowed from the Greek, and it means literally *word*, or reason, or rational principle. In Greek philosophy *logos* referred to thought and its utterance. Heraclitus was the first to use the term, and then later Philo of Alexandria, a Hellenized Jew, used the term to refer to a divine being who bridged the gap between God and the material world, even calling the logos "the first-born of God."[16]

John identifies the *logos* as Yeshua, Jesus of Nazareth. "The logos became flesh and made his dwelling among us" (1:14). Yeshua is truly

---

15 Cardin, "The Place of Place in Jewish Tradition,"210-216.

16 Copleston, *A History of Philosophy*, 458–462.

human, truly flesh. He is the ultimate image of God, imago Dei.[17] He is
the logos of God, existing with God before the world was made. As the
creed states, he was "begotten of the father before all worlds ... being of
one substance with the father." The incarnate Son makes visible the
logos—in him we see what we could not see. We are invited to follow
Jesus in life, to be transformed into his image (2 Cor. 3:18), and in
seeing him we see beyond him to the Father. The ordinary and physical
life of the Son reveals the transcendent God.

But look what else John is telling us in his poetic narrative. Before
John makes this identification of the *logos* with Jesus, he tells us that
this word is somehow expressed in creation. John writes, "Through him
all things were made." In this view, everything that exists in our material
world exists somehow as an expression of the *logos*. Similarly, Col.
1:16-17,

> For in him all things were created:
> things in heaven and things on earth, visible and invisible,
> all things have been created through him and for him.
> He is before all things, and in him all things hold together.

Stan Grenz refers to Col. 1:15-20 as a cosmology of creation and
redemption.[18] The *logos* in creation is a spoken word, and that word is
written into the nature of every created *thing*. "The Word within the
world and for the world," as TS Eliot put it.[19] In some sense, every
thing in creation, every person and every place, is a word that existed in
the mind of God, and then was spoken into being. And not merely
spoken in the past, but always *being spoken*. "The world, which is the
self-expressive utterance of the Divine Word, becomes itself a true
revelation, in which ... what comes is not truth concerning God, but

---

[17] Grenz argues that Romans 8:29 is the final exegesis of Genesis 1:26-17. "Jesus as the Imago Dei," 623.

[18] Ibid., 619.

[19] Eliot, "Ash Wednesday."

God Himself. This ... does not exclude the possibility of special revelations; rather, it is the condition of that possibility."[20]

All that exists is held together in the Word, coheres in him. The *logos* remains intimately involved in the things that are. They cohere in his life, and remain related to him. They are themselves a *logos* in the sense that they are his word writ on and into creation: they *speak* of him.

J.R.R. Tolkien, in his short paper, "On Faery Stories," builds on this theme, imagining the *logos* as the prism through which divine light passes, refracting to many hues, a splendid and multi-voiced diversity.

> "Dear Sir," I said—"Although now long estranged,
> Man is not wholly lost nor wholly changed
> Dis-grace he may be, yet is not de-throned,
> and keeps the rags of lordship once he owned:
> Man, Sub-creator, the refracted Light
> through whom is splintered from a single White
> to many hues, and endlessly combined
> in living shapes that move from mind to mind."[21]

The visible things speak of the invisible, of the *logos* that existed before creation. We may legitimately fix our eyes on the things that are, and enjoy them as God's word in creation. We commonly do this with landscapes, and see in deserts the otherness or distance of God, as we see in fruitful land his provision and providence. A sunrise becomes a promise of new life; a sunset becomes a portent of the coming world. Ordinary things become symbols that point beyond themselves: bread and wine become visible and outward symbols of an inward and spiritual grace.

Let's consider where this approach took Duns Scotus, the brilliant writer in the Middle Ages, and then we'll consider the implications for a sacramental perspective.

---

[20] Temple, *Nature, Man and God*, 478.

[21] Tolkien, "On Faery Stories."

Duns Scotus and Inscape

According to the Stanford Encyclopedia of Philosophy, John Duns Scotus (1265/66-1308) was one of the most important and influential philosopher-theologians of the High Middle Ages. "His brilliantly complex and nuanced thought, which earned him the nickname 'the Subtle Doctor,' left a mark on discussions of such disparate topics as the semantics of religious language, the problem of universals, divine illumination, and the nature of human freedom."[22] "Scotus" is a nickname: his family name was Duns, which was also the name of the Scottish village in which he was born.

The date of Scotus' birth is not known, but he was ordained to the priesthood in the Order of Friars Minor—the Franciscans—at Saint Andrew's Priory in Northampton, England, on 17 March 1291. The minimum age for ordination was twenty-five. It appears that he began his formal studies at Oxford in October, 1288, finishing them in June, 1301.

One of Scotus' concerns was individuation, and he rooted his reflection in the Incarnation. Scotus believed that the Incarnation is God's greatest work, and is not explained by anything outside God's own reality, including the fall. Rather, Incarnation is the "highest good" and was always intended by God. Everything without exception is rooted in the cause of creation, which is Jesus. Thus all things exist to be themselves, and to "do" themselves. This thought is clearly captured in "As Kingfishers Catch Fire," one of the very fine poems of Gerard Manley Hopkins.

> As kingfishers catch fire, dragonflies draw flame;
> As tumbled over rim in roundly wells
> Stones ring; like each tucked string tells, each hung bell's
> Bow swung finds tongue to fling out broad its name;
> Each mortal thing does one thing and the same:
> Deals out that being indoors each one dwells;
> Selves—goes itself; myself it speaks and spells,
> Crying *What I do is for me: for that I came.*

---

[22] Stanford Encyclopedia of Philosophy, "John Duns Scotus."

I say more: the just man justices;
Keeps grace: that keeps all his goings graces;
Acts in God's eye what in God's eye he is—
Christ. For Christ plays in ten thousand places,
Lovely in limbs, and lovely in eyes not his
To the Father through the features of men's faces.[23]

"Each mortal thing ... deals out that being indoors each one dwells." Hopkins captures Scotus' essential insight, moving far beyond the Greek ideal. For Scotus the ideal only exists in the real. Perfection is not according to some type that exists in the mind of God, but in his actual expression of it in the world, his speaking it into being. All things in their uniqueness say "yes" to God and his good word. Thomas Merton, a poet and mystic who appreciated the work of both Scotus and Gerard Manley Hopkins, displays Scotus' influence in his work. He writes,

No two created beings are exactly alike. And their individuality is no imperfection. On the contrary, the perfection of each created thing is not merely its conformity to an abstract type but in its own individual identity with itself.[24]

Thus it is in particularity that the love of God is most clearly expressed. God says, "I love this tree, this flower, this man," more than the idea of the thing. The particular thing is real, and upheld and embraced by God's ongoing work in creation. God's life is so fruitful that it "constantly, and inherently, expresses itself in the particularity of creation."[25] Poets like Carrie Newcomer capture this in song.

Holy is the dish and drain
The soap and sink, the cup and plate
And the warm wool socks, and the cold white tile
Showerheads and good dry towels
And frying eggs sound like psalms

---

[23] Hopkins, "As Kingfishers Catch Fire."

[24] Merton, *New Seeds of Contemplation*, 29.

[25] Sheldrake, *Spaces for the Sacred*, 24.

With a bit of salt measured in my palm
It's all a part of a sacrament
As holy as a day is spent ...[26]

Scotus gave the name *haecceitas*, or "thisness" to this individualizing form. Hopkins, interpreting Scotus, described thisness as *inscape*, the unique inner texture of a particular person or thing. Merton brings out the force of meaning by equating inscape to sanctity. To the extent that a created thing agrees with God's unique idea of it, answers the call written into its nature, it is holy. Holiness thus connects to "vocation" (from the Latin *vocare* for "voice") in two ways.[27]

First, God creates through the word; He speaks and things exist. And second, the things He creates respond to His present creative work, His moment by moment willing the world into existence through love, by *becoming what they are*.[28] Merton captures the force like this: "It is not humility to insist on being someone that you are not. It is as much as saying that you know better than God who you are and who you ought to be. How do you expect to arrive at the end of your own journey if you take the road to another man's city?"[29]

The Experience of Place

As we have seen, the *Imago* does not only indicate the nature of our making, but also our destiny: God created humanity to represent him in ruling the world.[30] Our vocation is both kingly, and priestly, and both roles are lived out in this world, empowered by the Spirit. We need to recover the sense of God's active presence in the world, where ordinary

---

[26] Carrie Newcomer. "As Holy as a Day is Spent."

[27] See Steven Garber's excellent treatment of vocation in *Visions of Vocation: Common Grace for the Common Good.*

[28] This confidence in the creative work of God in individuation is expressed in the work of Canadian psychologist David Benner.

[29] Merton, *New Seeds*, 101. St. Augustine expressed it differently: "Sin is seeking many good things, but never choosing the one thing you are called to."

[30] Middleton, *The Liberating Image*, 25-26.

things respond to God's call to *be what they are*, each place and each thing unique.

Because the Word was made flesh in Jesus, ordinary things are beacons of glory. Particular things say yes to God in their own unique texture and existence; at the same time, their particularity speaks of more. As in the Incarnation itself, this is neither a universalization of place nor a relativization of place: rather, God in Christ is making all things new, and we meet God in particular places. The incarnation implies that, "places are the seat of relations or the place of meeting and activity in the interaction between God and the world."[31]

We have come this far without attempting a definition of place. After doing considerable theological work, we can speak more artfully of our experience of place. We are ready for a definition.

David Canter offers that, "places ... are units of environment."[32] Canter is careful to distinguish between "place" and the objects that reside in an environment. I have blurred this distinction in making the connection to *haecceitas* and place, because place takes on the character of a whole through its arrangement of things, through its boundaries, and through our perception of place in its wholeness, its *gestalt*.[33]

Canter believes that our perception of place, and action are intrinsically linked. He argues that "any act is made in relation to the context within which the individual thinks himself to be."[34] This becomes obvious when considering the disposition of persons at Disneyland, versus a soccer game, versus a cathedral. The place in question does not determine response, but is conditioned by it.

Amos Rapoport uses a model with four variables to conceptualize the structure of an environment, including space, time, meaning and

---

[31] Torrance, *Space, Time and Incarnation.*

[32] Canter, *The Psychology of Place*, 2.

[33] Typically this discussion proceeds with reference to a genius loci, an old Roman idea that described a power than inhabited a place, giving it a special and peculiar quality. This conception, if used at all, needs to be redescribed with reference to ontology. See Mark Wynn, "Knowledge of place and knowledge of God," 155.

[34] *The Psychology of Place*, 1.

communication.[35] Bill McAlpine in his work suggests five components, divided by two kinds of awareness: awareness of self, and awareness of externals. The awareness of self includes one's own sense of identity as well as the lens and frames through which we see the world. The awareness of externals includes an appreciation of others present, an appreciation of the setting itself, and an appreciation of the activities that occur in a place.[36]

McAlpine notes that the dynamic interaction of these components makes any experience of place unique. He argues that "place is more than location; it is a meaningful integration of activity and persons within location."[37] He thus approaches the position of Edgar Casey. Casey argues that a place is more an "event" than a thing to fit into a category. "As an event, it is unique, idiolocal. Its peculiarity calls not for assumption into the already known ... but for the imaginative constitution of terms respecting its idiolocality (these range from placenames to whole discourses)."[38] Idiolocality, with reference to place, mirrors the *haaecitas* of Scotus with reference to things.[39]

McAlpine notes that whether intended or not, built environments evoke responses. Equally powerful, however, is our experience of the activities we associate with a place. Activities that occur in places we deem sacred have a special quality that is deemed essential by those who participate. It is not easy to separate the place from the activity, because, "ritual and custom has the incidental if not deliberate effect of strengthening attachment to place by reaffirming ... the enduring relationships between a people and their place."[40] Richard Twiss, the native Elder, describes how when a baby is born to a Navajo family, they bury the umbilical cord somewhere on the property. They believe this

---

[35] Rapoport, "Sacred Places, Sacred Occasions, and Sacred Environments," 75-82.

[36] McAlpine, *Sacred Space for the Missional Church*, 122.

[37] Ibid., 128.

[38] Casey, in Feld and Basso, *Senses of Place*, 12.

[39] In a similar way Yi-Fu Tuan remarks that "What begins as undifferentiated space becomes place as we get to know it better and endow it with value." *Space and Place*, 6.

[40] Relph, *Place and Placelessness*, 33.

action connects the person to the place; the ritual is about identity and God's work in that place.[41] Belonging is both to a people and a place.

If we regard places as "units of environment," as Canter suggests, how is one place separated from another? Places are *bounded*, and boundaries are socially constructed, sometimes literally by physical divisions, and sometimes by tacit agreement. In the suburbs, fences, shrubs, and sometimes pavements will separate one yard from another. The home itself is separated from the yard by walls. A neighbourhood is naturally bounded by major streets, sometimes by open space, and sometimes by natural features like hills or rivers.

A boundary, writes Caroline Westerhoff, is "that which defines and gives identity to all kinds of systems." Boundaries are constitutive to identity and "unless we can draw a line—a boundary—and say that something lies outside its domain, then we can speak about nothing that lies inside with deep meaning."[42] Westerhoff continues:

> Boundaries are lines that afford definition, identity and protection—for persons, families, institutions, nations ... A boundary gives us something to which we can point and ascribe a name. Without a boundary, we have nothing to which we can invite or welcome anyone else.[43]

Without boundaries there can be no sense of "place" as home, as site of hospitality, security and intimacy with local knowledge. "Without boundaries there is no locality, and therefore no sense of membership in a particular community, family, or neighbourhood which has an identity in distinction from other communities, families and neighbourhoods."[44]   Without boundaries, place identity is impossible.[45] But while boundaries are important, they must also be

---

[41] Richard Twiss, "A Theology of Place."

[42] Westerhoff, *Good Fences*, xi.

[43] Ibid., 7. Italicized in the original.

[44] Walsh and Bouman-Prediger, "With and Without Boundaries," 9.

[45] Place identity concerns the meaning and significance of places for their users and inhabitants, and in cities is sometimes denoted by urban character.

permeable: there must be known and appropriate ways to cross them. We knock at the door of a house.[46] At the local coffee shop, given certain hours, we can freely enter. Out in the country, boundaries are less defined, and we know a place more by an intuitive sense of its wholeness, by specific markers or by a history of experience there.

Neighbourhoods, like homes, have a special role in shared experience, and offer a particular kind of belonging. Neighbourhood is a place "that bridges the gap between privacy ... and the world beyond. It's not just about your experience, or my experience, it's about our experience ... It's an experience common to all."[47] In making this connection to common life the idea of neighbourhood connects to an older idea, that of parish. Parish is unique in our historical experience and in our stewardship of place.

Neighbourhood and Parish

How do we locate ourselves in a place? Neighbourhood defines a particular kind of placed experience. Simon Carey Holt suggests that the old practice of parish offers hope for a recover of placed-ness in local mission and ministry. "The term parish, derived from the Greek noun *paroikia*—meaning those living near or beside—was used from the second century to describe the intimate relationship between the congregation and its neighborhood."[48] Does "parish" offer us something special as the intersection of neighbourhood and place? Can "parish" help us recover a spiritual practice of place, an invitation to invest and dwell in our neighbourhoods?

"Strangers," Walter Brueggemann writes, "are people without a place." They are "displaced persons" because the "social system ... [has] assigned their place to another and so denied them any safe place of their own." In ancient Israel they are often people whose 'boundary

---

[46] Mircea Eliade draws attention to the important role of doors or gates: "The threshold concentrates not only the boundary between inside and outside but also the possibility of passage from one to the other." *The Sacred and the Profane*, 18.

[47] Holt, *God Next Door*, 13.

[48] Ibid., 81.

stones' have been moved." To be placeless is to live in the tenuous vulnerability of life without the bounded security of home and shelter.[49]

We live with a rip in our psyche: we long for a place where we truly belong, and are rooted. At the same time, there are many forces that erode our sense of place, and our ability to belong. Forces of globalization, for example, are invested in the homogenization of place to "space." Because what is universal is non-local, it is merely an abstraction, and can be freely manipulated in the name of profit: exported or imported.[50] We are tempted to view our neighbourhoods as something we consume, rather than a place to serve and invest. To the extent we are consumers we remain rootless, disconnected from both people and place.

The Gospel response is simple: to recover the practice of parish and become Jesus body, visible and local. Thus Lesslie Newbigin doubts that, "the geographical parish can ever become irrelevant or marginal. There is a sense in which the primary sense of neighbourhood must remain primary, because it is here that men and women relate to each other simply as human beings and not in respect of their functions in society."[51] In other words, it is in our neighbourhoods that we have the possibility of engaging richly. Rowan Williams comments that, "one of our problems is that we don't know where to find the stable relations that would allow us room to grow without fear."[52] If I am not sure I will be here tomorrow, why should I invest my life? If my neighbour is unsure that I will be here tomorrow, why should he tell me who he is and what he cares about?

Diana Butler Bass describes the recovery of the village church as a recovery of parish.[53] A parish was bounded space where a local church served its community. The pastor and people were intimately connected

---

[49] Walsh, "With and Without Boundaries," 8.

[50] The critique of the work of Milton Friedman in this regard is particularly helpful. Friedman is best known for his sloppy methodology in works like *The World is Flat* and *The Lexus and the Olive Tree*.

[51] Newbigin, *Sign of the Kingdom*, 64.

[52] Williams (paraphrase). "Faith and History."

[53] Bass, *Christianity for the Rest of Us*, 36-37.

in the life of the neighbourhood. Bass describes the village church, or parish, as God's house, with the church at the center, offering hospitality for pilgrims in a strange land.

This is an inclusive vision rather than exclusive. It doesn't "Christianize" the world by using blinders to difference, but neither does it divide the world into sinners and saints. (I've met a lot of sinners in church, and a few saints who never pass through the doors). Instead, the parish creates open space—a kind of "third place." There is no spiritual test to come in, no intellectual position to which one must agree. At the center is a core of people who know Jesus and who live out the Gospel so that others may belong, and one day believe. Conversion is about believing and belonging: it is both a story we commit to *and* a community we belong to.[54] Moreover, belonging, believing and behaving are not different stages but different dimensions of a single journey.

The parish does not exist in the insulated mode typical of many churches: it makes the concerns of the village its own concerns.[55] Neither does it exist in the typical evangelistic mode: its goal is not so much conversion (though this is a good thing), but rather the transformation of the neighbourhood.[56] Jeremiah 29:7, or "shalom" would be readily identified as a goal: the welfare of the village. "Place" is so much a partner in mission that Calvin College Professor Mark Mulder can write that, "a poor conception of place ... manifest in weak ties and affiliations," fed the flight of CRC churches from their Chicago neighbourhoods.[57]

My own discovery of parish occurred in the period from 2001 to 2005. My wife and I stepped outside the culture of the organized church, and suddenly we had time for our neighbors. With few structures to rely on and some unlearning to do, we began to listen in

---

[54] Murray, *Church After Christendom*, 35.

[55] In this way it connects to another old practice, that of the commons.

[56] Peter Block notes that, "The choice not to focus [on individual transformation] ... is because we have already learned that the transformation of large numbers of individuals does not result in transformed communities." *Community*, 2.

[57] Mulder, "Mobility and the (In) Significance of Place in an Evangelical Church,"16.

new ways. We saw the texture of our neighborhood. We learned a new dependence on the Spirit, and we saw God active outside church walls. Until this time, we had no way of really seeing our neighbourhood as a place God could dwell; no way of engaging the call of God there.

I recall one Saturday when some neighbors arrived to share a meal, and brought friends with them. We picked fresh beans and tomatoes from our garden. After dinner, one woman entered the kitchen to help clean up. As she worked she shared her story, and related growing up in a religious home with an abusive father. Suddenly she popped out with, "You're Christians aren't you—I can tell by your love." Brent Aldrich writes, "At the scale of the neighborhood, we can know by the senses of our bodies; we can meet our neighbors and strangers in common, shared spaces; and we can enter into and work towards the long work of God's transformation in our places."[58]

The automobile is a tool for mobility that often fragments our communities. In 1970 futurist Alvin Toffler commented that, "Never in history has distance meant less. Never have man's (sic) relationships with place been more numerous, fragile and temporary. Figuratively, we 'use up' places and dispose of them in much the same way we dispose of Kleenex or beer cans."[59] We drive through neighborhoods to attend a church across town, in a building often isolated from its neighborhood, an island surrounded by a parking lot, cut off from the fabric of community life. (More on this in chapter 7). Simon Carey Holt records the resentment created by commuter churches.

> Mark and Wendy have a deep affection for their neighbourhood [except for] the presence of a large church on the corner ... "Hundreds of people pour into it every Sunday. They come from all over the place, but none from the neighbourhood. Even the pastor lives somewhere else ..." They [noted] the poor level of maintenance on the building and the gardens. "It's like they don't care about the people who actually live here. In effect, they're lousy neighbours!"[60]

---

[58] Aldrich, "Eric Jacobsen—The Space Between."

[59] Toffler, *Future Shock*, 75

[60] *God Next Door*, 81

Holt notes that those who don't invest in a community take more than they give. Without a vision to redeem space and convert it to place, we unwittingly contribute to the destruction of local culture. But why is that important?

Local Culture – Who Cares?

Wendell Berry highlights the value of local culture through observing an old rusted out bucket nailed to a tree.[61] The bucket collects leaves and nuts and bird-droppings over the years, then the fibers break down and the collection turns into soil that returns to the earth and promotes growth. Berry sees in the bucket an analogy for how human community should develop:

> A human community, too, must collect leaves and stories, and turn them to account. It must build soil, and build that memory of itself —in lore and story and song—that will be its culture. These two kinds of accumulation, of local soil and local culture, are intimately related.[62]

Berry claims that in order to do this kind of work, a community must exert a kind of centripetal force on its residents, holding local soil and local memory in place. It must draw residents toward the center of community life, and it must encourage the next generation to return and make their contribution to the local culture. Tony Hiss argues that it is only as we experience a place from the inside that we begin to invest in it as our community.[63] The church in the neighborhood could exert this kind of influence on a neighborhood if it saw the value of the role. It would require a sense of its physical connection to the neighborhood: *a sense of parish and a sense of belonging.* "The 20th-century American dream was to move out and move up; the 21st-

---

[61] Hawaiian activist Eric Enos has said, "You can have culture in a petri dish. But we define culture as something that links us to a sense of place. This place, we live here."

[62] Berry, *The Art of the Common Place.*

[63] Hiss, *The Experience of Place.*

century dream seems to be to put down deeper roots."[64] Peter Block writes,

> The social fabric of community is formed from an expanding shared sense of belonging. It is shaped by the idea that only when we are connected and care for the well-being of the whole that a civil and democratic society is created ...[65]

Public spaces are critical to the quality of neighborhood life, because community building occurs in an infinite number of small steps.[66] Block notes that it requires that we "treat as important many things that we thought were incidental. An after-thought becomes the point; a comment made in passing defines who we are more than all that came before. If the artist is one who captures the nuance of experience, then this is whom each of us must become."[67] Stability is an endangered species. Without long term relationships, we withhold ourselves in ways that are costly to ourselves and to the quality of our communities.[68] Without personal investment, we don't garner the local knowledge that enables us to thrive in the places where we live.

In the year 2000 Robert Putnam published *Bowling Alone: The Collapse and Revival of American Community*, a fascinating treatment of social capital.[69] The central thesis of social capital theory is that relationships matter, and that social networks are a valuable asset in daily life. Interaction enables people to build communities, to commit themselves to each other, and to knit the social fabric. A sense of belonging and the concrete experience of social networks (and the relationships of trust and tolerance that can be involved) can bring great

---

[64] Crouch, "Ten Most Significant Cultural Trends of the Last Decade."

[65] *Community*, 2.

[66] See Amy Marshall's discussion of these issues in her new book, *Kingdom Calling*.

[67] Ibid.

[68] Mulder, "Mobility and the (In) Significance of Place in an Evangelical Church," 16-43.

[69] Putnam, *Bowling Alone*.

benefits. Trust between individuals becomes trust between strangers and then trust of social institutions.

Without this interaction, on the other hand, trust decays and this decay begins to manifest itself in serious social problems. There is now a range of evidence that communities with a good "stock" of such "social capital" are more likely to benefit from lower crime figures, better health, higher educational achievement, and better economic growth. We'll return to this concept in a discussion of two specific types of social capital in chapter five.

A Sacramental Vision

> *Rain rings trash can bells, and what do you know?*
> *My alley becomes a cathedral.*
> *Eyes can be arch ways, to enter or leave by ...*[70]

The visible things speak of the invisible, of the *logos* that existed before creation. We may legitimately fix our eyes on the places that are, and enjoy them as God's word in creation, whether they are direct expressions of creation or expressions of human place-making. We may also look through things to the Creator who spoke them into existence. Because God was made flesh in Jesus of Nazareth, ordinary things can conceal glory: bread and wine become visible symbols of an invisible and spiritual grace. Particular places invite us into God's ongoing work in the world.

In Christ God has redeemed all places, neither a universalization of place nor a relativization of place: rather, God in Christ is making all things new, and we meet God in particular places. Particular places express something of the divine in their own unique texture and existence; at the same time, their particularity speaks of *more*.

Sheldrake writes that discipleship "simultaneously demands a particular 'placement,' and a continual movement beyond each place in search of an 'elsewhere,' a 'further,' an even greater. A disciple is one who is called to a journey across boundaries ..."[71] In this image of journeying

---

[70] Cockburn, "Thoughts on a Rainy Afternoon."

[71] *Spaces for the Sacred*, 64. Italics in the original.

we catch a sense of the old practice of pilgrimage, but also of the longing for a wholeness and a home that can't be found in this broken world. Leonard Cohen sings,

> *You can add up the parts*
> *but you won't have the sum*
> *You can strike up the march,*
> *there is no drum*
> *Every heart, every heart*
> *to love will come*
> *but like a refugee.*
>
> *Ring the bells that still can ring*
> *Forget your perfect offering*
> *There is a crack, a crack in everything*
> *That's how the light gets in.*[72]

The old rabbis said that only the broken heart can be whole. The world is broken, but the brokenness reminds us that there is more, as darkness contrasts with light. How do we embrace the particular, while allowing the particular to lead us beyond? There is a sense of paradox here, of the presence of the kingdom as well as anticipation of a future fullness. The singular way of bringing these worlds together is in our celebration of the Table. There we look back in memory, embrace the presence of the Spirit in the gathered body of Christ, and anticipate the future healing of creation, and the uniting of all things in Christ. We use ordinary bread and wine to speak of the presence of Christ, of the sacrifice of Jesus and of his redemption, anticipating the restoration of all things.

Moreover, there is a Trinitarian reality in this practice. We who are many are one body. We partake of one loaf as separate individuals, and are united in our sharing. We become radically open to one another in our participation in the bread and the wine.[73] A symbol participates in the reality for which it stands: therefore the world, graced by God, is

---

[72] Cohen, "Anthem,"

[73] 1 Cor. 10:16.

the theatre of his glory. This phrase 'theatre of his glory' reminds us that, "all sacrament... begins with God's action."[74]

At the table we participate in a body that is both present and future, both visible and invisible. Through the Incarnation our experience is anchored firmly in the world of things and people and places. At the same time, people and places speak sacramentally, beyond themselves, of God's promised future. So Sheldrake notes that, "catholicity does not mean simply what is ubiquitous but what is whole and complete."[75] The Eucharist is an eschatological practice that looks forward to fulfillment, but it is also the realization of the future kingdom, an alternative geography where the universal body of Christ is wholly present in the local assembly.

Christ died to redeem all places, all cultures, all nations. The Church is called to be an ethical space: "a practice for making place for the fullness of all things and all people."[76] This use of the word "practice" indicates a preparation process for what is yet to come, but also a performance, the embodiment of the future reality in the present as a sign and a foretaste. The Eucharist calls us to become our words of faith and promise and act them out in the world. Rodney Clapp writes that,

> The Eucharist for its enactment requires [us to] gather and the physical bodies of the members of Christ must go through certain motions and assume particular positions ... bodily gestures communicating and reinforcing a wealth of tacit knowledge. To kneel ... to stretch out empty and receptive hands for the bread of life ... So the Eucharist leads us to say that corporality is the very mediation where faith takes on flesh and makes real the truth that inhabits it.[77]

---

[74] Inge, *A Christian Theology*, 89

[75] *Spaces for the Sacred*, 70. He uses the word here in the sense of *katholikos*, meaning universal or "in respect of the whole."

[76] Ibid., 74. Craig Dykstra defines practices as "patterns of communal action that create openings in our lives where the grace, mercy, and presence of God may be made known to us." *Growing in the Life of Faith*, 66.

[77] Clapp, *Border Crossings*, 74.

The ultimate symbol, and practice, of reconciliation is the Eucharist. As Philip Sheldrake points out, reconciliation does not homogenize people or environments, "but creates space for the diversity of human voices to participate ... a space of reconciliation invites all who inhabit it to make space for 'the other,"[78] for all of us together to be transformed into something new. Politics, in God's kingdom, is simply caring for the places in which we dwell and in which our neighbours dwell with us.

The Eucharistic table is not only at the center of our worship, but also at the center of our politics. At the table, we learn an economics of sharing. Yoder observes that "[Bread] *is* daily sustenance. Bread eaten together *is* economic sharing. Not merely symbolically, but also in fact, eating together extends to a wider circle the economic solidarity normally obtained in the family."[79] At the table we learn a politics of hospitality, welcoming the stranger and sharing our sustenance with each. At the table we learn a politics of dialogue, learning to listen together in a world that is increasingly marked by ideology and violence.

In contrast, globalism has become a new master-story, a false catholicity, a narrative uniting together people from all over the world in the same space-time. "The logic of global capitalism is blind to the significance of place, history, culture or religious identity to peoples' work and well-being."[80] As a result, serious engagement with the other is by-passed.

Place is storied, and people tell stories for a variety of reasons. Competing discourses, like that of space versus place, remind us that place has an ethic. In the tar-sands of Alberta, or in the water poor regions of Africa, the politics of place is all too real. In the next chapter

---

[78] *Spaces for the Sacred*, 168.

[79] Yoder, *Body Politics*, 20. Italics original.

[80] Ramachandra, "Christian Witness in an Age of Globalization," 5.

we consider the politics of place, where all the narratives are situated, and disputed: there is no pure seeing.[81]

---

[81] Competing discourses relative to place are contested. Pierce, Martin and Murphy. "Relational Place-Making," 55.

What Christ has done is take our broken priesthood into his and make it strong again. We can, you see, take it with us. It will be precisely because we loved Jerusalem enough to bear it in our bones that its textures will ascend when we rise; it will be because our eyes have relished the earth that the color of its countries will compel our hearts forever. The bread and the pastry, the cheeses, the wine, and the songs go into the Supper of the Lamb because we do: It is our love that brings the City home.[82]

//

When you're lovers in a dangerous time
sometimes you're made to feel
as if your love's a crime—
but nothing worth having comes without some kind of fight—
got to kick at the darkness 'til it bleeds daylight ...[83]

---

[82] Capon, *The Supper of the Lamb*.

[83] Cockburn, "Lovers in a Dangerous Time."

No Home Like Place

CHAPTER V

Place, Politics and Public Space

The Politics of Place

In 1717, the governor of New France granted lands encompassing a Mohawk cemetery in what would one day become Canada, to the Society of the Priests of St. Sulpice, an order based in Paris. Although the Order was supposed to hold the lands in trust, the seminary altered the agreement to make themselves the sole owners.

In 1868, a year after Canada's Confederation, the chief of the Oka Mohawks, a man who had himself been educated in the Sulpician seminary, discovered the betrayal and condemned the seminary for illegally holding the land. In 1869 the Mohawks attacked with a small armed force, after giving the missionaries eight days to hand over the land. Local authorities ended the stand-off with force. In 1936 the seminary sold the remaining territory for development, and left the area. The Mohawks protested and were ignored.

In 1961 the city of Oka built a private nine-hole golf course on a portion of the land. The Mohawks filed against its construction, but by the time the suit was heard much of the land had already been cleared. In 1977 the band filed an official land claim which was rejected in 1986 on technical grounds.

In 1988 the city of Oka began drawing up plans for an expansion of the golf course on land that still included a Mohawk burial ground and standing tombstones. In July of 1990, as bulldozers prepared to raze the burial grounds, the Mohawk First Nation armed themselves and erected a barricade.[1] A lengthy armed stand-off with Quebec Provincial Police began. Another group of Mohawks at the nearby location of Kahnawake blockaded the Mercier Bridge where it passed through their territory, sealing a major access point to a Montreal suburb. Quebec's minister of Indian Affairs, John Ciaccia, reacted to the crisis with surprise: "I never thought it would go so far."[2]

On August 8, Quebec premier Robert Bourassa invoked Section 275 of the National Defence Act to requisition military support in "aid of the civil power," a right available to provincial governments. On August 20, a company of the Quebec-based Royal 22e Régiment, (known as the "Van Doos," an Anglicized pronunciation of the French "Vingt-deux," or number 22) led by Major Alain Tremblay, took over three barricades and arrived at the final blockade leading to the disputed area. Additional troops and mechanized equipment mobilized at staging areas around Montreal, while reconnaissance aircraft staged air photo missions over Mohawk territory to gather intelligence.

The tense stand-off finally ended on August 29 when the Kahnawake Mohawks negotiated an end to their protest. The Quebec government rejected further negotiations, and on September 26 the Mohawks laid down their arms, dismantled their guns and threw them in a fire, ceremonially burning tobacco. Many were detained by the Canadian Forces and arrested by the Quebec Provincial Police.

In July 1992, 34 Mohawks involved in the stand-off were found not guilty and acquitted on charges ranging from weapons possession to assault and participating in a riot. In 1997, the federal government purchased the disputed land from the village of Oka. Instead of the village expanding a golf course, the Mohawks were allowed to expand their existing cemetery.

---

[1] The entire story was documented and later produced by Canada's National Film Board. http://www.nfb.ca/film/kanehsatake_270_years_of_resistance.

[2] http://hrsbstaff.ednet.ns.ca/mwebb/oka_crisis.htm.

In 2010, twenty years after the conflict, John Ciaccia commented, "We never learn from history, do we?" The former Quebec native affairs minister was at the center of the storm in 1990, at odds with his own government and the police. "The whole crisis could have been avoided with common sense and respect for the native community."[3]

Place is Storied

Reading this story today, and with vague memories of the images on TV in 1990, I am still stunned that this could happen in Canada so late in the 20th century. We consider ourselves civilized and enlightened, a model of justice in a dark world. A friend who lived near to Kahnawake in the 90's wrote to me,

> I was living in Chateauguay at the time, and have seen the ugly stupidity of brainwashed leaders. Some parents bought plastic guns for their kids to shoot at the "Indians."

> It was very intense. One day I got out of my car and started walking toward the barricade. A soldier asked where I was going. I told him I wanted to talk to the natives to tell them not all whites were against them. He told me that past a certain point he could not defend me anymore. It worked: I was hit with fear and backed out. To this day, I regret not having gone all the way. I always felt they were in their right to defend the land and the boundaries.[4]

It is easy to frame this story in terms of justice, or integrity, and simply write off the conflict as stupidity and prejudice. There was that, to be sure. But I wonder how much of the conflict was rooted in cultural attitudes to the land. For the whites, descendants of European immigrants, roots were relatively shallow. And there was no inherited story, no shared memory of care for the land. There were no rituals, like

---

[3] Wikimedia Foundation, LLC, "The Oka Crisis." http://en.wikipedia.org/wiki/Oka_crisis and http://hrsbstaff.ednet.ns.ca/mwebb/oka_crisis.htm. I wish I could report that things have changed, but in spite of good things like the appointment of Mark MacDonald as National Indigenous Anglican Bishop in 2007, the attitude of politicians to our First Nations people has changed little. A search for "Attawapiskat" reveals much.

[4] Andre Lefebvre, private correspondence. November 10, 2012.

that described by Richard Twiss in chapter four, of connection and identity. With such differences, and so little exchange of cultures, conflict is inevitable.

Place is first landscape, and then it is memory, and then it is story. Stories and memory are shared and so place is political.[5] Philip Sheldrake notes that it is appropriate to think of place as a text, layered with meaning. "Every place has an excess of meaning beyond what can be seen ... at any time."[6]

There is no "pure" seeing, and no pure "place," unmediated by history, politics, or religion. Even the surface of the moon is socially mediated. We tell stories about the moon, and have memories, perhaps of moon landings ("a small step for mankind,"). We may have knowledge related to etymology (ever heard of the "lunatic?") or related to literature and the tradition of romance ("moon-struck"), or related to science. The moon determines the tides and tides impact human communities. When I worked as a fishing guide in the tidal waters of British Columbia, the tides were a constant and necessary interest, with profound impact on local economies and transportation.

Place is storied, and people tell stories for a variety of reasons.[7] As Michel de Certeau expressed it, every story is a spatial practice. Stories are *placed*. In the real world of profits, scarcity and need, place is a political reality. In my Canadian context large corporations are investing

---

[5] A particularly poignant example is offered by Michael Northcott in the use of the first blue-planet photos of the earth from space. These images were later used by certain multi-national corporations to justify a unitary management of the earth's "commons" that would benefit powerful Northern interests at the expense of the South. "From Environmental U-topianism to Parochial Ecology," 71-72.

[6] Sheldrake, *Spaces for the Sacred,* 17. There is a hermeneutic of place that manifests in a conversation between landscape, memory, and a particular community. The political component comes through when the meaning of place is disputed, and even in such simple ways as who has access to a place, like the boss's office (see Cresswell, *In Place, Out of Place.*).

[7] The discipline of ethnography overlaps with that of human geography. See Moschella, *Ethnography as a Pastoral Practice.*

huge financial and physical resources in developing the oil-sands.[8] The environmental impact of extraction and processing is contested. Meanwhile, a new debate is raging around the Northern Gateway Pipeline, a story popularized by its prominence in the recent American election. Whose land is affected? Who really wants it, and who fears it? The bulk of the citizens in my province of British Columbia oppose it.[9]

And who tells the story of the land itself: the history, occupancy, and future? It certainly isn't our First Nations people, who were once the sole tenants of these large tracts of land.[10] The original caretakers of our land are shunted off to reserves, frequently the least valuable land, and the most difficult to cultivate.[11] Various groups are contesting the rights of Canada's government to determine the future of these lands and resources. "As competing discourses about places are contested (and, in their contestation, shaped and adopted by others), they become constitutive of new, shared place identities."[12]

Globalization, Sacramentality and Place

Place is contested space because humans have different values and goals and desires. Who defines "the good?" But place is also political because of corporate interests and global mapping, "globalization."

---

[8] See the documentary "Petropolis" http://www.petropolis-film.com. Recently new methods of extracting natural gas from shale are impacting communities. See The Nature of Things documentary "Shattered Ground" http://www.cbc.ca/natureofthings/ as well as "The Tipping Point" http://www.cbc.ca/natureofthings/episode/tipping-point.html.

[9] Which raises the question of power. The work of Foucault in exploring discourses of power is well documented, and his contribution to place theory is through historicism.

[10] This recent interview between activist Naomi Kline and one of the key voices in the "Idle No More" movement reveals much. http://www.commondreams.org/view/2013/03/06.

[11] This was seen very concretely in Canada in the summer of 1990 in Quebec, where a confrontation between the Mohawk Nation and a local government led to an armed standoff. In dispute was a small piece of heritage land that was also a burial ground and the local government wanted to extend a golf course. A NFB documentary relates the damning story: http://www.nfb.ca/film/kanehsatake_270_years_of_resistance.

[12] Pierce, et al., "Relational Place-Making," 55. Note the connection to post-colonial discourse.

There is no single accepted definition of globalization, but most agree it relates to the interconnected nature of the economic and cultural lives of the world's people. Vinoth Ramachandra writes, "Various global processes (at root, technological) uproot human activities from local contexts and re-attach them in complex ways in other contexts. Moreover a global civil society has emerged, alongside the nation-state system, comprising transnational actors of different kinds and with varying degrees of global influence."[13]

Global mapping is a complex phenomenon that has both positive and negative aspects. On the one hand it is a powerful democratizing force. Information technologies and social media are allowing for significant dialogue across cultures. On the other hand, the growth of a handful of giant multinational corporations means that unelected leaders wield enormous power. Post-development and human security theorists recognize globalization as a new form of colonialism and advocate relocalization and cultural pluralism in response.[14]

Globalization appears beneficial at first glance because it gives the appearance of overcoming the limits of both place and time. The universalizing of place and the free movement of goods is the goal of corporate and statist interests. A new debate is raging worldwide around water and the trend to privatization. Sources of fresh water in the world are limited, and placed. Reduced to profits, will the haves retain access while the have-nots lose it?[15] Zygmunt Bauman notes that, "The change from solid to liquid modernity is driven by the needs of the powerful, which means the economically powerful, whose ends are best met by an inversion of what once served them."[16] Leonard Cohen sings,

---

[13] Ramachandra, "Christian Witness in an Age of Globalization," 1. See also his outstanding work, *Subverting Global Myths*.

[14] Escobar, *Encountering Development*, xxiv-xxvi. In some debates the recognized need is for "epistemic decolonization."

[15] See "Blue Gold," Sam Bozzo, Purple Turtle Films, 2008. http://www.bluegold-worldwaterwars.com.

[16] Bauman, *Liquid Modernity*, 14.

Everybody knows that the dice are loaded
Everybody rolls with their fingers crossed
Everybody knows that the war is over
Everybody knows the good guys lost
Everybody knows the fight was fixed
The poor stay poor, the rich get rich
That's how it goes
Everybody knows[17]

Given the inequities between cultures, the tendency is for the powerful to dominate, through the media, with their images and symbols. The route is determined, and there seems no way to get off the road. Ramachandra thus identifies the "global village," in the sense of a mutually enriching exchange, as a myth.[18] While capital and consumer goods can freely cross borders, people cannot. Skilled workers and professionals are recruited from relatively poor countries, leaving unskilled workers behind, inhibiting development and growth in those places.[19] The wealth of a country lies less in the capital that flows into its coffers electronically than in its forests, rivers, biodiversity and indigenous knowledge.

Contrast older ways of being, ways that respected the harmony of local economies. Leanne Simpson, the First Nations academic, notes that, "Extraction and assimilation go together. Colonialism and capitalism are based on extracting and assimilating. My land is seen as a resource ... The act of extraction removes all of the relationships that give whatever is being extracted meaning."[20] Post-colonial discourse will offer additional nuance to the recovery of place as we include indigenous voices at the table. Our hope is to rediscover the strong connection between land and covenant. Over-emphasis on the latter as

---

[17] Cohen, *Stranger Music.*

[18] "Christian Witness in an Age of Globalization," 2.

[19] Zygmunt Bauman notes that there is a new stratification of the world population into the globalized rich, who overcome space and never have enough time, and the localized poor, who are chained to the spot and can only "kill" time. *Globalization,* 89.

[20] See this interview with Canadian indigenous elder Leanne Simpson in *YES* magazine. "Dancing the World Into Being." http://www.yesmagazine.org/peace-justice/.

a reality divorced from shalom, divorced from connection to the land, is a legacy of the dualism that abstracted place into space. The result is the marginalization of large groups of people who have been forcibly dispossessed of their inheritance.

Belden Lane describes the intimate connection between spirit and place, referencing the Latin *habitus*. Lane writes that this connection is hard to grasp for those of us living in a post-Enlightenment technological society. "Landscape and spirituality are not, for us, inevitably interwoven. We experience no inescapable link between our 'place' and our way of conceiving the holy, between habitat and habitus."[21] *Habitus* describes that habit of being that enters and honors the demands of its environs. We find it difficult to establish such a habit of being when our concern is simply to move quickly (and freely) as possible from one place to another. Lane continues that,

> We have lost the ability even to heed the natural environment, much less to perceive it through the lens of a particular tradition. Modern western culture is largely shorn of attentiveness to both habitat and habitus. Where we live—in what we are rooted—no longer defines who we are. We have learned to distrust all disciplines of formative spiritual traditions, with their communal ways of perceiving the world. We have realized, in the end, the "free individual" at the expense of a network of related meanings.[22]

Of course this "free individual" is a myth, existing only where there is wealth and power, and ubiquitous technological support. Zygmunt Bauman notes that there is a new stratification of the world population into the globalized rich, who overcome space and never have enough time, and the localized poor, who are chained to the spot and can only "kill" time.[23] Meanwhile, call-centers mushroom in Indian cities. Young educated Indians are trained to provide telephone services for the Western customers of transnational corporations. They learn to speak in British and American accents, and Indian names are Anglicized when

---

[21] Lane, *The Solace of Fierce Landscapes*.

[22] Ibid.

[23] *Globalization*, 89.

on call: Arvind becomes Andy, Sushila answers to Suzie, etc. This is depersonalizing precisely because it separates people from place.

The disconnect between people and place thus erodes human community by eroding humanity itself: we are reduced to "consumers" and our behavior is reduced to self-interest. The bottom line shifts from quality of life to profit margins. Even our most intimate relationships are commodified: witness the ubiquitous marketing of automobiles and travel using sex.

Ramachandra argues that globalism has become a new master-story. The narrative unites together people from all over the world in the same space-time.[24] "The logic of global capitalism is blind to the significance of place, history, culture or religious identity to peoples' work and well-being."[25] In this master-story humans are inter-changeable individuals where differences are unimportant. As a result, serious engagement with the *other* is by-passed.

In contrast, the very nature of the body of Christ is to make space in love for *the other*. True sacramentality is always ethical. Sheldrake writes that, "in its Trinitarian life, the Christian community (not exclusively but as a sacrament of human community) is a place oriented to a universality that does not depend on eliminating particularities."[26] Ethics is never merely a matter of behavior, but a way of being in the world that grows out of and is sustained in worship.

A sacramental sensibility does not affirm a sacredness of place naively, therefore, but affirms the need for transformation. The world is a gift, but fallen. A true sense of the sacredness of place begins with

---

[24] Post development and human security theorists advocate "planetization" and re localization in response to the colonializing forces of globalization. Moreover, they recognize the necessity of spirituality in resistance to globalizing narratives. (In some debates this is referred to as "epistemic decolonization"). Escobar, *Encountering Development*, xxiv-xxvi.

[25] "Christian Witness in an Age of Globalization," 5.

[26] *Spaces for the Sacred*, 74-75.

estrangement. The master-story of globalism is literally a Utopian ideal, a space that is no-place.[27] As Wendell Berry writes,

Every place had been displaced, every love
unloved, every vow unsworn, every word unmeant
to make way for the passage of the crowd
of the individuated, the autonomous, the self-actuated, the homeless
with their many eyes opened toward the objective
which they did not yet perceive in the far distance,
having never known where they were going,
having never known where they came from.[28]

Part of the damaged condition of the world is that we live with flawed identities with reference to God and the world. Place has its own politics.[29] We seek possession of places for private ends rather than the common good. We steal land, dispossess peoples, and abuse the land at will. Sheldrake offers that the Eucharist is a "practice of resistance to any attempt to homogenize human places."[30] It rejects a detached universalism. The value of places, like the value of people, is not merely as instances of a general type, but as each person or thing "does itself."

The victory of Christ on the cross reconciles us "in one body" to God. The ultimate symbol, and practice, of that reconciliation is the Eucharist. To become one bread is to be made food for the world. "As Louis-Marie Chauvet points out, the essence of bread is only realized when it is consumed; bread that is not food has not accomplished its purpose. Only bread as food, bread as meal, bread broken for sharing reveals the true being of bread ... The real presence of Christ is not a

---

[27] "Utopia," says the president of Nabisco Corporation, is "One world of homogeneous consumption ..." Quoted in Jerry Mander, "The Rules of Corporate Behavior." In Mander and Goldsmith, eds., *The Case Against the Global Economy*, 321.

[28] Berry, "A Timbered Choir."

[29] "As competing discourses about places are contested ... they become constitutive of new, shared place identities." "Relational Place-Making," 55.

[30] *Spaces for the Sacred*, 77.

static presence, but an active giving. Christ's presence becomes real in being given away for others."[31]

Consequently, reconciliation does not homogenize people or environments, "but creates space for the diversity of human voices to participate,"[32] where all of us together are transformed into something new. (Too often we have celebrated the monoculture of the church rather than embrace the beauty of diversity.)[33] Ramachandra notes that the counter-narrative of the Gospel collapses spatial barriers, but differently from globalizing capitalism. "We engage with each other through our ethnic/cultural heritages, not abandoning them for some mythical 'global culture'. Whenever we celebrate the Eucharist, we enact a counter-narrative of globalization that builds the global Body of Christ in every local assembly [thus, in every *place*]. It is the whole Christ, not some part of him, that is given to us in every local gathering that meets in his name (Matt. 18:20)."[34]

Virtual Space and Disciplines of Resistance

> *All of us sprung from one deep-hidden seed,*
> *Rose from a root invisible to all.*
> *We knew the virtues once of every weed,*
> *But, severed from the roots of ritual,*
> *We surf the surface of a wide-screen world*
> *And find no virtue in the virtual.*
> *We shrivel on the edges of a wood*
> *Whose heart we once inhabited in love,*

---

[31] Cavanaugh, "The Church as God's Body Language," 11.

[32] *Spaces for the Sacred,* 168.

[33] In *The Gospel After Christendom* Markus Weimer calls us to "overcome the morphological fundamentalism ... we need many new different styles and rhythms." Weimer, *The Gospel After Christendom,* 215.

[34] "Christian Witness in an Age of Globalization," 7. He notes that "Despite all the rhetoric about market efficiency and foreign aid, the net financial flows in the world economy are not from the rich to the poor but from the poor to the rich. Debt repayments, tariffs on exports and falling prices of agricultural goods caused by rich nations' farm subsidies mean that the low-income nations transfer to the rich nations around $30-50 billion a year more than what they receive in so-called aid."

Now we have need of you, forgotten Root
The stock and stem of every living thing
Whom once we worshiped in the sacred grove,
For now is winter, now is withering
Unless we let you root us deep within,
Under the ground of being, graft us in.[35]

In my younger years, church culture mediated place identity for me, where place was transparent in most of theology and practice.[36] Thus I had no way of really seeing my neighbourhood as a place God could dwell; no way of engaging the call of God to a place. The sacred could intersect with the concrete realities of my world, but that intersection was rare, or dramatic. Only the artists, and a few mystics, had a different sense of God's connection to the world. I couldn't see God hovering over the face of the waters, still creating.

The recovery of place has significance for more than the arts; it has rich missional significance. In fact, the recovery of *missio Dei* is directly related to a recovery of place. Without this way of seeing, the Incarnation becomes a doctrine that we embrace with our minds while refusing to know it in practice.[37] "Place" is so much a partner in mission that Mark Mulder can write that, "a poor conception of place... manifest in weak ties and affiliations" fed the flight of Christian Reformed churches from their Chicago neighbourhoods.[38] He notes that,

> the typical white flight issues of racial change and concerns over property values certainly played a role in the rapid departure of these CRC congregations. However, a more nuanced examination

---

[35] Guite, "Radix."

[36] Thus post-development theorists, noting that globalization is a colonizing imaginary, press for "epistemic decolonization."

[37] Charles Taylor might describe our practice of the incarnation as "excarnation." *A Secular Age.*

[38] Mulder, "Mobility and the (In) Significance of Place in an Evangelical Church," 16.

[offers] evidence about the historical importance that the concept of place played in the process of white flight.[39]

Apart from a vision of the world that recognizes place as a partner in redemption, we will fail to engage deeply in God's mission in the places where we live. Deep engagement is critical, because there is a grace that comes to us only through deep commitment. When we commit we deepen presence. As John O'Donohue put it,

> Though your choice narrows the range of possibility ... it increases the intensity of the chosen possibility. New dimensions of the chosen path reveal themselves; a new path opens inwards to depth and outwards to new horizons ... When we avoid [making those choices] we become victims of distraction.[40]

Numerous commentators are raising the specter of new communication technologies further eroding our ability to live in the places we dwell. In particular, the world-wide-web and the internet create a new kind of space.[41] One book raises many serious arguments involving these dangers. The new technology will change our approach to truth; it will change our language; it will erode our relationships; it will remove the "soul" from language and turn it into a *simulacra*—a mere shadow of the real.[42]

The text in question is not new, however, but was written before the time of Christ by Plato. *Phaedrus* was penned in the fourth century BC, and warned against the transition from an oral culture to a written culture. The warnings were overstated. Yet Plato rightly perceived that technology is never neutral, but arrives with its own practices. Practices

---

[39] Ibid.

[40] O'Donohue, *Eternal Echoes*, 89.

[41] Somewhere Graham Ward comments that the internet is the culmination of the modern city: the city that never sleeps. Phyllis Tickle in her book *Emergence Christianity* speaks with approval of cyber-churches.

[42] French cultural theorist Jean Baudrillard speaks of the hyperreal, a copy with no original. *Selected Writings*.

ground a *habitus*, a way of being in the world. Paul Virilio, in an interview in 1996, comments:

> We now have the possibility of seeing at a distance, of hearing at a distance, and of acting at a distance, and this results in a process of de-localization, of the unrooting of the being. "To be" used to mean to be somewhere, to be situated, in the here and now, but the "situation" of the essence of being is undermined by the instantaneity, the immediacy, and the ubiquity which are characteristic of our epoch. Our contemporaries will henceforth need two watches: one to watch the time, the other to watch the place where one actually is.[43]

Too near the truth. My iPhone locates me quickly. When I check into Facebook, I have the option of locating myself for my friends. But these devices also pull me out of my world, make demands of my limited fund of attention when I am trying to attend to the place I am in. The incessant demand to connect and be connected can leave us no time to rest, can keep us moving at such a pace that we can't simply "be" where we are. Stability is an endangered species.[44] As St. Vincent de Paul warned, "he who is in a hurry delays the things of God."

The promise of virtual space is seen by Jennifer Cobb as a counterfeit. She names the human need as that of "deep participation," which can't be limited to cognitive activity and interaction divorced from the physical world.[45] Similarly, Dodge and Kitchin argue that "cyberspace undermines the connection of place to identity and community by providing a space of identification free of location [and] based on affinities rather than on shared geography."[46]

These concerns are not unfounded. Humans have an incredible ability to be elsewhere than the space they physically occupy. We can live in interior worlds of our own making, and technology allows us to externalize those worlds. But those worlds are not *placed*. Technology

---

[43] Virilio and Oliveira, "Global Algorithm 1.7."

[44] See the discussion in Simon Carey Holt, *God Next Door*, 111 on "Nurturing Stability."

[45] Cobb, "A Spiritual Experience of Cyberspace," 402.

[46] Dodge and Kitchin, *Mapping Cyberspace*, 1.

can help us connect, but it can also be fragmenting, drawing us out of the world to a virtual space which is no-place. Our Western tendency is to dissolve all places into communication networks, transforming place into space.[47] William Deresiewicz warns that, "Facebook's premise is that [there] are, my friends, all in the same place. Except, of course, they're not in the same place, or, rather, they're not my friends. They're simulacra of my friends." While we should not invalidate human experience in virtual spaces, we need to distinguish between space and place: between simulation of place, and actual places.[48] Similarly, Giles Slade notes that the more technology mediates connection, the lonelier we become.[49]

Futurist William Knoke argues that we are entering a "placeless society" where the difference between near and far is erased and where the longing for a place to call home will only increase.[50] An article in the *UTNE Reader* cited research that multitaskers are worse at every kind of cognitive function. They were worse at distinguishing between relevant and irrelevant information and more easily distracted.[51]

We have noted above the dangers of the homogenization of place. "For the consumer with money, the illusion is created that all the world's peoples are contemporaries occupying the same space-time."[52] Difference is important, but only at the surface level. "Space remains segmented ... between the Minnesotans who enjoy mangoes in the dead of winter and the Brazilian Indians who earn forty cents an hour

---

[47] O'Donovan. "The Loss of a Sense of Place," 42.

[48] "The friendship circle has expanded to engulf the whole of the social world, and in so doing has destroyed both its own nature and that of individual friendship itself." Deresiewicz, "Faux Friendship."

[49] Slade, *The Big Disconnect.*

[50] Knoke, *Bold New World.*

[51] Deresiewicz, "Solitude and Leadership," 14.

[52] Cavanaugh, "The World in a Wafer," 187.

picking them."[53] That social media buttress de-localization is incidental, yet powerful in shaping our imagination through shaping our practice.[54]

New tools always create a demand that becomes a necessity, and new tools shape the user.[55] Dan Russ, speaking to the Dallas Institute in spring, 2000, offered a talk titled, "Babel: the Fear of Humanity and the Illusion of Divinity." He invited his listeners to consider that globalization, with all its complexity, "is merely a euphemism for technological imperialism which seeks to subjugate [humankind] and make it after the image of those who control the technology."[56] Russ noted that Babel was mankind's attempt to create the city of God in its own strength: a central place that was nowhere, *u-topos*, discarding both context and diversity to achieve power.

It is more important than ever that we know what we are choosing and why, and that we choose our tools according to our goals and our vision of the good life. For Christians, that means the kingdom of God. It means *re-membering* who we are: continuing to connect with the One who Fathers forth in beauty, learning to value what he values, and dwelling in the world he creates and upholds. "All living is local: this land, this neighborhood, these trees and streets and houses, this work, these people."[57] Love is particular: we name this person and love them. We invest in this place, in this soil and watch things grow.

In order to love well we need to make choices for attention. We need disciplines that will draw us deeper, carry us over the long haul toward the prize. We need disciplines of resistance: prayer and solitude will slow us down and reconnect us with the Center. And we need disciplines of engagement: justice and hospitality push us beyond the

---

[53] Ibid., 188.

[54] See in particular the work of Dallas Willard and James K.A. Smith. In *Desiring the Kingdom* Smith notes that consumer culture is one of the most powerful systems of formation in the contemporary world by shaping our practices and appealing to our affections.

[55] In this connection see Phyllis Tickle's discussion of cyber-churches in her book, *Emergence Christianity*, 151-155.

[56] Russ, "Babel." See also my Afterword in Volume One of the *Wikiklesia Project*, "Voices of the Virtual World."

[57] Peterson, *Christ Plays in Ten Thousand Places*.

ego toward the "other." Practices of earth care and gardening connect us with the land. Ragan Sutterfield writes,

> The problem with our role in creation is that we don't remember it. In our fallen state we have forgotten our place, both within God's will and love and also in our love and care for creation. We need to be reminded of who we are and what we are about. Practices and disciplines are our primary way of learning to remember, of being recollected to our place and call as creatures. I would like to offer farming, done well, as one of those disciplines.[58]

Farming as a discipline of resistance? Wendell Berry would affirm this view. While farming is still seen primarily as a rural engagement with land, "half the world *has become the City.*"[59] The reality of the world's peoples is now primarily an urban reality. The increase in interest in urban gardening represents a hopeful move toward re-placing the city.

Urban and Global Reality

We can't speak realistically about the places we live without addressing the built environment. Swanson and Williams call us to the reality of urban living in our millennium.

> On Wednesday, May 23, 2007, Shao Zhong, clutching a black plastic bag filled with all his possessions, shuffled off the train onto the platform of Beijing's West Railway station. He was from a small rural village in the Shaanxi province and had arrived at the city to work in a factory with several others from his village ... Shao's arrival in Beijing that morning tipped the global demographic scales from a rural to an urban majority. There are now ... more people living in cities than in rural areas of the world. Most important, this is an irreversible trend ...[60]

---

[58] Sutterfield, "Farming as a Spiritual Discipline," 5-6.

[59] Brugmann, *Welcome to the Urban Revolution*, 10.

[60] Swanson and Williams, *To Transform a City*, 25.

Urban living is becoming the norm in our world. In Australia 86 percent of the population live in cities; in the USA the number is 82 percent, and in Canada the number is 80 percent.[61] Yet Western history has tended to idolize rural and wilderness landscapes, connecting nature with the sacred, while denigrating the urban or built landscape as secular, and even demonic. Many students of Scripture assume that the Bible supports this view. Our next stop is a tour of the urban landscape.

---

[61] Statistics Canada, 2012. www.statcan.gc.ca.

Transformation, which includes both spiritual renewal and organizational restructuring, need not, in most circumstances, be conceived in revolutionary terms. Transformation implies changing of vital elements of the organization's value system which have been forged during its long history.[62]

///

"The shift is to believe that the task of leadership is to provide context and produce engagement, to tend to our social fabric. It is to see the leader as one whose function is to engage groups of people in a way that creates accountability and commitment.

"In this way of thinking we hold leadership to three tasks: Create a context that nurtures an alternative future, one based on gifts, generosity, accountability and commitment;

Initiate and convene conversations that shift people's experience, which occurs through the way people are brought together and the nature of the questions used to engage them;
Listen and pay attention ..."[63]

---

[62] Gibbs, *In Name Only*, 105.

[63] Block, *Community*, 88.

No Home Like Place

CHAPTER VI

The Urban Landscape

It's survival in the city
When you live from day to day
City streets don't have much pity
When you're down, that's where you'll stay.[1]

The classic Eagles song tells one side of the story. William Cronon notes that for many of us cities have "represented all that [is] most unnatural about human life ... a cancer on an otherwise beautiful landscape."[2] This dualistic view may have served a purpose in the preservation of parks and forests, but it has had the negative effect of limiting creative and redemptive engagement in our urban places. We must move beyond the duality of country good, urban bad.

But, what is a city? Is a city different than a town or a hamlet? Is a city defined by population, geography, or function, or some combination of these? In his book *The City Shaped*, Spiro Kostoff offers two popular definitions for the city, both dating back to 1938. "For L. Wirth, a city is a 'restively large, dense, and permanent settlement of socially heterogeneous individuals.' For Mumford, a city is a 'point of maximum

---

[1] The Eagles, "In the City."

[2] Cronon, *Nature's Metropolis*, 17.

concentration for the power and culture of a community.'"[3] Tim Keller defines city as "a walkable, shared, mixed-use, diverse area. It is a place of commerce, residence, culture and politics."[4] This is what we call a functional definition.

Broadly speaking there are three models of city, organized by function. Architect Kevin Lynch describes them as cosmic, practical, and organic. The "cosmic" city is designed to reflect the core of a belief system. Ancient Chinese capitals were laid out in perfect squares, with their twelve gates representing the months of the year. Ancient Roman capitals reflected similar concerns. The "practical" city is imagined after a machine, and grows as new parts are added and old parts altered. New York is a practical city.

The third type is the "organic" city. Here functions are arranged organically, with cohesion, access and function acting together. Streets may meander, and neighbourhoods and boroughs are joined together in the greater labyrinth. London, England is a good example of an organic city, as are Portland, Oregon and Vancouver, BC.[5]

Sean Benesh prefers an alternative approach to functionality, classing cities by the transportation technologies around which they organize: walking cities, transit cities and automobile cities.[6]

Why concern ourselves with the city? First, as noted above, the city is the place where most humans live, and this proportion will increase as the century unfolds. More to the point, the city is the place where most people will exercise their "skilled mastery" in this century. This will translate into place-making in the city. Jacques Ellul writes,

> The city dweller becomes someone else because of the city. And the city can become something else because of God's presence and the results in the life of a man [sic] who has met God. And so a

---

[3] Ibid., 26.

[4] Ibid.

[5] All three of these are also "multi-nucleated," or "polycentric," where dispersal and densification play off one another.

[6] Benesh, *The Multi-Nucleated Church*, 18-19.

complex cacophony raises its blaring voice, and only God can see and make harmony of it.[7]

Elsewhere Ellul notes that, "Because Christ is Savior and Lord of both creation and mankind, he is also Savior and Lord of man's works."[8] Our task in skilled mastery doesn't stop with farmers and craftsmen, but includes shaping the urban landscape, place-making in the city. This becomes only more important when we realize that our environments in turn will *shape us*. Will our environment make us more human, or less? Will our urban places help us to thrive, and offer us a context for *shalom*, encouraging practices that make space for the Kingdom? Even in the city, place-making is determined by a master-story.

Earlier we reflected on how forces of global capitalism privilege the universal in the name of profit. These same forces powerfully impact our large cities. Graham Ward writes that, "the major issues affecting a global city are increasingly less local, or even national—they are international. This is mainly because it is an international profile that the major cities of the world are competing for in order to attract investment."[9] Thus the ability to make choices is often suspended, transferred to multinational corporations where unelected leaders wield enormous power. As we noted above, Ramachandra identifies the "global village," in the sense of a mutually enriching exchange, as a myth.[10]

What, then, does characterize global cities? According to Ward, the answer is fear and anxiety. He writes that, "The global, post-secular city [London] is the home of the migrant soul. Citizens are caught between two public narratives: the potential violence of coexisting cultural

---

[7] Ellul, *The Meaning of the City*, 44.

[8] Ibid., 177.

[9] Ward, "Christian Political Practice and the Global City," 30.

[10] Ramachandra, "Christian Witness," 2. Graham Ward argues that one answer to the depoliticization of politics is the practice of cultural hermeneutics: the analysis, examination and interpretation of cultural practices.

differences, and the fear of the erasure of difference."[11] He notes that both these narratives are totalitarian and depoliticizing (they do not lead to engagement).

Ward argues that the alternative is a "practice of living that ... negotiates difference without assimilation."[12] This engagement is a politics of resistance rooted in a paradox. David Bentley Hart frames the paradox like this: "He is not the high who stands over against the low, but is the infinite act of existence that gives high and low a place."[13] The essential practice is the Eucharist, which "creates space for the diversity of human voices to participate."[14] The Church is an anticipation of the eschatological humanity, with the Eucharist a counter-narrative of globalization that builds the global Body of Christ in every *place*.

Cities are enormous factories for culture; culture in turn forms us into certain kinds of people. Still more, cities generate *cruciality*: they are crucibles for change more than other environments. But if this is true, why haven't we paid them more attention? At *Project for Public Spaces* they remark, "As much as we prize creativity in cities today, the cultural centers that we've built to celebrate it rarely hit the mark. Culture is born out of human interaction; it therefore cannot exist without people around to enjoy, evaluate, remix, and participate in it."[15]

In cities diverse kinds of people brush up against one another, and this can be confronting and confusing. It can also generate immense creativity. In the pressure of this environment people become open to new ideas and to change. Places can help or hinder our ability to manage change, and so place-making in the city is a critical vocation.

---

[11] Ward, "Christian Political Practice," 39.

[12] Ibid.

[13] Hart, *The Beauty of the Infinite*.

[14] Sheldrake, *Spaces for the Sacred*, 168.

[15] PPS, "Creativity and Placemaking: Building Inspiring Centers of Culture."

Seeking a Place in the City

There are numerous texts where we can anchor our reflection on the city, and most of them are in Isaiah and Jeremiah, prophets of the exile. The classic text to begin thinking about our relationship with our cities is Jeremiah 29:7. *"Seek the welfare of the city into which you have been called, for in its welfare you will find your welfare."* In this passage the exiles from Jerusalem are living in Babylon and are told that they will have to remain in exile for another 70 years. Jeremiah instructs them to seek the welfare—or shalom—of the city. [16]

We first referred to *shalom* in chapter 2, connecting shalom with covenant. Shalom is a rich biblical concept that generally appears in English as peace, a narrow form that does not capture the richness of meaning. Shalom is much more than absence of conflict; shalom is wholeness and prosperity, peace and justice—a community that is thriving in relationship to the Creator and to the land. To get a fuller sense of the meaning we need to look at the wider text of Jeremiah 29:4-7.

> Thus says the LORD of hosts, the God of Israel, to all the exiles whom I have sent into exile from Jerusalem to Babylon, "Build houses and live in them; And plant gardens and eat their produce. Take wives and become the fathers of sons and daughters, and take wives for your sons and give your daughters to husbands, that they may bear sons and daughters; and multiply there and do not decrease. Seek the welfare of the city where I have sent you into exile, and pray to the LORD on its behalf; for in its shalom you will have shalom."

When we look at the entire command and the promise, we remove the abstraction. Shalom is not a *spiritualization* of peace, a future peace in some heavenly realm. Rather, shalom is what happens when God's kingdom comes among us where we live. Moreover, the common good is in view, the welfare of the whole city. Kelly Kapic reminds us that, "Good theology is public theology. God calls his people to understand

---

[16] Some beautiful things are happening among a group calling themselves Urban Expressions in the UK. http://www.urbanexpression.org.uk.

and live in his extravagant love, and this inevitably includes concern for others in the public places."[17]

Jeremiah first tells them to build houses and plant gardens. He tells them to get married, have kids, and intermarry with the Babylonians. Then he turns his attention outward—outside of the walls of their individual houses and families, to what the city should be like. And note the priestly function of the exiles here: they are to "pray to the LORD on [the city's] behalf." There is no separation here between their engagement in the practice of place and their spirituality. Furthermore, in addressing the city itself the entire society is in view, from the individual household to relations with other households to the shape of public life.

Whatever shalom means by way of specific characteristics, we must acknowledge that it is a public or shared vision for life together in relation to God. Here we come full circle, as we found in the call to the rhythm of Sabbath. "In the purview of covenant, the stability of political life and the effectiveness of worship depend on Sabbath ... If life is not handed over to God regularly, with discipline and intentionality, then the [community] will end in destruction."[18]

In *To Transform A City*, the authors ask helpfully, "If God were to build a city from the ground up, what would it look like?"[19] They work out of Isaiah 65:17-25 to outline elements of the New Jerusalem. The city to be built by God is a place where:

- there is joy (v. 19)
- there is an absence of weeping (v. 19)
- there is no infant mortality (v. 20)
- people live out their full lives (v. 20)
- people build houses and live in them (v. 21-22)
- people will sow and reap (v. 21-22)
- there is fulfilling and meaningful work (v. 22)
- there is confidence that the next generation will have better lives (v. 23)

---

[17] Kapic, *A Little Book for New Theologians*, 89.

[18] Brueggemann, *Interpretation and Obedience*, 159.

[19] Swanson and Williams, *To Transform a City*, 56.

- people experience the blessing of God (v. 23)
- there is intergenerational family support (v. 23)
- there are rapid answers to prayer (v. 24)
- there is an absence of violence (v. 25)[20]

In a similar way Zechariah 8:4-5 offers a scene from the city of God: "[those] of ripe old age will sit in the streets of Jerusalem, each with cane in hand because of his age. The city will be filled with boys and girls playing there." Philip Bess argues that a sacramental approach to city-building involves six components:

1. a sense of verticality, in which height and depth are allowed sacred significance
2. concern for light (and shadow) as symbolic of the immateriality of the sacred
3. care for and delight in craftsmanship, redolent of the goodness of matter and its sacramental potential
4. the use of geometric ordering systems as emblematic of the order in creation
5. compositional and artistic unity, whether simple or complex
6. a sense of hierarchy, of sacred things being exceptional in their grandeur or their humility[21]

While this list is helpful, I offer caution on the final element. Hierarchy exists in nature, but should be avoided in the church. The Body moves within the fellowship of the Trinity, in mutuality and interdependence. The fundamental reality at the heart of Godself is relational, not hierarchical, and this is mirrored in humankind created in God's image.

In considering the built environment, we are no longer merely reflecting on what is, but on *what might be*. Bess distinguishes between sacred *presence*, and sacred *anticipation*. In the latter case an object may be sacred when offered up in hope of God's presence. A building may be erected as a response or as an offering. This is both an anticipatory and transformative response. Yi-Fu Tuan notes that, "Humans not only

---

[20] Ibid.

[21] Bess, *Till We Have Built Jerusalem*, 54.

submit and adapt, as all animals do; they transform in accordance with a preconceived plan ... Seeing what is not there lies at the foundation of all human culture."[22] In seeking God's kingdom in the city we are praying for and imagining a good future, a future for all humankind. Henry Drummond admonished, "To make cities—that is what we are here for. To make good cities—that is for the present hour the main work of Christianity. After all, though men [sic] make cities, it is the cities which make men."[23]

We create our buildings, then our buildings create us. The culture we create then forms us in turn. Joel Kotkin offers that there are three critical functions that every city must provide: sacred space, security, and a commercial market.[24] In the urban environment we must constantly balance commerce and simplicity, human thriving and access, beauty and functionality, maximizing limited space and resources in ways that enhance shalom. Place-making in the city therefore must utilize wisdom (the "ripe old age" of Zech. 8:4) to make space for human community, such that there is safety and laughter: places to work and to play and to grow.

Place in the urban environment, is both private and public, but architects of place must give special attention to public space: to the commons. Eric Jacobsen writes of the commons that the words civic and commons, "represent important aspects of our shared life that have been badly obscured, undergoing subtle transformations from being concrete notions to abstractions."[25] Michael Northcott notes that the word commons "traditionally refers to land areas or other natural resources managed communally by local people in ways which provide livelihood for local people while conserving the resource for the benefit of all, and for succeeding generations."[26]

---

[22] Tuan, *Escapism*, 6.

[23] Quoted in *To Transform a City*, 31.

[24] Kotkin, *The City*, xvi.

[25] Jacobsen, "Redeeming Civic Life in the Commons," 37.

[26] Northcott, "From Environmental U-topianism to Parochial Ecology," 73.

Before we consider the commons more closely, we need to revisit the concept of boundaries. Urban environments are places which are defined in special ways by boundaries and space: the space between buildings. Earlier we noted that places are bounded. In the suburbs, fences, shrubs, and sometimes pavements will separate one yard from another. A neighbourhood is naturally bounded by major streets, sometimes by open space, and sometimes by natural features like hills or rivers. Public space may be bounded in a variety of ways, but without boundaries there is no sense of place. Without boundaries, place identity is not possible.[27]

But while boundaries are important, they must be permeable: there must be known and appropriate ways to cross them. We knock at the door of a house.[28] At the local coffee shop, given certain hours, we freely enter. Public, or common, spaces have few restrictions: all may belong, so long as they respect the right of others to belong. Let us now consider the nature of public space and make a more formal connection to belonging.

The Nature of Public Space

One of the dangers in placing a strong emphasis on relatedness is that we may reinforce the irrelevance of place: place as a mere container, exchangeable, an inert environment where things might as well happen in one container as another. But we have seen that place is a critical partner in human relatedness. Our engagement with place can help or hinder our ability to connect and to thrive, and nowhere is this more true than in the commons.

The commons is a "space between," a transitional place, an environment defined in special ways by boundaries and open space. Note that here we are using "space" not as an abstraction of place, but to denote a physical transition point and a symbol. A doorway, or an

---

[27] Place identity concerns the meaning and significance of places for their users and inhabitants, and in cities is sometimes denoted by urban character.

[28] Mircea Eliade draws attention to the important role of doors or gates: "The threshold concentrates not only the boundary between inside and outside but also the possibility of passage from one to the other." *The Sacred and the Profane*, 18.

archway, both symbolizes and potentially enacts a physical movement from one place to another. Physical transition points are so important to belonging that they have become metaphors for human transitions, as when Victor Turner coined the concept of *liminality*: threshold places.[29] Let's consider how transitional places are formed.

Buildings are constructed to enclose space for certain activities, and then valued for the amount of square footage that they enclose. The outside space is used for parking and signage. What is neglected is the way that buildings shape the public realm. Architect Colin Rowe helped to bring this to light, using ground figure renderings (the view from above) to draw attention to the shapes created by the *space between* the buildings.[30] Buildings are related to one another by their wider context, and by the intention of the designer, who must discern the right relationship between places.

In long gone days, urban design sought to make the public realm attractive, a pleasant place to interact with neighbors. Research is showing that when people encounter a space functioning as a commons, they tend to gather there. *Soul of the City*, a project funded by the Knight Foundation, asked critical questions in relation to attachment to place.[31] What makes a community a desirable place to live? What draws people to stake their future in it? Their research found that there are three main qualities that attach people to place: openness (welcoming), aesthetics (beauty and green spaces), and social offerings—opportunities to interact. Two of these criteria are social, and the other is physical.

"Good inhabitance is an art requiring detailed knowledge of a place, the capacity for observation and sense of care and rootedness."[32] Recently a group in Tacoma, Washington asked this question: "Beautiful places inspire love. But what if our love inspired beautiful

---

[29] We ritualize the physical and social transition in marriage with the common use of an archway.

[30] "Redeeming Civic Life in the Commons," 38.

[31] http://soulofthecommunity.org.

[32] Orr, *Ecological Literacy*, 130.

places?"[33] Inhabitation is a matter of being, "not merely *at* our destination but fully in it."[34] Inhabitation requires attention, intimacy and even love of a particular place—only then do we discern, and respect, the integrity of that place. Note that this requires a *commitment* to place: place, like people, reveals its secret to those who care, those who are seeking *shalom*. Shalom is intimately tied to a covenant lifestyle.

In *The Gospel After Christendom* Troy Bronsink relates a story of engagement in a neighborhood known nationally for the sexual exploitation of children. A member of the church organized a daily prayer rite known by CU@2. In partnership with other churches and agencies a network was formed where phone and watch alarms were set for 2 PM. A five part prayer was then offered, for healing and liberation for the victims of exploitation; that coalitions against this would be strengthened; that perpetrators hearts would be broken and their lives transformed; that politicians and law enforcement officials would engage; and that their own neighborhoods would be strengthened to confront this tragedy. Through Facebook the initiative went international, and the effort helped Troy's community to refine its own sense of call. Moreover, those in the neighborhood who were not connected to a church could still participate in the mission.[35]

In Scripture justice referred to the fulfillment of responsibilities that rose out of particular relationships within the covenant community.[36] "Each relationship has its specific obligation, and all relationships ultimately are bound by relationship to God ... When the demands of various relationships are fulfilled, justice or righteousness prevails and there is *shalom*, 'peace' or 'welfare.'"[37] Yahweh's covenant love, or *hesed*, was expressed through steadfast love and loyalty. We are

---

[33] Post at the Parish Collective Facebook group, Nov. 21, 2012. http://www.parishcollective.org.

[34] Casey, *The Fate of Place*, 121.

[35] Bronsink, "Our P(art) in an Age of Beauty," 146.

[36] Anderson, *The Eighth-Century Prophets*, 43.

[37] Ibid.

to exercise skilled mastery by place-making in ways that honor the call to *do shalom*.

Our obligations to Yahweh are to be manifest in every relationship in our city. The challenge is that, "people move in and out of ... communities before deep roots are established."[38] Northcott notes, "The modern city celebrates and facilitates mobility at the expense of settlement, movement at the expense of place."[39] This is both a social and a theological issue. When the condition of our places undermines our ability to belong and to thrive, the church can speak and act. In many cities in North America the only sense of place that remains is a private one in the face of the disintegration of the commons.

How then can our urban landscape facilitate belonging? Craig Handy notes that criticism of contemporary built culture often manifests a romantic notion that we need to restore traditional town squares. He acknowledges that there are lessons to be learned in studying historical practices, but a better answer is to confront the conditions of Modernity and its spiritual and philosophical mapping. Handy issues a call to renew the built environment in ways that foster human community and interaction.[40] As Peter Block reminds us, "The social fabric of community is formed from an expanding shared sense of belonging. It is shaped by the idea that only when we are connected and care for the well-being of the whole that a civil and democratic society is created."[41]

The challenge is to balance the private and common components of human life. Places which assist in our belonging must be hospitable places. Recall the earlier reference to George Eliot, "A human life, I think, should be well rooted in some spot of a native land ... a spot where the definiteness of early memories may be inwrought with affection, and kindly acquaintance with all neighbours, even to the dogs and donkeys, may spread not by sentimental effort and reflection, but as

---

[38] Pohl, *Living Into Community*.

[39] Northcott, "A Place of Our Own," 122.

[40] Handy, "The Good Life," 16.

[41] Block, *Community*, 19.

a sweet habit of the blood ..."[42] Such a place requires only the most basic structure, and this sends us back to our discussion of boundaries.

In *Becoming Human* Jean Vanier notes that "as humans we are caught between competing drives: the drive to belong, to fit in and be a part of something bigger than ourselves, and the drive to let our deepest selves rise up."[43] Vanier notes that belonging is necessary for our growth to maturity, and that belonging is a necessary mediation between an individual and society. For our purpose here, we note that belonging is the essence of the Trinity. "Interpersonal relatedness belongs to the very being of God ... No one can be made whole except by being restored to the wholeness of that being-in-relatedness for which God made us and the world and which is the image of that being-in-relatedness which is the being of God himself."[44] Personhood is a relational quality.

Boundaries have a parallel function for place as for persons. "Murphy Creek" names an identity, just as "Joe" (and not Bob) names a person. External space becomes place, a physical location with definable properties, partly by what is internal to the place, and partly through boundaries. Similarly, the self is a location for personal identity. Without boundaries, there is no clear "self" and so no personal identity.[45] We have an internal architecture and personal boundaries that must be respected in order to thrive in human community. Similarly, physical architecture can and should mediate healthy belonging.

Healthy belonging allows for individuals to be wholly themselves, yet in community. Urban places and the commons play a powerful role in belonging, balancing independence with relatedness, and supporting healthy boundaries. We need common space, and private space: open space, and closed (personal) space. Closed space is usually where we are renewed and where the inner life is fostered. However, open (shared)

---

[42] Eliot, *Daniel Deronda.*

[43] Vanier, *Becoming Human,* 18.

[44] Newbigin, *The Open Secret,* 70.

[45] We recall the Athanasian Creed: "That we worship one God in Trinity, and Trinity in Unity; Neither confounding the persons nor dividing the substance." Without boundaries, substance is confused and identity is not possible.

space—a commons—is a necessary balance where there is a different kind of life exchange.[46]

These two broad categories of space first describe a rhythm of life that is represented in the Trinity: inward in love, outward in mission. Inward and outward are complementary movements that require a transition. In human experience the moments and places of transition are critical. Again and again the narrative of Scripture highlights stories of transition, usually in the form of a journey from one place to another.

Just as belonging mediates socially, place mediates physically and symbolically.[47] We need places of encounter, places that are transitional and allow random yet intentional engagement, between strangers who might become friends. Handy writes that, "Places of transition are moments of balance and a source of wealth. In them we meet, welcome, and learn from one another ... Places of encounter are the soil from which compassion, civility, and community can grow, if cultivated."[48]

Civic Life and Social Capital

This returns us to the earlier discussion of social capital. Putnam defined social capital as follows: "Whereas physical capital refers to physical objects and human capital refers to the properties of individuals, social capital refers to connections among individuals— social networks and the norms of reciprocity and trustworthiness that arise from them."[49]

Why is social capital important? First, social capital allows citizens to resolve collective problems more easily. Second, social capital greases the wheels that allow communities to advance smoothly. "Where people are trusting and trustworthy, and where they are subject to repeated

---

[46] "Let him who cannot be alone beware of being in community; let him who is not in community beware of being alone." Bonhoeffer, *Life Together*, 82.

[47] "The Good Life," 17.

[48] Ibid., 18.

[49] Putnam, *Bowling Alone*, 19.

interactions with fellow citizens, everyday business and social transactions are less costly."[50]

Michael Woolcock, a social scientist with the World Bank (and Harvard), distinguished between bonding social capital, which denotes ties between people in similar situations, such as immediate family, close friends and neighbours, and bridging and linking social capital, which encompasses more distant ties, including reaching out to unlike people in dissimilar situations. Bonding social capital is evident in most Christian communities, but on its own it can reinforce the inwardness of a community, and tend toward a monoculture.[51]

> Bonding capital is good for under-girding specific reciprocity and mobilizing solidarity ... Bridging networks, by contrast, are better for linkage to external assets and for information diffusion ... Moreover, bridging social capital can generate broader identities and reciprocity, whereas bonding social capital bolsters our narrower selves ... Bonding social capital constitutes a kind of sociological superglue, whereas bridging social capital provides a sociological WD-40.[52]

Bridging social capital is increasingly necessary as we seek to discover a new imagination for God's people in this new social location.[53] Community empowerment, group formation, civil society strengthening, coalition building are integral components of bridging social capital and social development interventions, all of which are significant in the recovery of place. Collaboration between diverse groups will be necessary for us to recovery a thriving common life that

---

[50] Ibid., 288-89.

[51] Eddie Gibbs writes that "the church's message of reconciliation is directed toward itself, with a view to bringing about a transformation which is evident both in the church's internal life and its engagement with the world." *In Name Only*, 107.

[52] Woolcock, "The place of social capital in understanding social and economic outcomes," 13-14.

[53] Craig Goodwin relates one such story on VIMEO. https://vimeo.com/54341053.

is rooted in place.[54] Sabina Panth of the World Bank writes, "Bridging allows different groups to share and exchange information, ideas and innovation and builds consensus among the groups representing diverse interests."[55] Consensus is critical in place imagination, since dominant motifs (chapter 4) differ widely and can reinforce engagement or detachment.

In a pluralistic and multi-cultural society, we need to find ways to build the trust that allows collaboration between otherwise siloed agencies and disconnected groups. Where we can identify common purpose, bridging diverse groups can allow us to share resources, knowledge of place, and will to engage that are otherwise lost.[56] For example, a non-profit society housing women in transition can benefit by working together with a local church and an artist's collective to establish a stronger sense of place in the neighbourhood. A housing cooperative that has noticed increased gang activity could utilize the gifts of local artists to mentor graffiti painters in an expression that enhances the neighbourhood rather than detracts and defaces local buildings. In the Philippines, an effort at bridging disparate groups for the purpose of collective action was successful in improving the management of the Kalahan Forest Reserve.[57]

The Fresno Model with Place at the Center

The Fresno model grew out of efforts to build trust among diverse stakeholders. At left we offer an adaptation to display the various stakeholders who participate in place-making.

---

[54] Wilfred Drath asks, "When there is shared work among people who make sense of that work and the world from differing worldviews, how can those people accomplish the leadership tasks while holding those differing worldviews as equally worthy and warrantable?" In answer he proposes a "third principle." See Drath, *The Deep Blue Sea*, 156-162. For a general discussion of adaptive leadership see the work of Ron Heifetz, Peter Senge and Margaret Wheatley.

[55] Panth, "People, Spaces, Deliberation." http://blogs.worldbank.org/publicsphere/bonding-vs-bridging. Italics original.

[56] Several of the chapters in *The Gospel After Christendom* are helpful in this regard. See also Samir Selmanovic in *An Emergent Manifesto of Hope.*

[57] Dahal, "Bridging, Linking and Bonding Social Capital in Collective Action."

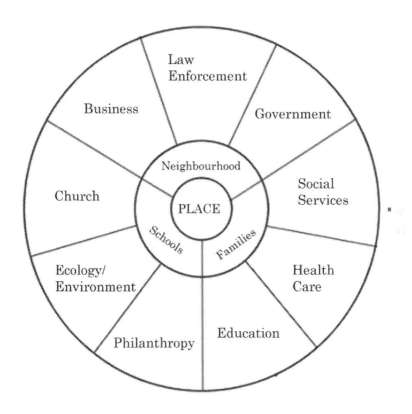

In order to leverage the knowledge base of diverse people groups we need places of encounter, where we can build bridging social capital—places that are transitional and allow both random and intentional engagement. We also need new leadership types to engage in collaborative work, a poetic leadership[58] that is rooted in new imagination about places and the potential of common life in our

---

[58] Hjalmarson, "Poetic Leadership, Mission and Theological Reflection." Unpublished paper. http://www.nextreformation.com. See also Part II of Peter Block, *Community*. Block writes that, "Communal transformation requires a certain kind of leadership, one that creates conditions where context shifts: From a place of fear and fault to one of gifts, generosity, and abundance; From a belief in more laws and oversight to a belief in social fabric and chosen accountability; From the corporation and systems as central, to associational life as central; From a focus on leaders to a focus on citizens; From problems to possibility." *Community*, 87-88.

communities. We need renewed imagination for the church as parish, thriving in the public sphere in the beauty of diversity. New, welcoming, placed communities are becoming more common, thriving between an old culture that is dying and a new one that is now being birthed.

Places of transition and the metaphor of liminality connect us to the next subject as we near the close of this exploration: pilgrimage, and the possibility of Holy places. The great stories of Scripture are paradigms of pilgrimage: Abraham leaving Ur for an unknown destination; Israel leaving Egypt for the land of Promise; Jesus ascension and eventual return as King reigning in the New Jerusalem; the disciples sent out into neighbourhoods and towns. The paradox on offer is that leaving the place we love can allow our return in a richer engagement. Sometimes we discover the texture and beauty of a place when we leave it.

June, 1923: the French paleontologist Teilhard de Chardin was
traveling on muleback in the vast wilderness beyond the Great Wall,
west of Peking. He saw it from a distance: the Ordos, the Inner
Mongolian desert. He saw from the mule what he had often seen in
Egypt years before: "the burnt stones of the desert
and the sand of the dunes in the desert."

The scant rain that reaches the Ordos falls in thunderstorms.
During one storm, Teilhard wrote a letter. "Of this part of the journey,
the crossing of the Arbous-Ula will remain in my memory as the finest
stage. The innumerable strata of this savage mountain, a forward
bastion of the Ula-Shan on the right bank of the Yellow River, bend
gently into two long concentric folds which seem to
unfurl over the eastern solitudes."

"Throughout my whole life," he noted later, "during every minute
of it, the world has been gradually lighting up and blazing before my
eyes until it has come to surround me,
entirely lit up from within."[59]

///

Pilgrimage, done properly, is one of the best-known antidotes to
Gnosticism. Gnosticism runs screaming at the sight of a muddy boot.
When wise men prescribe pilgrimage, there's a fair chance that the
diagnosis on the notes is "Gnostic."[60]

---

[59] Dillard, *For the Time Being*, 8-13.

[60] Foster, *The Sacred Journey*, 19.

No Home Like Place

CHAPTER VII

Re-placing the World through Pilgrimage

It was the spring of 1980 and I had begun attending Trinity Baptist church near the Osborne Village area of Winnipeg. Trinity's building was erected by stone-masons in 1909. The graceful arches of the chancel looked out onto a tree-lined street. Inside were sweeping, curved benches, stunning panes of stained glass, and an impressive pipe organ. When I arrived the church was experiencing renewal. The mixture of old and new, hymns and choruses, tradition and future hope was palpable.

The paradox of old and new, an anchor cast into the future, was present not only in the spiritual and emotional orientation of this group of pilgrims, but also in the place itself. Here was a building that had been rooted to the spot for seventy years. Set in its context, a mixed neighbourhood of apartments and homes and small shops, most of them dating back fifty years, it had the appearance of timelessness. It was connected to a tradition both in architecture and in faith. It was a sacred place, present to both heaven and earth: a symbol that mediated something more than the beauty of stones, wood and glass. God was very much alive in this place, as evidenced by laughter and tears, and the joy and expectancy of God's people.

And here by the water
I'll build an altar to praise you,

Out of the stones that I've found here,
I'll set them down here, rough as they are—
Knowing you can make them holy.[1]

But wait a minute: this chapter is on pilgrimage. Moreover, this book is written amidst the recovery of *missional* practice, when we all know that buildings tend to draw us inward and root an *attractional* and inward focus.[2] How does a static building, rooted in place, connect to the experience of God, and to a dynamic practice that involves movement from one place to another? There are multiple layers of connection, and we'll begin with some general reflections on the history and practice of pilgrimage.

The Recovery of Pilgrimage

Pilgrims are poets who create by taking journeys.[3]

We have seen how salvation, God's restoration project, involves not just people, but *place*. Moreover, we have seen how salvation is both historical, and embodied. We are saved, not *out of* history, but *in* history. By extension, we are not saved *from* places, but *in* and *through* places.

The Winnipeg story I shared above is rooted in a place where there is rich memory of meeting with God. Trinity Baptist Church are a people with history. They are rooted in a tradition of architecture, as well as a tradition of faith. People who have participated in the life of the congregation are people who are on a journey with God, a journey that incorporates a present location and a future destination in ongoing pilgrimage.

Roots, a journey, and a future destination in a story authored by God: these are the elements of pilgrimage. Roots always involve place, as does any journey. There is a starting point, and an end goal, and places in between. It is the metaphor of in-between, of journeying, that

---

[1] Croegaert, "Here By the Water."

[2] This word and frame was popularized by Frost and Hirsch in 2003, and is generally understood to describe the opposite of incarnational practice.

[3] Attributed to Richard H. Niebuhr.

makes up the heart of pilgrimage. By virtue of being *in-between*, pilgrimage constitutes a *liminal* experience.[4] By virtue of passage through real places, it is sacramental. It situates us between two worlds: this one we see now, and a future world yet to come. In pilgrimage, as in sacred places, two worlds meet. Phil Coniseau remarks on the meaning of pilgrimage:

> Pilgrimage is the kind of journey ... that moves from mindless to mindful, from soulless to soulful travel. It means being alert to the times when all that's needed is a trip to a remote place to simply lose yourself, and to the times when what's needed is a journey to a sacred place, in all its glorious and fearsome masks, to find yourself.[5]

Today religious traditions are recovering pilgrimage. Why now, in this strange post-modern, post-Christendom location? It may be precisely because we are entering a post-*everything* location, a time when the synthesis of the past five hundred years is collapsing, and the experience of dislocation is both inward and outward, personal and cultural.[6] The practice of pilgrimage is an ancient practice that invokes memory, and both embodies and ritualizes our sense of displacement, being caught in between two worlds. Eugene Peterson notes, "We necessarily live much of our lives in exile, so to be able to spot the people and places that re-establish our true identity is so important."[7]

Moreover, it is exactly our recovery of place that makes pilgrimage possible. In her poetic and complex history of walking, Rebecca Solnit writes that, "Pilgrimage is premised on the idea that the sacred is not

---

[4] Victor and Edith Turner coined this term to speak about transitional phases in primitive cultures and connected pilgrimage to rites of passage as well as the *axis mundi* of faith. *Image and Pilgrimage in Christian Culture*, 34.

[5] Coniseau, *The Art of Pilgrimage*, 22.

[6] Thomas More writes, "Stanley Hopper's solution for our sense of mythic vertigo is a new appreciation for the role of imagination. He recommends that we replace theology, the rationalistic interpretation of belief, with theopoetics, finding God through poetry and fiction." *Original Self*. New York: Harper Perennial, 2001.

[7] Peterson, *The Wisdom of Each Other*, 85. Italics original.

entirely immaterial, but that there is a geography of spiritual power."[8] Making the connection between spiritual life and the physical journey, she notes that it is the pilgrim who goes on an actual journey, acting it out with both body and imagination "in a world whose geography has become spiritualized."[9]

"Why now" must also be answered in terms of the dissolving boundaries between Christian traditions. This dissolution and new emerging center has been well described in the popular work of Phyllis Tickle (*Emergence Christianity*) as well as by Diana Butler Bass (*Christianity After Religion*). The impact of dissolving boundaries is that we Protestants are recovering aspects of our faith that we have neglected. Sheldrake describes the Catholic and Protestant tendencies in terms of two strands of biblical tradition, one rooted and the other transcendent.

> The Abrahamic strand includes the prophets, St. Paul and the Protestant Reformers. The primary symbol is the word, our critical sense is hearing and the fundamental dynamic is a movement towards an eschatological Kingdom. The physical world, images and ritual need to be questioned ... In contrast, the Catholic tradition, associated with Moses or the Gospel of John, places its emphasis precisely on being located. The location is primarily in a human community which is the carrier of the tradition. The kerygma is mediated through place, local particularities and the sacramental space of community.[10]

Sheldrake notes that Protestantism, in the spirit of Martin Luther, also concentrated on the "sacred community" of the church, and downplayed the physical locations that might be understood as a *sacramentum* of that community.[11] Rudolph Bultmann well represented the tradition when he remarked that "Luther has taught us that there are no holy places in the world, that the whole world is a profane

---

[8] Solnit, *Wanderlust*, 51.

[9] Ibid.

[10] Sheldrake, *Spaces for the Sacred*, 61-62. Italics original.

[11] Ibid., 62.

place."[12] In contrast, Calvin was more comfortable with the notion that the world is a *theatrum gloriae Dei*—"a theatre of wonders in which God's glory becomes apparent. The loci communes, the ordinary places of the world itself, become the stage on which divine revelation is acted out."[13]

The Incarnation and the New Temple

> I want very much to believe that every tourist is at least
> in part a pilgrim,
> but the evidence is against it.[14]

There is a certain approach to life, a particular posture, that dominates in our culture: it's the posture of the tourist. In these days most people travel, but their reasons for travel vary greatly. The tourist and pilgrim look the same externally: hat for shade, backpack and camera, water bottle and lip gloss, maybe a staff. But in the character of the journey everything is different. The challenge we face as followers of the Incarnate One is to move from the posture of tourist, to the posture of pilgrims.

Tourists are escaping life; pilgrims are embracing it. Parker Palmer notes that, "In the tradition of pilgrimage ... hardships are seen not as accidental but as integral to the journey itself."[15]

---

[12] Ibid., 62. But while this broadly represents the Lutheran tradition, Bonhoeffer is a clear exception, rejecting a two-spheres approach to the world. See in particular his *Ethics*, 62-75.

[13] Ibid., 63. This needs nuancing, conveniently provided by William Dyrness in *Poetic Theology*, 217-224. In Calvin's view "worship was everywhere, but nowhere in particular."

[14] Foster, *The Sacred Journey*, 109.

[15] Palmer, *Let Your Life Speak*, 18.

Tourists are trying to forget; pilgrims are trying to remember.[16] Tourists are looking for bargains, and aren't really *seeing* at all; and they hate to be surprised.

Pilgrims love to be surprised, and are looking to see. Dennis, one of those pilgrims who loves the Celtic tradition, writes of his experience in Ireland.

> Perhaps it is because of the centuries of Christians who gathered in intensive prayer and learning on that tiny isle that Iona has a reputation of being a thin place. As one recent pilgrim noted, "It has been said that the millions of prayers offered over the centuries echo in the very stones of the walls and the presence of God resonates from the ground itself." This was certainly a sense I had, both while wandering around the island with Beth, and when worshiping in the Iona Abbey with other pilgrims.[17]

Like Dennis, many people believe that sacred ground persists. Is it because this is the way we humanly experience sacred memories connected to place, or because there is something ontologically different about certain places? Or is this either/or choice missing the point, and the more helpful path is a sacramental view?

We also need to acknowledge a paradox: sometimes it is in leaving a place that we discover its deep nature. We require perspective in order to see clearly, and with depth. A single eye cannot triangulate. It requires stereo vision to perceive depth, and analogically perception in life comes through diversity of experience in places. The experience of being at home in a place is frequently enhanced by displacement. The rich reflections on the meaning of place in the work of Heidegger and

---

[16] My wife and I watched "The Way," recently, a movie based on a modern pilgrimage on the Camino de Santiago de Compostela. The story is built around a man whose son died walking the Way, and he makes the pilgrimage partly in desperation, and partly to honor his son. The Camino dates back a thousand years.

[17] Private correspondence, March, 2012.

Derrida came through a profound experience of displacement.[18] T.S. Eliot, in *Little Gidding* (V) describes the circular nature of knowledge, a knowing that is perspectival.

> *We shall not cease from exploration*
> *And the end of all our exploring*
> *Will be to arrive where we started*
> *And know the place for the first time.*[19]

As we begin this discussion we recall the definition offered by Torrance: the incarnation implies that "places are the seat of relations or the place of meeting and activity in the interaction between God and the world."[20] Let's also recall that creation is a word spoken by Christ, and then upheld by God in its particular form in the world. As a result, the visible things speak of the invisible, of the *logos* that existed before creation. Particular places express something of the divine in their *idiolocality*, their unique texture and existence; at the same time, their particularity speaks of more. God was made flesh in Jesus of Nazareth and ordinary things conceal glory: bread and wine become bridges to the invisible, physical symbols of an invisible and spiritual grace.

In chapter three we discussed Jerusalem and the temple. We listened to Jesus words to the woman at the well in John 4: "a time is coming and now is, when neither here nor in Jerusalem you will worship the Father." We affirmed with New Testament scholars that Jesus is the new Temple, the new meeting place of heaven and earth.[21] By extension, this dwelling is now in the church (1 Peter 2). We also noted that Jesus words to the Samaritan woman do not make place

---

[18] "The transitory nature of Place is a concept that has occupied Derrida from youth. He evokes the experience of de-colonization to illustrate his ideas. At the synagogue where his father would bring him as a child, it is clear from the design that it was first an Islamic mosque. It is a mosque again, reconfigured in the wake of de-colonialism." From the introduction to Derrida's *Elsewhere*. A film by Safaa Fathy. http://icarusfilms.com/new2001/derr.html. For a lucid analysis of Heidegger's later thought on place see Jeff Malpas, *Heidegger's Topology*. Cambridge: MIT Press, 2006.

[19] Eliot, *Four Quartets*.

[20] Torrance, *Space, Time and Incarnation*, 52.

[21] Wright, *How God Became King*, 236.

irrelevant, nor question the reality that God chooses some places to uniquely reveal Godself.

But it is important to note just what was occurring in the Incarnation itself. We referenced Walton's work on Genesis 1 as the inauguration of a cosmic temple. Let's now translate this spatialization of temple as creation and cosmos to the *God who inhabits* the temple. In the Incarnation, God inhabits his temple. Sacred place then coheres in the person of Jesus: where Jesus is, is the Most Holy place. The man Jesus is the place in all space and time where God meets with humankind, and humankind meets with God.

Jesus, in becoming man, enters a bounded space: an ethnically, socially conditioned and gendered place, and then radically subverts these boundaries. Sheldrake comments that, "The Body of Jesus Christ is [always] 'in the present' in the sense that it is ethnic, social and gendered in specific contexts of space and time. But it is also unstable. The instability is expressed in the Gospels in a number of ways such as the displacements of the Transfiguration, Eucharist, Resurrection and Ascension."[22]

Jesus does not remain: He who descended, later ascends. At his ascension and the sending of His Spirit, Jesus becomes the *complex* Body of the Church. What was local in one body becomes everywhere present. The Body of Christ becomes truly itself not by being bound in the Incarnation but in the Eucharistic moment: by indwelling Jesus Christ, who is everywhere present in His body. "The Eucharistic community is both a historical body and a mystical body."[23] Now let's relate this back to the temple inauguration theme.

Place and the World-Temple

In his earthly life Jesus was God occupying his temple. God's temple was the world. At the ascension the Body was no longer located in this world, and then at Pentecost Jesus sent forth the Spirit. Suddenly God again occupied the temple, but in an entirely new way.

---

[22] *Spaces for the Sacred*, 85.

[23] Ibid., 86.

NT Wright describes the scene at Pentecost, demonstrating how this event is the fulfilling and renewing of the Temple:

> Luke, telling the story of the day of Pentecost, tells it in terms that would awaken these old stories of God filling the Temple with his glorious presence. The rushing of a violent wind filled the house where the apostles were sitting, and flaming tongues of fire came to rest on each of them. That phrase is so well known that we lose, perhaps, its immediate and vivid force. Imagine a dragon with a red, fiery tongue reaching out to lick you ... and everyone in the room is being licked with fire. That's the picture. And Luke, writing the story, wants us to think: this is the glory of the Lord coming back to fill the Temple! This is the pillar of cloud and fire coming to lead the people through the wilderness! This is the restoration we've all been hoping for!

> Pentecost wasn't just the fulfilling and renewing of Torah. It was the fulfilling and renewing of the Temple. The apostles are constituted as the new, true Temple: not now a building of stone and timber, of bricks and mortar, but as a community of living, breathing, worshipping human beings.[24]

God returns to his temple, but in a way no one could have imagined. The Body of Christ is the Body *catholic*: everywhere present by the indwelling Spirit. What does this mean in terms of the temple? The temple is all creation, and we now constitute the presence of the Deity. Our bodies are the shrine. Where *we* are present, God is making Godself known, and inviting all to enter his rest.

But while this reality of God's presence in the world-temple in His body is just below the surface, an explicit New Testament theme is our residence as priests in the temple. Walton's work brought out the broader *telos*, or direction, of the biblical narrative: our destiny is to rule an earthly kingdom with Christ. Meanwhile we serve as priests in the temple, which is at the center of God's work in the cosmos. This sense of the world as God's temple is demonstrated in Isaiah:

> Heaven is my throne,

---

24 Wright, "New Law, New Temple, New World," 2-3.

> And the earth is my footstool.
> Where is the house you will build for me?
> Where will my resting place be?
> Has not my hand made all these things,
> and so they came into being?
> declares the Lord. (Isa. 66:1-2)

God rests in His world-temple, and in the living priesthood of Christ, scattered throughout creation in His body. Christ in his sacrifice raises man to God, and then is everywhere present by His Spirit and in His body. In redemption, the world is restored as God's creation and human beings resume their priestly vocation.

There are further implications. In the cosmic temple inauguration, the veil symbolized the separation between heaven and earth. As the writer to the Hebrews makes clear, Jesus has opened the way for us through the curtain by his body. The Latin word "profanum" means "outside the temple." Before the Incarnation, the world was divided between sacred and profane. But now that God inhabits his temple though his body, the old division is gone: all the world is potentially sacred space. Frost and Hirsch write that, "In Judaism, there is a distinct activity called *kavanah*. It is cultivated in order to maximize the inwardness of our actions. It means to pay attention, to direct the mind and heart in order to maximize the levels of intentionality in our actions ..."[25] The goal in *kavanah* is to find access to the sacred in the deed itself. As the old hymn expresses it,

> Blest are the pure in heart,
> For they shall see our God;
> The secret of the Lord is theirs;
> Their soul is Christ's abode.
> He to the lowly soul
> Doth still himself impart;
> And for his dwelling and his throne
> Chooseth the pure in heart.
> Lord, we thy presence seek;
> May ours this blessing be;
> Give us a pure and lowly heart,

---

[25] Frost and Hirsch, *The Shaping of Things to Come*, 133.

A temple meet for thee.[26]

Holy Places, Holy Intention and the Sacred

Sam Gill, in his essay, "Territory," cited Mircea Eliade as the most influential thinker to refocus the study of religion toward territory.[27] Eliade was a Romanian historian of religion, fiction writer, philosopher, and professor at the University of Chicago, and it is his framework that gained currency when religious studies came into being as a field. In Eliade's thought, sacrality varies from time to time and place to place. He believed that anything in the world has the capability of becoming sacred. Until a certain event occurs in what previously was homogeneous space, a place remains profane. "Every sacred space implies a *hierophany*, an irruption of the sacred that results in detaching a territory from the surrounding cosmic milieu and making it qualitatively different."[28] Eliade is describing an opening from one ontological level to another. Significantly, Eliade believed that when an object became sacred, it did not cease to be itself.[29]

A critical feature of Eliade's approach to sacrality is the concept of the center, the zone of the sacred, "the zone of absolute reality."[30] This zone is expressed symbolically in temples, palaces, sacred cities, etc. At the center, heaven and earth meet: the *axis mundi*. In this location communication from one cosmic level to another was made possible, and the break was disclosed through a visible symbol like a ladder, a pillar, a bridge, etc. thus designating the axis as the center of the earth.

Eliade offers us a language and framework that can be useful, but we have no sure way to answer the ontological question. Moreover, he assumes a dualism (sacred/profane) that is transcended in a biblical theology of creation. In the biblical world the *axis mundi* moved from

---

[26] König, "Blest are the Pure in Heart."

[27] Gill, "Territory," 289-313.

[28] McAlpine, *Sacred Space for the Missional Church*, 78.

[29] Eliade, *Sacred and the Profane*, 21.

[30] Ibid., 36-47.

the temple in Jerusalem, to Jesus own body, to the Body of Christ. It may be helpful to answer the broader question of holy places with reference to a particular experience of the sacred, and return to our discussion of the sacramental. Places are partners in redemption, and our built environment can be curated to mediate the knowledge of God.

Directly related to the idea of direction-intention (*kavanah*) is the idea of the hallowing of the everyday. It is built on the Hebraic understanding that there are effectively only two realities in the world: the *holy* and the *not-yet-holy*, and that the missional task of God's people is to make the *not-yet-holy* into that which is *holy*. This is done by the directing of the deed *toward* God (and not away from Him) and by the level of intentionality and holiness with which we perform our daily tasks. It is important to note that any and every deed, no matter how seemingly profane or trivial, can become a place of holiness when performed with the right intention and with the appropriate holy direction. Frost and Hirsch quote Buber in *Mamre*,

> One should, and one must, truly live with all people and things, but one must live with all these in holiness, one must hallow all which one does in one's natural life. No renunciation is commanded. When one eats in holiness, when one tastes the flavor of the food in holiness, then the table becomes an altar.
>
> When one works in holiness, he raises up the sparks that hide themselves in all tools. When one walks in holiness across the field, then the soft songs of all herbs, which they voice to God, enter into the song of our soul. When one drinks in holiness to each other with one's companions, it is as if one read together in the Torah. When one dances the roundelay in holiness, brightness shines over the gathering. When a husband is united with his wife in holiness, then the Shekinah rests over them.[31]

Buber describes a missional holiness. It works to change the world, to sanctify it, and is active in every sphere of life. It recognizes the potential holiness of places and partners with God in the redemption of the world.

---

[31] Buber, *Mamre*, 78.

God reveals Godself in the world: but this does not make the world self-revelatory of God. Instead, the cosmos is God's temple, the place where God makes Godself known. God is at work in the world in His body, and also by his Spirit. The Spirit hovers over the world, going before us to reveal the Creator. Sacraments are "those rents in the opacity of history where God's concrete engagement with the world becomes visible."[32] Sacraments represent the occasion of a duality in experience: at once ordinary, material and visible, and extraordinary and spiritual.

The incarnation has implications not only for the material, but for the particular. God chooses particular places to reveal Godself. Places, like ordinary things, are caught up into God's purpose in history.

The concept of a sacrament is rooted in the symbolic: that the symbol not only *re-presents* something but in some way actually *participates* in the event which it re-presents. More than memory and hope are involved: there is a gracious presence of God. A special word is used in Luke 22:19 for "remembrance," that has been the focus of much discussion in the Anglo-Catholic traditions. "The sacramental act of *anamnesis* draws the Church into a transformative encounter with the risen Christ in the present."[33] Memory in this view connotes more than cognitive recalling: the performance is a recapitulation. In Japanese the word for memory means "implanted in the body:" the memory of Christ resides in the Body of Christ, and is a participation in the life of Christ – past, present, and future—by the Holy Spirit.[34]

In times of exile we face the unique danger of loss of memory and loss of community. In that void, we are apt to believe the promises of the Empire to give us a home, to bring us security, to provide meaning and to offer unlimited consumption in an eternal Now. Who needs memory when life is so good today? Who needs community when we have everything we need?

God's people have faced other times like this. In Joshua 24 the generation who saw God's wonders in the desert have died off. The

---

32 Gorringe, "Sacraments,"165.

33 Gittoes, *Anamnesis and the Eucharist*, 2.

34 Lacey, "Eucharist as the Intersection Between Memory and Forgetfulness," 55.

people have lost their sense of identity because they don't have those old memories. A renewal of covenant is necessary, and part of that renewal is the renewal of memory. What does Joshua do? He recounts the story of God's loving faithfulness, going back to Abraham. Then he calls the people to make a choice (verse 15). In light of their determination, Joshua calls them to remove the idols from among them. He calls them to a heart commitment, a commitment of their entire being. Then he does two things which are significant: he writes the words of their commitment in a book, and he sets up a large stone (verse 26). He symbolizes the events of the covenant concretely for all to see, and for an ongoing memory.

"Tell all his wonderful acts," is more than a simple refrain in David's song (1 Chron. 16:9b); it is the fundamental work of the people (*liturgia*). Apart from memory we have no stories and without stories we have no identity. Lacking identity we have no way to renew covenant, and no way to move forward as a people. And we must renew covenant, because we continually compromise and falter and fail. Walter Brueggemann writes,

> Only through the practice of memory will new possibility emerge. Without some form of memory, this sentence you are reading would make no sense ... Without memory we become imprisoned in an absolute present, unaware of the direction we have come from, and therefore what direction we are heading in. Without memory there can be no momentum, no discernible passage of time, and therefore no movement or velocity. [35]

All these things come together in the New Testament at the Lord's Table. The story of Passover is brought into the present, and the memories of deliverance and the hope for a just future become one story. "This is the new covenant in my blood. Do this in memory of Me." That this remembrance is enacted in a particular place should not escape our notice.

---

[35] Brueggemann, *Hopeful Imagination*, 56.

The Shrine and Pilgrimage

> What the church needs is not better arguments,
> but better metaphors.[36]

John Inge, in his discussion of holy places, focuses on the concept of the shrine. He describes a shrine as the destination of a pilgrimage, and uses the definition of John V. Taylor: a shrine is, "a permanent reminder that this is not a human-centred universe: it revolves round God and for God."[37] By "permanent" Taylor implies something either very enduring, like a mountain, or built to endure, like a stone church. Recall our earlier statement that roots (memory), a journey (present experience) and a future destination are the elements of pilgrimage. Inge discusses the shrine under three related headings: past event, present experience, and future hope.

The shrine is the focus of pilgrimage first by its ability to visibly and concretely hold past events in fixed memory. The beautiful stone building erected on Nassau Street in 1909, and occupied by worshippers to this day, is a constant reminder to present pilgrims of the heritage of faith given to them. It points to a larger story, of which they only see one chapter. In this sense it is both local and particular, and trans-local, calling to deeper memories of the settlers of Winnipeg, and to their fathers before them, back to the journey of the patriarchs. It reminds them of the faithfulness of God and of his provision for his people through the centuries.

The shrine is the focus of pilgrimage second in its ability to transcend time and place in facilitating an encounter with God in present experience. Inge's discussion on this point extends for seven full pages and revolves around the Eucharistic celebration. We will rehearse some of our earlier discussion here where it is relevant.

The shrine is a place of Eucharistic celebration, and the Eucharist offers a counter-narrative to globalization. As Cavanaugh noted, "the Eucharist refracts space in such a way that one becomes more united to

---

[36] Attributed to CS Lewis.

[37] Inge, *A Christian Theology of Place*, 103.

the whole the more tied one becomes to the local."[38] If this is true, then the shrine itself is caught up in this transcendence and partakes of an alternative geography. But are not such attempts to privilege the local as expressing a cosmic story subject to sectarianism? Cavanaugh answers this charge by arguing that the Eucharist is not a place as such, but a story which performs certain spatial operations on places.[39]

Referring to de Certeau's discussion of spatial stories, Cavanaugh notes that stories move from one space to another and construct spaces through the practices of characters who trace an itinerary through the story. But this is a concrete *practice*, not a detached vision. "The itinerary implies not seeing but going ... a story is not simply told but performed."[40] The shrine, then, like pilgrimage itself, partakes of an alternative geography, telling a cosmic story. As Inge phrases it, "the shrine is caught up with the reality of which it is symbolic."[41] This is more likely to be seen where the congregation participates in a local practice that is rooted in a larger tradition. But even where this is lacking, the connection to the larger story is brought out in the stories we share, and in the feasts we hold in common with the wider church. Christmas, Epiphany, Easter, Pentecost: these connect us to other assemblies, local and trans-local, as well as to the history of redemption.

Finally, the shrine is the focus of pilgrimage as an eschatological sign. It is God and God's kingdom we desire. The fullness of that experience is not found in this world, but by the Spirit we have a foretaste of the coming kingdom. The shrine—often a simple church building—also points to more, to the Jerusalem that will come. The "more" we desire is not here; but this place becomes a sacrament of the future, the presence of the Spirit in the gathering of God's pilgrim people. At the common table what was broken is renewed in wholeness.

Even with the destruction of the temple, Israel's primary shrine, Jerusalem retained her importance. Jerusalem anchored not only memory, but hope: God's future kingdom would be established on earth

---

[38] Cavanaugh, "The World in a Wafer," 190.

[39] Ibid., 191.

[40] Ibid.

[41] *A Christian Theology of Place*, 108.

in fulfilment of the promise. God's covenant with land and people had not changed.

In the writings of Justin Martyr the first Christian reference to "holy land" appears. Justin tells us that when Christ returns he will distribute the land to His people as an eternal possession. Christian hope is firmly centered on the establishment of Jesus as king in Jerusalem. At this early stage in Christian history, "hope for the future [was] rooted in the land promised to Abraham and in the words of the prophets about the glorification of Jerusalem."[42]

The theme of restoration is taken up later by Irenaeus in his refutation of Gnosticism. He teaches that the final act of redemption will be the establishment of God's kingdom on earth. Irenaeus speaks of the promise of the land, the return of the exiles and the restoration of the temple.[43] Irenaeus clearly rejects a spiritualized interpretation of prophetic promises.

It is not until Origen in the third century where this literal fulfillment is rejected in favor of a "spiritual" one. Origen's approach is allegorical, seeking a deeper significance than the literal sense. "By the time of Constantine's conversion ... Christians had ceased to associate salvation with the land in a physical sense."[44] Curiously, it was this shift that cemented the practice of pilgrimage. With the literal sense of land traded for the allegorical, and with future hope displaced from earth to heaven, believers sought connection with their roots in a physical journey, to the places where Christ and the saints had actually lived. It was Cyril of Jerusalem who firmly established Jerusalem as the center of Christian piety, and Cyril believed in the intrinsic sanctity of holy places.

Is every church building a shrine? Is every journey to meet with other believers around the table a sort of pilgrimage? What might we gain if we took this point of view? Inge notes that the influence of a shrine is attractional or centripetal. "Shrines gather in a particular manner ... the experiences, language, and thoughts of the Christian

---

[42] Wilken, *Palestine in Christian History and Thought*, 58.

[43] *A Christian Theology of Place*, 94.

[44] Ibid. 95.

community ..."[45] In this day we have seen how the attractional church now struggles to become outward focused, engaged in the life of the neighbourhood. Buildings that are isolated from their context have come to symbolize colonial and oppressive forces.

But buildings can also symbolize an alternative future, in the stories of stone and glass and altar, and through the kingdom practices of a people with their hearts open to God and to the stranger. Where buildings are made to endure, and where they are also beautiful, they speak of the *moreness* of the kingdom.[46] Who determines what "beauty" is with regard to the places we gather? Evangelical churches have tended to shape space around the horizontal experience—community and immanence—while sacramental churches have tended to shape space around the vertical—mystery and transcendence. I affirm with McAlpine that "churches should thoughtfully and intentionally consider and create sacred spaces,"[47] with less concern for functional efficiency. There is a renewed interest in sacred architecture in this generation in part because we are escaping the hyper-rationalism of Modernity and finding renewed opportunity to acknowledge mystery and beauty. My memories of Trinity Baptist Church would be very different had the congregation gathered in a gymnasium.[48]

Even an ancient stone building can be alive in spirit and act as a place of refuge. Where a building becomes the center of a parish, it can act as an island in a stormy sea, where a diverse community gathers to be refreshed, to remember the gospel story, to learn the language of the kingdom, and to dream together of ways to counteract the forces that subvert the local. A refuge can become a launching pad for engagement, anchoring the dance of gathering and dispersion. For many a building connotes immobility, but where pilgrims gather a place becomes a shrine. Instead of merely fixity, a building can be a still point:

---

[45] Ibid., 114.

[46] See William McAlpine's discussion of Rudolph Otto's conception of the holy in *Sacred Spaces for the Missional Church*, 74-76.

[47] Ibid., 175.

[48] An intriguing example is offered by Eugene Peterson in the story of gathering a young church in a basement space that imaginatively became "the catacombs." *The Pastor*, 105.

And do not call it fixity,
Where past and future are gathered.
Neither movement from nor towards,
Neither ascent nor decline. Except for the point, the still point,
There would be no dance, and there is only the dance.[49]

Critically, we need symbols more than ever, and there is a recovery of symbolic language and practice underway in a world where images are becoming increasingly important.[50] Many local churches have lost the sense of sacred space—space not as a location, but as *axis mundi*—and their buildings are mere buildings. McAlpine comments that for Mircea Eliade, the discovery of a sacred place is equivalent to the creation of the world: "nothing begins or culminates in the absence of a fixed point, a center, found in the sacred place."[51]

As the Christian story loses coherence, a recovery of the church building as symbol, as with the recovery of liturgical practice, may help us to embody our faith, and thus make it visible as it is rooted it in the local.[52] Buildings are physical places that should also story and embody the truth of our journey.[53] Buildings themselves are rarely a problem: where a community ceases to embody the truth of pilgrimage and loses its vital connection to the Spirit, the building becomes an empty wineskin, a monument to history. But pour in fresh wine, and our physical places are renewed.

---

[49] Eliot, *Four Quartets.*

[50] Jacobsen names this ability for buildings to connect us symbolically with history "semiotic" memory. *The Space Between*, 74.

[51] *Sacred Space for the Missional Church*, 147.

[52] See in particular William Dyrness discussion of the importance of symbol in our knowing and our making (*poesis*) in *Poetic Theology*, 52-57.

[53] A beautiful example is offered by Eugene Peterson in the story of the imagination, design and construction of a gathering place for Christ the King Presbyterian church. *The Pastor*, 167.

Is the Whole World "Thin?"

The ancient pagan Celts, and later, Christians, used the phrase "thin places" to describe places that seemed to bridge heaven and earth, like the wind-swept isle of Iona, or the rocky peaks of Croagh Patrick. As the Celts put it, heaven and earth are only three feet apart, but in thin places that distance is even shorter.

Eric Weiner, writing for the *New York Times* in March, 2012 asks this question: "Why isn't the whole world thin?" Reaching for an answer, he proposes this: "Maybe it is but we're too thick to recognize it. Maybe thin places offer glimpses not of heaven but of earth as it really is, unencumbered. Unmasked."[54] Consider the world through the eyes of singer-songwriter Peter Mayer:

> *This morning outside I stood*
> *And saw a little red-winged bird*
> *Shining like a burning bush*
> *Singing like a scripture verse*
> *It made me want to bow my head.*
> *and i remember when church let out—*
> *how things have changed since then,*
> *everything is holy now.*[55]

"Everything is holy now." We return to a question we raised much earlier in relation to sacrament. If all the world is holy, is anything holy? Does this word, which really means set apart, lose all meaning in such a view? A sacramental understanding offers a mediating view of sacred places: places become sacred through God's action in them, or when our vocation is expressed with *kavanah*—holy intent. All the world is sacred as God's creation, but thin places exist only in potential, and this potential does not exist apart from the Body, the living presence of God in the temple. A sacred place is created in the interaction of God, people, and place. A thin place is really an event, the not-yet-holy becoming holy, where place as the seat of relations is intimately involved in God's interaction with persons.

---

[54] Weiner, "Where Heaven and Earth Come Closer."

[55] Mayer, "Holy Now."

Many of us can describe the experience of thin places. I have listened to stories that describe an experience of thin place on the island of Iona, at Northumbria, in Oxford, but also in Boston, Minneapolis, Portland, Toronto, Vancouver and Mexico City. While thin places probably do not exist apart from people, those who describe this experience are usually on a journey with God, and there are marker stones on that journey: events, connected with particular places. As part of their personal pilgrimage, they return to those places expecting that God will meet them there. They are not usually disappointed.

Re-Placing the World Through the Arts

Renewed attention to the beauty of the places we gather can help us recover the symbolic sense of the sacred that enhances our worship and mission. Truly place is meant to be our partner in mission. We have lived in the world with words; according to Hebrew tradition, God created the world in song. We inhabit our world in walking; God teaches us to dance. Dance is a communal activity, and requires both physical motion and sensitivity to context.

Sacrament and symbol are critical to our being placed in the world, because the first battleground is the imagination. As Richard Rohr points out, "The mind only takes pictures using the film with which it's loaded."[56] Artists understand symbol, and the arts help us to re-enchant the world. The role of the artist will be critical in helping us recover place. To the artist and the arts we now turn.

---

[56] Rohr, *Everything Belongs*, 66.

One afternoon, before anything was made, God the Father, God the Son, and God the Holy Spirit sat around in the unity of their Godhead discussing one of the Father's fixations. "From all eternity, it seems, he had had this thing about being. He would keep thinking up all kinds of unnecessary things—new ways of being and new kinds of beings to be."

And as they talked, God the Son suddenly said, "Really, this is absolutely great stuff. Why don't I go out and mix us up a batch?" And God the Holy Spirit said, "Terrific! I'll help you."

So they all pitched in, and after supper that night, the Son and the Holy Spirit put on this tremendous show of being for the Father. It was full of water and light and frogs; pine cones kept dropping all over the place, and crazy fish swam around in the wineglasses.

There were mushrooms and mastodons, grapes and geese, tornadoes and tigers—and men and women everywhere to taste them, to juggle them, to join them, and to love them.

And God the Father looked at the whole wild party and said, "Wonderful! Just what I had in mind! Tov! Tov! Tov!" And all God the Son and God the Holy Spirit could think of to say was the same thing: "Tov! Tov! Tov!"

And for ever and ever they told old jokes, and the Father and the Son drank their wine in *unitate Spiritus Sancti*, and they all threw ripe olives and pickled mushrooms at each other per *omnia saecula saeculorum*. Amen."[57]

---

[57] Capon, *The Romance of the Word*, 177

CHAPTER VIII

Re-placing the World through the Arts

Today, like every other day, we wake up empty
and frightened. Don't open the door to the study
and begin reading. Take down a musical instrument.
Let the beauty we love be what we do.
There are hundreds of ways to kneel and kiss the ground.[1]

Renewed attention to the beauty of the places we dwell can help us recover the symbolic sense of the sacred that enhances our worship and mission.[2] Truly place is meant to be our partner in redemption: our neglect of this truth has made us and God's mission in the world the poorer. We have lived in the world in black and white; God creates in color. We have lived in the world with flat screens; God creates in three dimensions. We have lived in the world with words; God creates in song. We inhabit our world in walking; God teaches us to dance.[3]

---

[1] Rumi, "The Essential Rumi," 36.

[2] William Dyrness notes that the Reformation replaced the practices of the lower body with those of the upper body: emphasis shifted from the whole body to the head. Adoration had been the goal; now thinking was the goal. "Poetic Theology and the Everyday Presence of God," 19.

[3] See a wonderful reflection on the meaning, poetry, and history of walking in Rebecca Solnit, *Wanderlust: A History of Walking*.

According to Hebrew myth, God created the world in song; and according to the Hebrew Scriptures, he so delights in his creation that he dances over us (Zeph. 3:17)!

The role of the artist will be critical in helping us recover place. First, because the artist helps us to see our seeing, lifts the veil on the glory in the ordinary things and intuits the whole in the parts. Second, because the artist helps us move toward embodiment, dances us from the realm of abstraction toward incarnation. Third, because the artist is not content with the world as it is. The artist embodies longing, hungering for beauty and reaching for more in reaching for the kingdom.

Fourth, the artist lives in that place "between the sea and the foam," and understands the limits of rationality and the need to bow before mystery. In part this is a recognition of limits, often discovered in relation to a particular medium, and in part it is a sacramental sensibility. In order to recover place we must re-vision the old stories, and re-enchant the world. Wendell Berry writes,

> The incarnate Word is with us,
> is still speaking, is present
> always, yet leaves no sign
> but everything that is.[4]

The Role of the Artist

The first of these roles, that of "seeing our seeing," I have already addressed in this book. Lifting the veil on ordinary things is both a theological and an artistic task. We need more than good sermons to aid us in this: we need new stories, music, dance, film, theatre, paintings and more. We need to engage the entire souls of people, who are much more than cognitive beings. What we commonly call discipleship, Harvard philosopher Elaine Scarry assigns to "the pedagogical role of beauty."[5]

---

[4] Berry, "Sabbaths," IX.

[5] Scarry, *On Beauty and Being Just*, 6-7. She writes that "the willingness to continually revise one's own location in order to place oneself in the path of beauty is the basic impulse underlying education."

Growing out of the Enlightenment, rationalism became reductionistic. Grenz notes that, "We cannot simply collapse truth into rational certainty. Rather we must make room for mystery—as a reminder that God transcends human rationality [and] at the heart of Christianity is a personal encounter."[6] Not only did we break things down into their smallest components in order to understand function, we then reduced things *to* their components: a chair is *nothing but* pieces of word, or a collection of fibers. This objectification resulted in fragmentation and loss of meaning. *Things* became disconnected from life and from the sacred, and inevitably, the same was true of people. T.S. Eliot asks,

> *Where is the Life we have lost in living?*
> *Where is the wisdom we have lost in knowledge?*
> *Where is the knowledge we have lost in information?*[7]

The arts tend to move in the other direction, away from reduction and fragmentation toward meaning and reconnection, and toward intuiting the whole from the parts. Moreover, the end of Newton's hegemony has opened space for a new imagination. Experiments done by physicist David Bohm in the 1970's demonstrated that "separate objects, entities, structures, and events in the visible or explicate world around us are relatively autonomous, stable, and temporary "subtotalities" derived from a deeper, implicate order of unbroken wholeness."[8] A similar idea has been popularized in the butterfly effect. Life is connected at deep levels. This understanding can help us see the places we dwell. Place is not merely a container, nor a collection of objects, nor simply a "unit of environment," but something more like an event. Place exists uniquely in time as an expression of the creative activity of God in the world.

In Tacoma, a group of neighbourhood residents, artists, and a local art school conspired together to curate "Love Tacoma Lane." The background of the project is that McGranahan Architects designed a

---

[6] Grenz, *A Primer on Postmodernism*, 169.

[7] Eliot, "Choruses from 'The Rock.'"

[8] Bohm, *Wholeness and the Implicate Order*, 48.

high-rise mixed use building for a local developer, and the project was suspended after the downturn in the economy. The site is only one block away from the Municipal building. Seong Shin notes that the fenced lane is used by "citizens who decide to walk to work every day, neighbors who determine to shop and play locally, and new urban dwellers who selected this particular area to live."[9] She writes,

> Because I believe in Albert Einstein's definition of INSANITY, "Doing the same thing over and over again and expecting different results," I wanted to try a small project in a different way. The first project location is at St. Helens and 6th Ave, 108 feet long Pedestrian Fenced Walkway. The vision is to reclaim and beautify a previously developed site that has been neglected over the years, and work together as a community to provide a canvas for neighbors, passersby and visitors to create temporary, interactive art that lifts the holiday spirit. It has been an exciting, creative and experimental ride.[10]

The installation was announced on Facebook, and then also on the Parish Collective website.[11] Despite its best intentions, the church has often failed to offer people practices and language that would help them recognize and celebrate the sacred where they live. Sometimes we have communicated that God's primary interest is in what happens on Sunday mornings. Dwight Zscheile writes that, "In the incarnation, God entrusts Godself to the hospitality of the world."[12]

This is much easier to do when a church sees its role as rooted in the neighbourhood, anchoring a parish (recall the discussion in chapter 4). Troy Bronsink relates a story of community engagement through the arts. They designed a ritual for Ash Wednesday, organizing a flash mob in the busiest station of Atlanta's transit system. An artist for the

---

[9] Unpublished public announcement supplied by Seong Shin to the writer. December, 2012.

[10] Ibid.

[11] https://www.facebook.com/TacomaLoveLocks.

[12] Zscheile, *People of the Way*, 77.

community designed a logo that read "Submit your sins here" to wrap around coffee cans. Troy tells the story:

> The cans were distributed to pubs and coffee shops across town, with instructions to stay posted for a "flAsh Requiem" on Ash Wednesday. On Fat Tuesday we collected the cans and burned the submissions. We mixed the ashes with oil, and the next day visitors to the website were instructed to join us at 5 PM at the MARTA station ... When we arrived Bill, Dan and Nancy were playing a requiem on cello, classical guitar and flute. Without any sermon or formal announcement we began marking a cross on one another's foreheads with ashes saying, "From dust you have come. To dust you shall return. Go with the grace of God." Strangers met up with us and joined in the ritual. Blurring contexts pushed participants into a translation dilemma, and reconstructing ancient rituals forced us to reexamine the traditional forms.[13]

Churches which are embedded in and committed to a place can engage imaginatively in common life in ways that acknowledge the sacred.[14] Eric Jacobsen helps us understand this role with his distinction between embedded churches and insular churches, a frame which helps us move beyond the rigid dichotomy of incarnational and attractional.[15] Churches built prior to WWII are embedded because "they facilitate direct connections between the interior space of the church building and the public space of the wider society."[16] Often these buildings extend to the sidewalk and have little or no parking lot.

---

[13] Bronsink, "Our P(art) in an Age of Beauty," 146-147.

[14] Sometimes the "parish" needs to give way to "place" just as art can sometimes appear as "craft." In indigenous communities reclaiming the land and ritual and craft are often interwoven. See this interview with Canadian indigenous elder Leanne Simpson in *YES* magazine. "Dancing the World Into Being." March 5, 2013. http://www.yesmagazine.org/peace-justice.

[15] Some interesting work was done in this regard by Drew Goodmanson and the SOMA communities. A "triperspectival" ecclesiology was advanced, with "missional" occupying the middle position between attractional and incarnational. "Building a Church Movement of Gospel Centered Communities," 3-4. Fitch and Holsclaw in *Prodigal Christianity* define one of the conditions of post-Christendom as "post-attractional."

[16] Jacobsen, *The Space Between*, 190.

Insular churches, on the other hand, were built after WWII and are insulated from direct contact with the community that surrounds them. These buildings tend to include a large parking lot that acts as a buffer between the space inside and the world outside, often sitting on lots that exceed five acres in size. These buildings, oriented to commuter traffic, are rarely *placed* in the sense we have been developing in this book. Jacobsen notes that one distinction between the two types of building is found in their doors. Embedded churches tend to have elaborate, symbolically rich doors that communicate the ethos to all who pass by. The doors guard thresholds, which are really *liminal* space, whereas insular churches have doors that are merely functional, and do not mark a significant transition.

Moving Toward Embodiment

The second role of the artist in the recovery of place, that of moving toward embodiment, I have addressed in several locations here. It would be helpful if I could include a short film on place, or perhaps an original song.[17] Alas, words are the limits of a written medium. The websites referenced at the close of this book offer other expressions that extend this project, and I encourage every reader to find or develop local expressions that will assist in the recovery of place.

However, it has been part of my careful method in this book to incorporate poetry as a means of reaching beyond the merely rational, beyond what can be expressed conceptually, to that realm in the human spirit that responds viscerally and intuitively. In one of his most popular pieces John Denver sings,

> *Life in the city can make you crazy*
> *For sounds of the sand and the sea*
> *Life in a high-rise can make you hungry*
> *For things that you can't even see ...*[18]

---

[17] https://vimeo.com/51492378.

[18] Denver, "Fly Away."

As one poet expressed it, "Poetry is the language of what it is not possible to say."[19] This is beautifully illustrated by John Bohannon in a TED Talk—a talk that is also a dance—filmed in November, 2011 in Brussels. The title of his presentation is "Dance vs. Powerpoint, a Modest Proposal."[20] John demonstrates that the collaboration of physicists with artists extends vision as if by stereoscopic sight.

In a similar way, adding music to words multiplies their power, actually creating something new, like a marriage between two people creates a third reality in the world. We are moved by music; music reaches beyond the intellect to our affections and will. It is an alternate way of *knowing* the world, and thus of redeeming it. It is not naively that JRR Tolkien pictures the creation of the world in song in his epic work, *The Silmarillion*.[21] And in another Eastern tradition, Rumi writes,

In your light I learn how to love.
In your beauty, how to make poems.
You dance inside my chest,
where no one sees you.
But sometimes I do,
and that light becomes this art.[22]

Longing, Beauty, and Mystery: Re-Enchanting the World

The third and fourth roles of the artist offer the hope of re-placing us in the world by naming our longing, revealing beauty, and acknowledging mystery. This is accomplished in several ways: by offering new language; by re-enchanting the world through the new telling of old stories; by revealing and paying attention to beauty; and by exposing the limits of rationality and helping us to bow before mystery.

---

[19] Alves, *The Poet, The Warrior, The Prophet*, 96.

[20] http://www.ted.com/talks/
john_bohannon_dance_vs_powerpoint_a_modest_proposal.html.

[21] Tolkien, *The Silmarillion*, 4-5.

[22] Rumi, "Sometimes I do."

What is it in humanity that longs for beauty?[23] Jim Croegaert writes,

Moon hanging lonely
Up there in the sky
Looking so holy
Like a host held up high
And off in the distance
There's a train going by
Why does it move us
And cause us to sigh
Why do we hunger for beauty?[24]

The creation itself longs for liberation from its bondage to decay. "Not only so, but we ourselves, who have the first-fruits of the Spirit, groan inwardly ..." (Rom. 8:23). Scripture names this inner knowledge, the awareness that there is so much more to come: more freedom, more wholeness, and the fullness of beauty and life that was intended for every person and place. CS Lewis reminds us: "We do not want merely to see beauty, though, God knows, even that is bounty enough. We want something else which can hardly be put into words—to be united with the beauty we see, to pass into it, to receive it into ourselves, to bathe in it, to become part of it."[25]

The invitation is to enter the story: to join with God in the outworking of God's purposes in redemption. Kenneth Bailey addresses the issue of serious theology through narrative in his work on Middle Eastern culture. He writes,

Today, Jesus is naturally seen by Christians as the Son of God and Savior of the world. But have we thought of him as a serious theologian?

---

[23] In a related article Robb Shoaf explores the connection to pedagogy. "Pedagogy Employs an Old Friend," 36-42.

[24] Croegaert, "Why Do We Hunger for Beauty?"

[25] Lewis, "The Weight of Glory."

Jesus was a metaphorical theologian ... That is, his primary method of creating meaning was through metaphor, simile, parable and dramatic action rather than through logic and reasoning. He created meaning like a dramatist and poet rather than like a philosopher.[26]

One cannot read the New Testament and escape the sensation of living in a very big story. Our churches live within stories and narratives that make meaning for them, and that story was powerfully subverted by Modernity. But the best stories open us to God at work in the world and connect us with our deep hopes and with the coming kingdom. Michael Frost writes, "If the root of art is storytelling, then the taproots are longings. Longings for such things as truth, beauty, romance, adventure. We long to find the true north that will guide us through this life and into the next ..."[27]

What is it in the great stories that draw us in? In *The Secular Age*, Charles Taylor asks what occurred between 1500 and 2000—the modern age of Western society—when in 1500 it was impossible not to believe in God while in 2000 it became possible? His answer: disenchantment, which led to secularism. Disenchantment "leaves us with a universe that is dull, routine, flat, driven by rules rather than thoughts, a process that culminates in bureaucracy run by "specialists without spirit, hedonists without heart."[28]

Look at the architecture and icons of medieval cathedrals and medieval art in museums in Europe and you'll see *enchantment*. Taylor argues that the cumulative impact of Renaissance humanism (humans are the center), the Enlightenment (the mind is the center), and the scientific revolution made it possible to explain the mystery and majesty of the world without God. Disenchantment discards the sacred,[29] but

---

[26] Bailey, *Jesus Through Middle Eastern Eyes*, 279.

[27] Frost and Banks, *Lessons from Reel Life*, iii.

[28] Taylor, *A Secular Age*, 26

[29] An alternate take on this is in the work of Stanley Hopper. Thomas Moore describes his argument for theopoetics: "finding God through poetry and fiction, which neither wither before modern science nor conflict with the complexity of what we know now to be the self." *Original Self.*

205

the New Testament, especially the nativity stories, offer an enchanted world. Today it is mostly Hollywood that offers enchantment. As Ivan Illich noted, "Neither revolution nor reformation can ultimately change a society, rather you must tell ... an alternative story."[30]

The stories of the bible place us in a real and enchanted world, one where God is intimately at work, and where we are invited to become partners in redemption. Our stories, our music and dance, our poetry and art should similarly place us in the world, engaged as kings and priests, hallowing the world and offering it back to God. "It is at the level of the imagination that the fateful issues of our new world-experience must first be mastered ... Old words do not reach across the new gulfs, and it is only in vision and oracle that we can chart the unknown and new-name the creatures."[31]

Enchantment presupposes the limits of rationality. Clark Pinnock reminds us that the Bible is a book of stories, but theology has failed to orient itself this way. Agreeing with James K.A. Smith, Pinnock notes that "Theology has been enamored by the rationalist ideal on the (dubious) assumption that people are basically rational beings who need to be appealed to with abstract arguments. This is not only untrue in relation to people, it refuses to take seriously the plain fact that in Christianity truth is in the story."[32]

If theology is built on logic and reasoning, then all one needs to understand theology is a clear mind and a will to work hard. But if, for Jesus, stories and dramatic actions are the language of theology, then our task is very different. We enter an adventure that is a risky joint-venture with God.[33] We are mystics, not managers, and poets, not engineers: lovers in a dangerous time. Even the creative process itself, in the mirroring of Trinitarian reality, is a mystery.[34]

---

[30] Dale, et al., *The Rabbit and the Elephant*, 150.

[31] Wilder, *Theopoetic*.

[32] Pinnock, *Tracking the Maze*, 182.

[33] The theme of participation has been under-explored in the missional conversation, but is becoming more prominent. See Craig Van Gelder and Dwight J. Zscheile, *The Missional Church in Perspective*, 109.

[34] See the discussion of Dorothy Sayers creative Trinity at the close of chapter 3.

The Lifted Veil

All names fall short of the shining of things.[35]

In the last chapter we explored the possibility of thin places, and the potential of any place to become thin, a meeting place of heaven and earth, a sacramental event where the future kingdom explodes in and through the physical reality of our world. For some of us this experience will occur around the Eucharistic table; for others it will occur unexpectedly, when the veil is lifted and we discover the glory of God barely masked in ordinary things.[36] The Table is ultimately situated in the temple of God's creation. But whether obviously sacramental or less so, the outcome is the same: a renewed body and spirit, and a hopeful glance toward the far country, which in such moments seems a little less far.

When we recall such places and events, we say to one another, "Did not our hearts burn within us?" C.S. Lewis remarks that we name such places Nostalgia and Romanticism and Adolescence, but the experience marks us with such sweetness that "when, in very intimate conversation, the mention of it becomes imminent, we grow awkward and affect to laugh at ourselves."[37] These experiences are a secret longing we cannot hide, but neither can we relate them. We cannot tell them because hidden there is a desire for something that has never appeared in our experience. Neither can we hide them because our experience constantly suggests the nearness of it. What comes through these experiences is so much more than the event or place suggested: in those places are glimpses of a destination we cannot know until we reach it. Inge writes, "In the same way as the resurrection of Christ is the first fruit, as the Eucharist is a foretaste of the heavenly banquet prepared for all humankind, so those moments speak to us in a sacramental sense

---

[35] Matthiesson, quoted in Charles Foster, *The Sacred Journey*, 97.

[36] One of those moments arrived for me in my first reading of Tolkien's Lord of the Rings in 1982. His picture of the creation of the world through song in *The Silmarillion* is a wonderful example of the Holy imagination.

[37] Ibid.

of our destination and the manner in which everything will, in God's good time, be in its place."[38]

We long to return to those places. In those places, we are most ourselves, and most alive. As Simone Weil reminds us, "The love of the beauty of the world ... involves ... the love of all the truly precious things that bad fortune can destroy. The truly precious things are those forming ladders reaching toward the beauty of the world, openings onto it."[39]

Notice that the ladders Weil describes are not ladders to heaven, but ladders to something hidden in the world. The beauty we reach for in created things is more than merely a reflection of something else, it is an *ikon*. As Jean-Luc Marion has observed, the icon lets the visible image be "saturated" by the invisible, pointing beyond itself.[40] Every ikon (Greek: *eikon*) takes its norm from what the apostle Paul applies to Christ, the ikon of the invisible God (see Colossians 1:15). Without a vision of the surpassing beauty and glory of Christ we will always be tempted to disordered affections. Until we become lovers we are not deeply converted. As St. John of the Cross sings,

> *Your eyes in mine aglow*
> *Printed their living image in my own;*
> *Only look this way now*
> *as once before: your gaze*
> *leaves me with lovelier features where it plays.*[41]

We become what we worship. This is axiomatic in Christian circles; but that isn't quite right. James K. A. Smith hits closer to the mark when he says that we become what we love,[42] because "worship" in our Christian culture connotes bending the knee, but not always action in the world, and not always intimate connection. Smith has it right, but

---

[38] Inge, *A Christian Theology of Place*, 76.

[39] Weil, "Love of the Order of the World," 180.

[40] Marion, *The Idol and Distance*.

[41] St. John of the Cross, "Spiritual Canticle," XXXII.

[42] Smith, *Desiring the Kingdom*, 33-34.

let me change the word to one that connotes worship but is less corrupt: *we become what we adore* ...[43]

> I am my beloveds,
> And he is mine.
> He feeds his flock among the lilies. (Song of Songs 6:3)

---

[43] Newberg and Waldman explore the formation question from the perspective of brain science in How God Changes Your Brain. "Contemplating a loving God strengthens portions of our brain—particularly the frontal lobes and the anterior cingulate—where empathy and reason reside. Contemplating a wrathful God empowers the limbic system ..."

Gardener

When Mary Magdalene
Saw Christ at dawn
In the tomb-haunted grove
She thought he was
The gardener
Then saw he was the Christ.
But still she was mistaken
Not seeing that
The gnarled, deep-rooted olives,
The flowers in the rock,
The rock itself
Were rooted in his flesh.

For Christ was gardener of that place
But hid his workman's hands,
The flowers of his flesh,
Lest the young church see
Persephone, Osiris,
Or only wild Pan,

And not the God
Beyond the world
Who made it
For His flesh, and ours,
And tends in each new Adam
The garden of His earth.

—Loren Wilkinson, April, 1980

CHAPTER IX

Re-placing the World through Biking, Baking and Gardens

We become what we worship. Speaking of adoration returns us again to the Great Commandment. We are to love the Lord with our *all*—and somehow in that loving we are transformed and *made whole.*

The Online Etymology dictionary[1] has a lot to say about the English word "holy." At its heart, it may once have meant "that which must be kept whole" or "that which is inviolate." The sense of truth here is lost in a culture that has long dichotomized heaven and earth, sacred and secular. Holiness in popular religion connotes mostly morality. Secularization is not something we witness out there in the world: it is alive and well in most churches.[2]

We have seen that technology and urbanization are not evil in themselves, but they are forces that tend to distance us from the earth. Few of us still participate in the once ubiquitous reality of working with soil and cultivating living things. Wendell Berry writes that, "The word health belongs to a family of words, a listing of which will suggest how

---

[1] www.etymonline.com.

[2] I am reminded of Richard Rohr's jibe that the Great Commandment is not "thou shalt be right," but "thou shalt love."

far the consideration of health must carry us: heal, whole, wholesome, hale, hallow, holy."[3]

A friend has belonged for more than ten years to a local community-supported farm. Last summer he ran into a pastor there, who like him was picking her week's share of cucumbers. "This is some of the holiest ground I know," she said. He could only agree. But what makes the ground of an ordinary farm holy? Not its tremendous spiritual/edible abundance, but the precursor to that abundance: the *kavanah* (that is, intention—see Chapter 6) with which it is farmed. We can't rule out that some places may be innately holy, but usually we make holy places together.

Holiness is something we both make and discover.

The explicit theme of this chapter is *re-placing* the world. While part of the requirement is a renewed imagination, my intention here is to provoke action, because in truth we only learn what we practice. I hope to launch the reader into a pilgrimage of her own. It may be a literal journey; but it should also be one that is richly undertaken *in place*. As noted above, we are taught to break apart problems, to fragment the world. This makes complex tasks and subjects more manageable, but we pay a hidden, enormous price. We can no longer see the consequences of our actions; we lose our intrinsic sense of connection to a larger whole. Berry reminds us that action implies place and connection.

> There can be disembodied thought, but not disembodied action. Action—embodied thought—requires local and communal reference. To act, in short, is to live. Living "is a total act. Thinking is a partial act." And one does not live alone. Living is a communal act, whether or not its community is acknowledged ...[4]

Re-placing ourselves in the world will require concrete practices of engagement, practices that are in every sense subversive.

---

[3] Berry, *The Art of the Commonplace.*

[4] Berry, *What are People For?*

Biking, Baking and Gardens

It may seem odd that I am about to close a book on place with a discussion of biking, baking and gardening. Yet these are three of the most spiritual practices we can muster at this late date in the dying gasp of Modernity. These practices slow us down, help us to locate ourselves, and open space for others. Wendell Berry writes,

> A person who is growing a garden, if he is growing it organically, is improving a piece of the world. He is producing something to eat, which makes him somewhat independent of the grocery business, but he is also enlarging, for himself, the meaning of food and the pleasure of eating.[5]

Gardens: the Bible is full of them, and its pages open and close—in Genesis and Revelation—with stories placed in gardens. How fitting that the first great title for God is given to us not in terms of a distant transcendence but in terms of his intimate role in creation: "And God planted a garden in the East" (Gen. 2:8). And then Mary's first sight at the open tomb echoes a world renewed: she sees Jesus as the gardener (John 20:15).[6] Loren Wilkinson writes,

> *Then the planet will spin in a Sabbath dance*
> *(And the dancing place will be the heart).*
> *Fruit will burgeon from scattered seeds*
> *And garden and town be clean as a fleece*
> *Early in the morning, on the first day of the week.*[7]

We who are created in God's image can do no less than imitate his work. In imitating God we discover a myriad of relationships that remain otherwise transparent to us. We discover, in a word, *ecology*. Ecological thinking is connected: this depends on that. The environment becomes critical. Soils vary tremendously—that would

---

[5] Ibid.

[6] Murray Pura expounds on these thoughts in his lovely book, *Rooted: Reflections on the Gardens in Scripture.*

[7] Wilkinson, "Imago Mundi."

make a good parable, don't you think? In gardening we are forced to slow down, to learn the unforced rhythms of grace, the importance of seasons,[8] and the lessons of the mustard seed. In other words, we learn nearly all the basics of spiritual life in the garden.[9] Pollan notes that,

> Gardening is a painstaking exploration of place; everything that happens in my garden—the thriving and dying of particular plants, the maraudings of various insects and other pests—teaches me to know this patch of land more intimately, its geology and microclimate, the particular ecology of its local weeds and animals and insects. My garden prospers to the extent I grasp these particularities and adapt to them.[10]

In Windsor, Ontario, the Downtown Windsor Community Cooperative (DWCC) reaches into neighborhoods by creating community gardens. Gardens are a venue for building relationships, where strangers become friends. "Gardens draw out leaders, enhance the quality of life, and break down walls between neighbours [creating social capital]."[11] Moreover, the DWCC has identified food security as an active need in their town. Several organizations and residents are interested and motivated to collaborate on launching urban gardens on unused property.

Gardens, like any cultivated place, remind us once again of the need for boundaries. "An essential tension is lost when gardens do not have porous, even promiscuous openings onto the world beyond their boundaries ... They offer ... a measure of seclusion that is not occlusion."[12] Boundaries must keep the garden "intrinsically related to the world that they keep at a certain remove." In this sense gardens offer a wonderful practice of hospitality.

---

[8] Parker Palmer relates seasons to spiritual pilgrimage in *Let Your Life Speak*, 95-109.

[9] I am thinking not only of the Parable here, but of Rumi's lovely poem, "The Seed Market."

[10] Pollan, *Second Nature*, 3-4.

[11] Cameron, "Downtown Windsor Community Cooperative." Unpublished paper.

[12] Harrison, *Gardens*, 56-57.

Baking: Why grow things if not to cook them, bake them, share them and eat them? Actually there are several good reasons. Some people garden just for the joy of it: to be outdoors in all weather and watch things grow. Some garden to share casual time with friends; many a good garden roots a living community of people. But many of us garden because we love to eat, and gardening allows us the satisfaction of watching things grow and the joy of later consumption. We used to think dancing leads to sex; well, maybe not. But gardening leads to baking.

Baking starts with bread. The communion liturgy from *Small Boat, Big Sea* offers that Jesus is our companion and vindicator. The Old French word *compaignon* translates literally as "one who breaks bread with another," from the Latin *com*—"together with" and *panis*, "bread."

> **The Leader Reads**—On the night of his betrayal Jesus our companion Took bread Broke it Gave it to his followers Eat My body is broken for you
>
> **Then All Read**—We break this bread with those who: hunger for justice, dream of a land free from occupation, long to live life free from fear, search for food and water each day, long for companionship.[13]

Baking starts with bread, and bread begins in the garden or the fields. If you are like Mary Ruth, you go to the flour shop and purchase a twenty-pound sack of wheat, take it home, and run it through the grinder. You can't get organic flour any fresher, and the bread it makes—*magnifique!* Individual grains offer their texture to the whole, and become the hope of glory in single loaves.

Clemens Sedmak closes chapter one of *Doing Local Theology* with the image of the local theologian as village cook. He argues that doing local theology is like cooking with local ingredients. He chooses this image because it offers a nuance and a "feeling" that a definition cannot convey (it also offers texture and taste!). He builds on the image to remind us that Jesus feeds us, was often at dinner parties, and was himself the bread of life. He notes that, "The theologian is not free to

---

[13] http://smallboatbigsea.org.

cook anything he or she likes, but is part of a community that provides ingredients and shares the food." To Clemens, "Food is, next to language, THE local cultural product par excellence ..."[14]

If Sedmak is right, then theory and practice are uniquely intertwined for those who love to cook, and those who love to eat. This intercourse of delight and dining makes baking a wonderful opportunity to engage in place making.

Five winters ago we still had a wood stove. Situated downstairs in an older house, when the temperature went below freezing, it was really the only way to keep the house comfortable. Every morning in December and January, I stoked a fire in our woodstove. Once a week, usually on Monday mornings, I did some baking. It helps to recall another old word here: *hearth*. The hearth, the center of the home, where the warmth is located, and where all the baking happens. It involves work: holy intention. This is similar to the English word *heart*: the center of relational life, and of the affections.[15] Relational life connects us to the larger story of the indwelling Spirit, and *perichoresis*. Baking and stoking fires are all about spirituality. Let me tell you the story in words from my journal.

> Monday morning, 7:30 AM. I build a fire in the woodstove. The embers are still live from the night before. By 9 AM the warmth spreads gradually upwards through the house, until by 11 AM the upper wood floor is warm to the touch, and acts like a slow heat sink, spreading the warmth evenly upstairs.

> I have to add wood or stir the fire every hour or so. Every time I approach the fire I feel the warmth. On a cool day, it's a very sensual experience, but also mystical: every piece of wood is transformed, becoming one with the fire. The coals glow, and the flames and coals radiate heat. Steve Bell writes, 'The whole soul becomes Christ's, just as the iron in the burning coal becomes fire as if it were burning—everything is fire, everything is light!'[16]

---

[14] Sedmak, *Doing Local Theology*, 19.

[15] Etymologically, these two English words are not related.

[16] Steve Bell, quoting Father John of Kronstadt, Russia. Steve's song "Burning Ember" is storied around this image. Online: http://stevebell.com/2010/10/burning-ember.

I leave the fire for my office at the other end of our home. Alternating my study with music and worship, my choice is Steve Bell and one of his older albums: 'Burning Ember.' I didn't see the synchronism until Tuesday. I feel the presence of the Lord as I study: it's a rich experience, and it keeps my being centered in Christ.

Stoking the physical fire takes effort. I split some wood in the morning, and sometimes have to revisit the pile around dinner time. I have to stir the fire at least hourly to keep the heat at maximum. If the cat is in the house, she is inevitably somewhere near the woodstove, melted into a small black puddle.

Stoking the spiritual fire takes similar focus and intention. If I don't spend at least a few times in worship during the week, I am like a neglected fire: radiating little light and little warmth, not likely to be a resting place for lonely animals, not likely to be tuned to God, and not likely to be doing good theology.

In the evening I go out to buy the ingredients for our Christmas cake. The recipe was my mother's, passed on to her daughters, and from my eldest sister to me. It's a 'light' cake as opposed to dark, a familiar recipe and rich with texture and flavor.

The process involves three major stages. Mix the ingredients and cook the loaves; soak the loaves in Napoleon brandy; set them aside wrapped in cheesecloth and soak them in brandy weekly until Christmas. The loaves are mostly fruit, dates, raisins and nuts. We mix all this in the largest bowl we have, which is probably an eight liter capacity. To finish we add a half cup of brandy to the mix. Into the pans it goes, bakes for about two hours at 250 F, and then on racks to cool overnight. The next morning I brush the loaves with brandy, then wrap them in cheesecloth.

Did I tell you about the Napoleon brandy? I don't drink hard liquor, but the fragrance of this stuff is incredible. It's aged in oak for seven years. The most obvious scent to me is apricots, and the golden color gives the same impression. (It runs around 40% alcohol, so you could probably use it in your lawnmower.) Soaking the cakes in spirits helps the flavors ripen and mature, and by Christmas time the flavor—and the aroma—is heavenly. Take a small sip of brandy and you feel the fires of creation on your tongue.

These cakes are a lot of work, and they are far from instant. We shouldn't really cut into the first cake for four weeks. Brandy and Christmas cakes get better with age. They are a celebration of fruitfulness and the gifts of God in the world. They are an act of submission to the seasons, and to the land. They require us to honor mystery: fullness comes, we know not how. Similarly, stoking fires is a lot of work. But the benefits are a warm and hospitable place that may become a dwelling place for God.

Hospitality: Why do we grow things and then cook them? So we can nurture our own bodies, and share the wealth with friends. Hospitality places us in the world, in community with others. We create space for friendship, and so create places to welcome God. Wendell Berry reminded us above that action in the world implies both place and others. Elsewhere he notes that, "an authentic community is made less in reference to who we are than to *where* we are. I cannot farm my farm as a European American—or as an American, or as a Kentuckian—but only as a person belonging to the place itself."[17] Belonging references a people and a place. Gardening and farming, as placed and embodied practices, teach us this as few other practices can.

Moreover, hospitality is a circle dance. Gardening and baking lead naturally to hospitality. Hospitality leads to the necessity of baking, and the possibility of communal gardens. Hospitality opens the possibility of sacred encounter. At the common table, strangers become friends. Redemptive communities root both memory and hope. Hospitality is forward looking, to a great Table at the center of the world, where all tribes and nations and tongues gather to celebrate and to worship. In A Happy Ending, published out of The Story[18] in Sarnia, Ontario, they write:

---

[17] Berry, *Sex, Economy, Freedom and Community*, 180. Italics mine.

[18] www.thestory.ca.

The table is a place of unending first starts. (Matthew 18:21-23)

The table is a place where doubt is validated and questions carry no penalty. (John 20:26-28)

The table is a place where the divide between the sacred and secular dissolves. (1 Corinthians 8:1-7)

The table is the place where our deepest wounds are healed. (1 Peter 2:23-25)[19]

They note that our commission is to be party planners: "to invite any and all, to serve well and plenty, until each has their fill and all the leftovers are collected (John 6:1-14)."[20] The Bible closes not only with a garden, but with a feast.[21] To some this will feel worldly, but detachment is not a Christian ideal. As Elizabeth Newman writes,

> True freedom does not lie in detachment from our created place and time (Gnosticism) nor in mastering creation. Rather, freedom results from living in communion with God and others. Hospitality is but another way of naming this communion.[22]

In the incarnation, God entrusts Godself to the hospitality of the world.[23] Inagrace Dietterich reminds us that human ideals of community emphasize sameness, comfort, and closeness, and minimize distance and difference. But Christian communities are shaped by faith in Christ, and offer a space where "[hostility] is converted into hospitality, strangers into friends, and enemies into guests [offering] both protection and freedom."[24] Our faith offers a counter-narrative to

---

[19] Manafo, *A Happy Ending*, 13.

[20] Ibid.

[21] See in particular Tony Campolo, "The Kingdom of God is a Party." http://www.tonycampolo.org/doc/crystalcathedral/The_Kingdom_of_God.pdf.

[22] Newman, *Untamed Hospitality*, 97.

[23] Zscheile, *People of the Way*, 77.

[24] Dietterich, In Guder, et al., *Missional Church*, 180.

the gospel of globalization, where the local and particular conditions of life are brought into conversation with the peace of the gospel.

Biking and Walking

> A suburban parish priest, if he takes no steps to resist the pattern of his days, will find himself car-cursed and chairbound by the age of thirty-five ... I [needed exercise and] took up walking.

> I have been delighted with it ... But walking has turned out to have intellectual as well as physical benefits. I am as much the victim of placelessness, as much the prisoner of canned environment, as the next person. It has, therefore, been a delightful and metaphysical surprise to be introduced to place again. I have, for example, rediscovered what a hill is. The automobile is the great *leveler*. I had lived in Port Jefferson for eight years as a parish priest, and I thought I knew it as a place ... But it wasn't until I walked up East Broadway for the first time that I, as a person, met the village as a place.

> Port Jefferson is just far enough away from New York City to have remained a small town, but it is also close enough to have felt the impact of developers. More than half my parish lies outside the village proper ... the housing developments have come in [and] the repeating fronts of the five basic houses give it away: it is *noplace*.

> Port Jefferson, on the other hand, is someplace—though, to tell the truth, it is not what it could be. It is untidy, distracted, and radically uncertain about just what place it is. But it is a place.[25]

Port Arthur and Port Jefferson have much in common. A city in transition, it doesn't quite know its own mind. And like Robert Capon, I discovered Port Arthur only when I began walking in it. By car I knew the general lay of the land—the map, if you will. But in walking I discovered the texture. I found people who hang out in an area bounded by an old church on one corner and a bank on the other. I discovered that one corner was preferred for the unbounded view of Lake Superior. I found that the hill is gradual until Court Street, and then becomes a

---

[25] Capon, *The Romance of the Word*, 42-43.

challenge for four or five blocks. And I found the many little shops that are hidden away, but known and loved by the college crowd. And of course, there are the pubs, which offer a good lunch at a good price, and promote that sense of neighbourhood by gathering patrons who return often. Rebecca Solnit writes, "Walkers are 'practitioners of the city,' for the city is made to be walked. A city is a language, a repository of possibilities, and walking is the act of speaking that language, of selecting from those possibilities."[26]

If Paul Virilio is correct that speed is the primary form of violence in modernity, then slowing down is the counter-discipline required to live in God's shalom. Biking and walking are the recommended methods.

In the era of the world-wide-web, globalization and automobiles, many of us live—nowhere. And we inhabit nowhere to get to no-place.

The inside of a car is typically nowhere. We drive through space, not places, and pass signs that mean nothing. Distance has become time. We stop to eat, passing from nowhere—into nowhere.

Thanks to the phenomenon of McDonaldization,[27] the restaurant on the road offers us sacraments of placelessness.[28] Music floats mindlessly in the dead space. We order. It's the same food we ate when we left, served by the same waitress. We get back to the car to race against the nothingness that wears at us. T.S. Eliot writes,

Between the idea / And the reality—
Between the motion / And the act—
Falls the Shadow ...[29]

When I step onto my bike, the vulnerability of the method forces me to pay attention. And vulnerability is not merely incidental, but key to the method of the missionary. Jesus entered our world vulnerably.

---

[26] Solnit, *Wanderlust*, 190.

[27] A term coined by George Ritzer in 1993.

[28] I recommended James K.A. Smith for a discussion of cultural liturgies, those forming practices that are ubiquitous, transparent, and counter-Christ.

[29] Eliot, "The Hollow Men."

When he sends out the disciples, he makes them dependent on those who will receive them (Luke 9, "Take nothing for the journey.") Just as vulnerability makes for good theology,[30] so vulnerability makes us attentive to place.

Earlier we noted that churches that are developed with walkability as a key value encourage us to be stakeholders in the places we live. We are less likely to be tourists where we are personally invested. Walkability "elevates the chance for investment in the local neighborhood that otherwise might be missing if the church is built and grows based upon the auto-based commuter mentality."[31] Portland, Oregon, a city with 1000 neighbourhoods, uses PDX20 as a development standard. "A 20-minute community is defined as everything you need for life within a 20-minute walk."[32]

In contrast, the commuter is the consumer and tourist, viewing the world through a pane of glass, and not entering into the lived story of the neighbourhoods they visit. The slower pace of biking or walking invites the attitude of the pilgrim.[33]

In *The Practice of Everyday Life*, Michel de Certeau describes the spatial practice of walking in the city. He references the "erotics of knowledge,"[34] and opposes the walker and the voyeur. The voyeur views the city from high above, the city at a distance, and becomes the "all-seeing eye."[35] To de Certeau this "seeing at a distance" is totalizing, colonizing, theoretical.

At the opposite extreme, the walker enters the labyrinths and textures of the city without knowing them. She follows the "thicks and thins" of the urban text, writing without the ability to read. She is the practitioner. De Certeau writes that the walker escapes "the imaginary

---

[30] *Doing Local Theology*, 10.

[31] Benesh, *Metrospiritual*, 156-157.

[32] Portland Church Planting. http://www.portlandchurchplanting.org/p/20-minute-communities.html.

[33] Coniseau, *The Art of Pilgrimage*, 16. See the discussion in chapter VII.

[34] De Certeau, *The Practice of Everyday Life*, 91.

[35] Ibid., 93.

totalizations produced by the eye ... the everyday has a certain strangeness that does not surface."[36] Is it possible to move beyond this duality of theoretical and practical as a walker? Perhaps this is a peculiarly theological task. The walker may become the reflective practitioner, one who carries the vision in their feet. Instead of driving through neighbourhoods, we can learn to invest in them.

Walking is a practice that converts space to place. Recall the distinction Eric Jacobsen offered above between embedded churches and insular churches. Churches built prior to WWII are embedded because "they facilitate direct connections between the interior space of the church building and the public space of the wider society."[37] Often these buildings extend to the sidewalk and have little or no parking. These sorts of buildings invite walking traffic, and are natural locations for coffee houses, drop-in centers, and daily classes of all sorts. They more easily facilitate community life.

In *God Next Door*, Simon Carey Holt describes walking as a form of prayer.

> I walk my neighborhood almost daily and pray as I do. I've never been one for prolonged periods of kneeling or sitting in silence. I prefer the stimulation of sight, sound, even smell, as I pray. In her delightful book, *Wanderlust: A History of Walking*, Rebecca Solnit describes walking as "ideally, a state in which the mind, the body, and the world are aligned, as though there were three characters finally in conversation together, three notes suddenly making a chord."
>
> My walking prayers are invitational; prayers inviting the Spirit of God to do a particular work of grace in the lives of those who inhabit the neighborhood with me, and in the neighborhood itself. I pray for those of my neighbors I know by name and those I recognise only by sight. As I walk by, I pray for the owners of the café across the laneway. Their youngest child has been in hospital the past month and faces the possibility of major surgery. I pray for the owner of the small clothing business that operates alongside the café. In all of the times I've passed during business hours, I've

---

[36] Ibid.

[37] Jacobsen, *The Space Between*, 190.

never seen a customer. I often say hello but he is guarded in his response; I've not been game to formally introduce myself. I pray, too, for the young man who works the night shift in the 7-11 convenience store at the end of the street. A recent immigrant from South Africa, he seems lonely. His face lights up whenever I walk in.[38]

In the end, prayer, place and devotion merge and become one. Our priestly task finds its fruition when we know a place well enough to suffer with it and lift it to God.[39]

May God restore our broken priesthood for the sake of the world.

Conclusion

Then he brought me back to the door of the house; and behold, water was flowing from under the threshold of the house toward the east, for the house faced east.

By the river on its bank, on one side and on the other, will grow all kinds of trees for food. Their leaves will not wither and their fruit will not fail. They will bear every month because their water flows from the sanctuary, and their fruit will be for food and their leaves for healing." (Ezek. 47:1,12)

In the Body of Christ, God indwells the world-Temple. This picture of the Temple-Garden occurs again at the close of the canon in Revelation 22. The message to us seems clear. Worship is not a doorway out of the world, nor a way to an abstract communion with God, but a *way into the world* through an alternative vision and way of life. Participation at the common table invites us into the life of God who was broken for us to renew wholeness; it teaches us to offer all of life to God, how to eat, and how to live. "The bread when lifted up and blessed, thrusts our vision both forward toward all of God's gifts and

---

[38] Holt, *God Next Door*, 111.

[39] Clemens Sedmak notes that theology is taught and written, danced and sung, sculpted and painted, dreamed and cried. He could also have added, "walked." *Doing Local Theology*, 11.

backward toward the bread we had for breakfast, to the gifted and social nature of our existence, to the interconnectedness of worship and life."[40]

God's story has always been told of both a people and a place—Israel and the land. The narrative never changed; but we lived into a world that could no longer hear the story as it was told. In this clearing in the dying days of Modernity, we are once again discovering that "place" is always a participant in the story God is authoring. The mystery is that we co-author the story with God: we are genuine participants, first in God's own life, and then in his vulnerable engagement in the world.

God invests in people and a *place*. His kingdom is both a rule and a *realm*. A recovery of place will be strengthened by a recovery of parish: an inclusive vision of God's mission in a particular place that he loves, and that we love along with him. The sacraments of place are bread and wine, but also land and hearth. Bread and wine are born on the land, and prepared in the hearth. The essential practice is hospitality. "At the scale of the neighborhood, we can know by the senses of our bodies; we can meet our neighbors and strangers in common, shared spaces; and we can enter into and work towards the long work of God's transformation in our places."[41]

We have spoken of the need to recover a sacramental way of seeing. The geography of the Eucharist invites us to inhabit the concrete particularities of this world. The pilgrim moves from place to place, inviting worship in the world-temple. There is no desire to experience homogenized space. Instead, the goal is to inhabit places, and to discern in what ways God is dwelling there; to discern "presence," and to participate in God's work. Moreover, this local engagement is always ethical space. Inagrace Dietterich calls us to solidarity with the hungry:

> Recognizing their own hunger, their own need for forgiveness and reconciliation, Christians stand in solidarity with the hungry, the dispossessed and the marginalized. Nourished and strengthened in a new relationship with Jesus Christ, those who break bread together are drawn into and participate in his ministry of

---

[40] Ibid.

[41] Aldrich, "Eric Jacobsen—The Space Between." http://erb.kingdomnow.org.

conquering need, overcoming alienation, and accepting the despised.[42]

The victory of Christ on the cross reconciles us "in one body" to God. The ultimate symbol, and practice, of that reconciliation is the Eucharist. Any meal can be Eucharistic: creating space for a diversity of voices, where all who come are transformed into something new. The Table provides soil for cultivating the life of Jesus in a place, a relational context where our words and actions can take root in deeds of love and acceptance.

> *And though the good is weak, beauty is very strong.*
> *Nonbeing sprawls, everywhere it turns into ash whole expanses of being,*
>
> *It masquerades in shapes and colors that imitate existence*
> *And no one would know it, if they did not know that it was ugly.*
>
> *And when people cease to believe that there is good and evil*
> *Only beauty will call to them and save them*
> *So that they will still know how to say:*
> *this is true and that is false.*[43]

---

[42] "Missional Community," 165.

[43] Milosz, "One More Day."

Appendix
Prayers, Liturgies, Resources

A Prayer for the City

This prayer of dedication was discovered by Simon Carey Holt.
It was prayed by a Benedictine as he moved into his 'cell.' Simon copied
it into his journal:

Lord, this cell is to be my home.
May your holy power furnish it
in peace and decorate its four walls
with holiness so that your sacred
presence will also abide here.

Lord, it is not large or grand
but it is to be my living place.
May I find within its close quarters
refreshment and your sacred space.
May your spirit of prayer
be my frequent guest and welcome housemate.
May the spirit of praise
guide every task and deed performed here.
Lord, this cell will be a place for living,
sleeping, praying; it will be a shrine and

a place for healing.
May my door stand open to all who are in need—
as a sign of the posture of my heart.
May peace, love and beauty flow out from
this cell of mine in all four directions
and up and down.
May your silent echo be heard
by all of those who lives surround me.
The birds of the air have nests;
foxes have dens;
May this cell of mine
be blessed by you, my God
as a home for me ...
and for you as well. Amen[1]

---

[1] Holt, *God Next Door*, 89-90.

Urban Liturgy––Urban Expression, UK2

We draw near to God, Creator, Redeemer and Sustainer.

Relationship

We believe that, in Jesus, God is revealed locally, and that we should be committed to our local community or relational network and active members of it.

Call to mind where you live.
Imagine that you're in a balloon floating over the roofs and parks,
people and traffic,
houses and flats.
Hear the sounds of where you live; breathe its air; feel its life and stay with this as long as you like.
This is where God has invited you to live.
Notice what part of the neighbourhood is uppermost in your mind.
What's calling out for transformation today? Silently offer that to God.

God
we come before you just as we are
with all our frailties and vulnerabilities
our baggage and prejudices
our hopes and dreams
our life and love
and we offer it all to you.
Take all we are and hope to be.
Use us here where you've brought us
and help us to be like Jesus.
Use our hands, our eyes, our ears,
our words, our silences,
our work, our rest
our hearts and minds,
and let your kingdom come
in the lives of all who live
next door and round about,
in this street and square
in the whole neighbourhood.

---

2 http://www.urbanexpression.org.uk.

Confirm in us your invitation
to be your people here.
Deepen our commitment to it.
In our experience of the
heights and depths of life here
help us to know your surging and renewing love.
Lord, in your mercy
Let your kingdom come!

A Good Friday Liturgy: I Witness, 2008 - The Story, Sarnia, Ontario

(Curator & musician(s) off to the side as to not obstruct the view of the images & tree)

Image: Eye on Record

OPENING

Is mystery more important than knowledge? When we mix confusion with wonder, sorrow with hope, is our end goal to know all the facts and have a grasp on the situation or is there something else, something just beyond our reach, something we know, yet don't fully understand?

Today we find ourselves embroiled in a paradox of emotions – we both celebrate and mourn Christ's death.

Today is about pain, suffering, sorrow, degradation and the brutality of sin.

Today we find ourselves at the foot of a tree, our eyes recording information, our brains and souls organizing this data the best it can, creatively filling in the gaps with homemade and borrowed symbols, experiences, ideas and images.

Today we leverage these things in an attempt to decipher what has happened. We need to do this in honesty, and admit that we are not able to look at the cross objectively since each of us is covered in the fingerprints of our upbringing and contexts. The risk we take is that our fears, pre-suppositions and agendas will be exposed, and at worst, or maybe best, challenged.

Today we gaze at the cross, and ask the question: What does a dying God look like? What does He look like from where you sit? What has He looked like from the vantage point of those who have come before us?

Today we're going to hopscotch through symbols and imagery of the last 2000 years. We will eaves drop on people who were working out their theology out loud through art, and hopefully today, we will be able to immerse ourselves in what is both the highlight of the Christian calendar but at the same time our darkest hour.

Scripture: Luke 23:33-46

BLOW OUT CHRIST CANDLE

Response: Hymn: Wonderful Cross[3]

---

[3] Melles ,*A Happy Ending.*

A Prayer for Pentecost – St. Benedict's Table, Winnipeg, Manitoba

Veni, Sancte Spiritus, reple tuorum corda fidelium,et tui amoris in eis ignem accende.

Come Holy Spirit, fill the hearts of the faithful and kindle in us the power of your love.

Father, we are at Pentecost and we thank you for the work of the Holy Spirit in our lives. As the first lesson captures the wild, visual and somewhat traditional perception it holds, we are also aware of its power to guide, comfort and inspire us. Keep us open and responsive to the leading of the Holy Spirit—in our vocations, in the sacred spaces where we invite friendship, enjoy family life and embrace community. May we be among those "who call upon the Name of the Lord and are saved."

Let us pray to the Lord, hear us Lord of glory.

We thank you for this season where our landscapes transform into a mute gospel by filling up our senses or by offering surprises of that bulb or perennial we forgot we planted.

In a time when we are constantly being reminded to be kinder to the earth, make us effective stewards of the green spaces entrusted to our car, make us intentional in our daily commute, and wise in the services and products we endorse.

As we move into summertime, may our routines and calendars be less hectic, and more relaxed and our spirits open to rest and rejuvenation. Take us to the lake, the beach, or the backyard to celebrate our personal vistas and unwind in a world wound so tight that we often forget to give our bodies rest, to slow the pace, to smell those flowers and to breathe.[4]

---

[4] "Pentecost: Vespers." In *Beautiful Mercy: A Book of Hours.* Winnipeg: St. Benedicts Table Publishing, 2010.

Prayer for CREATION

God of heaven and earth. God who sees us. God who hears our cry.

We thank-you for creating us and creating this world.

We know you are not done, and that this world is far from the good that you intended.

Thank-you for being a God who does not give up and who pursues his purposes till completion.

We are hard up now because it feels at times like you are not around, like creation is getting worse.

Sometimes it feels like we are getting worse and less in tune with you.

Give us comfort and peace in knowing that one day you will redeem all of creation.

Give us comfort and peace in knowing that one day these problems will disappear.

Give us comfort and peace in knowing that you care more than we do and are passionately pursuing your purpose in us and throughout all your creation.

May we be your creation, and may you look at our lives and say it is good.

May we be good to your creation, and good to each other

May we long for the image of God in our lives in everything we do.

God of heaven and earth. God who sees us. God who hears our cry.

Teach us to create and redeem along side of you.

Teach us to see your creation behind everything, good and bad

God of heaven and earth. God who sees us. God who hears our cry.

Have mercy on us. Amen.

IMAGINING A NEW ECONOMY

God forgive us for not truly living in your kingdom.

Whether it be through our money, time and relationships

We always tend to make it about us

We never think twice

Before following blindly what we think is normal

God forgive us for being addicted to our cash-flow
For feeling secure when we have money in the bank
For feeling valuable when we buy new things
For feeling powerful when we show off
God forgive us for living by our own rules
For living by our own values
For dictating what we think we deserve
For trying to control outcomes
Free us to live the way you created us to be
Free us to live generously
Remind us of our insurmountable value
Remind us that love doesn't come through things
Give us dreams that start with you
Give us dreams that aren't selfish
Give us dreams that help the world
Give us boldness to live backwards to this world
Give us boldness to live without idols
Give us boldness to proclaim with our lives
The kind of life that you made possible. Amen.[5]

---

[5] *A Happy Ending.*

Breaking Bread - Small Boat, Big Sea, Sydney, Australia

Screen 1
Jesus, Our Companion & Vindicator

Middle English: from Old French compaignon, literally "one who breaks bread with another," based on Latin com- "together with"'+ panis "bread."

Leader Reads—On the night of his betrayal Jesus our companion Took bread Broke it Gave it to his followers Eat My body is broken for you.

All Read—We break this bread with those who: hunger for justice, dream of a land free from occupation, long to live life free from fear, search for food and water each day, long for companionship.

Screen 2
ORIGIN mid 16th cent. (in the sense [deliver, rescue]): from Latin vindicat- "claimed, avenged," from the verb vindicare, from vindex, vindic- 'claimant, avenger.'

Leader Reads—On the night of his betrayal Jesus our vindicator Took wine Gave it to his followers Remember My blood is poured out for you Drink This is a new promise All who come to me will have life.

All Read—We drink this wine with those who: see too much blood flow, watch loved ones die, are judged by their race or skin colour, carry in their blood the stigma of HIV/AIDS, long for someone to dry their tears.

Leader Reads—Come, eat, drink, you who hunger and thirst, For a deeper faith, for a better life, for a fairer world, For healing and wholeness—Come.

[Invite people to take and eat the bread after they have dipped it in the wine.]

Source: http://www.freshworship.org/node/375.

Online Resources and Journals

Mars Hill Audio Review—http://www.marshillaudio.org

Project for Public Places—http://www.pps.org

New Geography—http://www.newgeography.com

Parish Collective—http://www.parishcollective.org/

Abundant Communities—http://www.abundantcommunity.com/

Better Cities and Towns—http://www.betttercities.net/

The Art of Neighboring—http://artofneighboring.com/resources

This is Our City—http://www.christianitytoday.com/thisisourcity/

Placemakers—http://www.placemakers.com/

Civitate—http://www.civitate.org/

Qideas—http://www.qideas.org/cities/

YES Magazine—http://www.yesmagazine.org/

Image Journal—http://imagejournal.org/

Books & Culture—http://www.booksandculture.com/

Humanities—http://www.neh.gov/humanities

Examples of Communities Engaged in Place

CANADA
    Awaken—Calgary, AB
        http://www.awakenchurch.ca/
    Downtown Windsor Community Collaborative—Windsor, ON
        http://www.bettertogetherwindsor.ca/
    Little Flowers Community—Winnipeg, MB
        http://littleflowers.ca/
    Westminster Church—Winnipeg, MB
        http://westminsterchurch.org/
    Love Ottawa—Ottawa, ON
        http://missiono.ca/
    The Journey—Ottawa, ON
        http://thejourneyottawa.ca/
    Nieucommunities—Vancouver, BC
        http://www.nieucommunities.org/where/vancouver/
    Grandview Calvary Baptist Church—Vancouver, BC
        http://gcbchurch.ca/
    The Story—Sarnia, ON
        http://www.thestory.ca/
    Neighbourhood Life—Calgary, Edmonton, AB
        http://neighbourhoodlife.com/

USA
    Bread and Wine—Portland, OR
        http://www.breadandwine.org/
    Nieucommunities—San Diego, CA
        http://www.nieucommunities.org/
    Soma—Tacoma, WA
        http://somatacoma.org/
    Theophilus—Portland, OR
        http://theophiluschurch.com/
    The Simple Way
        http://www.thesimpleway.org/

General Index

Index of Names

Index of Scripture References

Bibliography

Alves, Rubem. *The Poet, The Warrior, The Prophet.* London: SCM, 1990.

Austin, Richard. *Hope for the Land: Nature in the Bible.* Abingdon: Creekside, 1988.

Bailey, Kenneth. *Jesus Through Middle Eastern Eyes: Cultural Studies in the Gospels.* Downers Grove: IVP, 2008.

Barth, Karl. *Dogmatics in Outline.* San Francisco: Harper Perennial, 1959.

Bartholomew, Craig. *Where Mortals Dwell: A Christian View of Place for Today.* Grand Rapids: Baker Academic, 2011.

Bass, Diana Butler. *Christianity for the Rest of Us: How the Neighborhood Church Is Transforming the Faith.* New York: HarperCollins, 2006.

Baudrillard, Jean. *Selected Writings.* Cambridge: Polity, 1988.

Bauman, Zygmunt. *Globalization: the Human Consequences.* Cambridge: Polity, 1998.

_____. *Liquid Modernity.* Cambridge: Polity, 2000.

Benesh, Sean. *Metrospiritual: The Geography of Church Planting.* Eugene: Resource, 2011.

Berger, Peter. *The Sacred Canopy: Elements of a Sociological Theory of Religion.* New York: Anchor, 1967.

Berry, Wendell. *Sex, Economy, Freedom and Community: Eight Essays.* New York: Pantheon, 1994.

_____. *A Timbered Choir:The Sabbath Poems 1979-1997.* Washington, DC: Counterpoint, 1999.

_____. *The Gift of Gravity.* Ipswich: Golgonooza, 2002.

_____. *The Art of the Common Place:The Agrarian Essays of Wendell Berry.* Washington, DC: Counterpoint, 2002.

_____. *The Mad Farmer Poems*. Berkeley: Counterpoint: 2008.

Bess, Philip. *Till We Have Built Jerusalem: Architecture, Urbanism and the Sacred*. Wilmington: ISI, 2006.

Block, Peter. *Community: The Structure of Belonging*. San Francisco: Berrett-Koehler, 2008.

Bohm, David. *Wholeness and the Implicate Order*. Boston: Routledge & Kegan, 1980.

Brueggemann, Walter. *The Land*. Philadelphia: Fortress, 1977.

_____. *Hopeful Imagination: Prophetic Voices in Exile*. Philadelphia: Fortress, 2004.

Buber, Martin. *Mamre: Essays in Religion*. Melbourne: Melbourne University Press, 1946.

_____. *On Judaism*. New York: Schocken, 1967.

Capon, Robert Farrar. *The Romance of the Word: One Man's Love Affair with Theology*. Grand Rapids: Eerdmans, 1996.

Casey, Edgar. *Getting Back Into Place: Toward a Renewed Understanding of the Place World*. Bloomington: Indiana University Press, 1993.

_____. *The Fate of Place: A Philosophical History*. Berkeley: University of California Press, 1997.

Copleston, Frederick. *A History of Philosophy, Vol.1: Greece and Rome From the Pre-Socratics to Plotinus*. London: Continuum, 2003.

Cresswell, Timothy. *In Place, Out of Place: Geography, Ideology and Transgression*. Minneapolis: University of Minnesota Press, 1996.

Clapp, Rodney. *Border Crossings: Christian Trespasses on Popular Culture and Public Affairs*. Grand Rapids: Brazos, 2000.

Copleston, Frederick. *A History of Philosophy, Vol.1*. New York City: Continuum, 2003.

Cousineau, Phil. *The Art of Pilgrimage: The Seeker's Guide to Making Travel Sacred*. Newburyport: Conari, 2000.

Crawford, Michael B. *Shop Class as Soulcraft: An Inquiry into the Value of Work*. New York: Penguin, 2009.

DeCerteau, Michel. *The Practice of Everyday Life*. Berkeley: University of California Press, 1988.

Dietterich, Inagrace. "Missional Community: Cultivating Communities of the Holy Spirit." In *Missional Church*, edited by Darrel H. Guder, 142-182. Grand Rapids: Eerdmans, 1998.

Dillard, Annie. *Holy the Firm*. New York: Harper & Row, 1977.

_____. *For the Time Being*. Toronto: Penguin, 1999.

Dodge, Martin and Robert Kitchin. *Mapping Cyberspace*. New York: Routledge, 2001.

Durning, Alan. *This Place on Earth: Home and the Practice of Permanence.* Seattle: Sasquatch, 1996.

Dykstra, Craig. *Growing in the Life of Faith: Education and Christian Practices.* Louisville: Geneva, 1999.

Eliade, Mircea. *The Sacred and the Profane: The Nature of Religion.* New York: Harcourt, Brace & World, 1959.

Eliot, George. *Daniel Deronda.* London: Oxford Paperbacks, 2009.

Eliot, T.S. *Four Quartets.* London: Faber & Faber, 1960.

_____. *Collected Poems: 1909 to 1962.* London: Faber & Faber, 2002.

Ellul, Jacques. *The Technological Society.* New York: Random House, 1967.

_____. *The Meaning of the City.* Grand Rapids: Eerdmans, 1970.

Escobar, Arturo. *Encountering Development: The Making and Unmaking of the Third World.* Princeton: Princeton University Press, 2012.

Fitch, David and Geoff Holsclaw. *Prodigal Christianity: 10 Signposts into the Missional Frontier.* San Francisco: Jossey-Bass, 2013.

Foster, Charles. *The Sacred Journey: The Ancient Practices.* Nashville: Thomas Nelson, 2010.

Frost, Michael and Robert Banks. *Lessons from Reel Life: Movies, Meaning and Myth-Making.* Cambridge: Open Book, 2001.

_____ and Alan Hirsch. *The Shaping of Things to Come:Innovation and Mission for the 21st-Century Church.* Peabody: Hendrickson, 2003.

Garber, Steven. *Visions of Vocation: Common Grace for the Common Good.* Downers Grove: IVP, 2014.

Gibbs, Eddie. *In Name Only: Talking the Problem of Nominal Christianity.* Wheaton: Bridgepoint, 1994.

Gill, Sam. "Territory." In *Critical Terms for Religious Studies*, edited by M. C. Taylor, 298-313. Chicago: University of Chicago Press, 1998.

Gittoes, Julie. *Anamnesis and the Eucharist.* London: Ashgate, 2013.

Gorringe, Timothy. "Sacraments." In *The Religion of the Incarnation: Anglican Essays in Commemoration of Lux Mundi,* edited by Robert Morgan. Bristol: Bristol Classical, 1989.

Guite, Malcolm. *Sounding the Seasons.* London: Canterbury, 2012.

_____. "Descent; A Christmas Poem." *Malcom Guite*, December 25, 2012. Online: http://malcolmguite.wordpress.com/ 2012/12/25/descent-a-christmas-poem/.

Gunton, Colin. "Trinity, Ontology and Anthropology: Towards a Renewal of the Doctrine of *the Imago Dei.*" In *Persons, Divine and Human: King's College Essays in Theological Anthropology,* edited by Christoph Schwobel and Colin E. Gunton. London: T&T Clark, 1992.

Harrison, Robert P. *Gardens: An Essay on the Human Condition.* Chicago: University of Chicago Press, 2010.

Hart, David B. *The Beauty of the Infinite: The Aesthetics of Christian Truth.* Grand Rapids: Eerdmans, 2003.

Hastings, Ross. *Missional God, Missional Church: Hope for Re-evangelizing the West.* Downers Grove: IVP, 2012.

Heidegger, Martin. *Poetry, Language, Thought.* London: Harper Colophon, 1971.

Herbert, George. In *The Works of George Herbert*, edited by F. E. Hutchinson. Oxford: Oxford University Press, 1967.

Hjalmarson, Leonard and John LaGrou. *Voices of the Virtual World.* Wikiklesia Press, 2007.

Holt, Simon Carey. *God Next Door: Spirituality and Mission in the Neighborhood.* Melbourne: Acorn, 2007.

Hopkins, Gerard Manley. "As Kingfishers Catch Fire." In *Gerard Manley Hopkins: The Major Works*, 129. Oxford: Oxford University Press, 2009.

————. "Pied Beauty." In *Gerard Manley Hopkins: The Major Works*, 132. Oxford: Oxford University Press, 2009.

Hooykaas, R. *Religion and the Rise of Modern Science.* London: Scottish Academic, 1973.

Inge, John. *A Christian Theology of Place.* Farnham: Ashgate, 2003.

Jacobsen, Eric. *The Space Between: A Christian Engagement with the Built Environment.* Grand Rapids: Baker Academic, 2012.

Knoke, William. *Bold New World: The Essential Road Map to the Twenty-First Century.* New York: Kodansha, 1996.

Kotkin, Joel. *The City: A Global History.* New York: Modern Library, 2005.

Lane, Belden. *The Solace of Fierce Landscapes: Exploring Desert and Mountain Spirituality.* Oxford: Oxford University Press, 2007.

Levenson, Jon D. *Sinai and Zion: An Entry into the Jewish Bible.* Minneapolis: Winston, 1985.

Longfellow, Henry Wordworth. *The Complete Poetical Work of Henry Wordworth Longfellow.* Charleston: Bibliolife, 2010.

Lowery, Richard. *Sabbath and Jubilee.* St. Louis: Chalice Press, 2000.

Malpas, Jeff. *Heidegger's Topology: Being, Place, World.* Cambridge: MIT Press, 2006.

Mander, Jerry. "The Rules of Corporate Behavior." In *The Case Against the Global Economy*, edited by Jerry Mander and Edward Goldsmith, 81-91. San Francisco: Sierra Club, 1996.

Marion, Jean-Luc. *The Idol and Distance: Five Studies*. New York: Fordham University Press, 2001.

Martens, Elmer. *God's Design: A Focus on Old Testament Theology*. Grand Rapids: Baker, 1986.

McAlpine, William. *Sacred Space for the Missional Church: Engaging Culture through the Built Environment*. Eugene: Wipf and Stock, 2011.

Merton, Thomas. *New Seeds of Contemplation*. New York: New Directions, 1972.

Middleton, Richard. *The Liberating Image: The Imago Dei in Genesis 1*. Grand Rapids: Brazos, 2005.

Milosz, Czeslaw. *New and Collected Poems: 1931-2001*. New York: HarperCollins, 2001.

Moltmann, Jürgen. *God in Creation: A New Theology of Creation and the Spirit of God*. Minneapolis: Fortress, 1993.

More, Thomas. *Original Self: Living with Paradox and Originality*. New York: Harper Perennial, 2001.

Muggeridge, Malcolm. *Jesus Rediscovered*. New York: Doubleday and Co., 1969.

Murray, Stuart. *Church After Christendom*. Bletchley: Paternoster, 2005.

Newman, Elizabeth. *Untamed Hospitality: Welcoming God and Other Strangers*. Grand Rapids: Brazos, 2007.

Norris, Kathleen. *The Cloister Walk*. London: Penguin, 1996.

Oduyoye, Mercy Amba. *Beads and Strands: Reflections of an African Woman on Christianity in Africa*. Maryknoll: Orbis, 2005.

Orr, David. *Ecological Literacy: Education and the Transition to a Postmodern World*. Albany: SUNY, 1992.

Oswalt, Conrad. *Secular Steeples: Popular Culture and the Religious Imagination*. Harrisburg: Trinity Press International, 2001.

Palmer, Parker J. *Let Your Life Speak: Listening for the Voice of Vocation*. San Francisco: Jossey-Bass, 2000.

Peterson, Eugene. *The Wisdom of Each Other: A Conversation Between Spiritual Friends*. Grand Rapids: Zondervan, 1998.

Pinnock, Clark. *Flame of Love: A Theology of the Holy Spirit*. Downers Grove: IVP, 1996.

———. *Tracking the Maze*. Eugene: Wipf and Stock, 1998.

Pohl, Christine D. *Living Into Community: Cultivating Practices That Sustain Us*. Grand Rapids: Eerdmans, 2011.

Pollan, Michael, *Second Nature: A Gardener's Education*. New York: Grove, 1991.

Putnam, R. D. *Bowling Alone: The Collapse and Revival of American Community*. New York: Simon & Schuster, 2000.

Pura, Murray. *Rooted: Reflections on the Gardens in Scripture.* Grand Rapids: Zondervan, 2010.

Relph, Edward. *Place and Placelessness.* London: Routledge, 1976.

Rohr, Richard. *Everything Belongs: The Gift of Contemplative Prayer.* New York: Crossroad, 1999.

Runyon, Dave and Jay Pathak. *The Art of Neighboring: Building Genuine Relationships Right Outside your Door.* Grand Rapids: Baker, 2012.

Santmire, H. Paul. *Brother Earth: Nature, God and Ecology in Time of Crisis.* New York: Nelson, 1970.

_____. *The Travail of Nature: The Ambiguous Ecological Promise of Christian Theology.* Minneapolis: Fortress, 1985.

Sayers, Dorothy L. *The Mind of the Maker.* New York: HarperCollins, 1978.

_____. *The Zeal of Thy House.* Eugene: Wipf and Stock, 2011.

Sedmak, Clemens. *Doing Local Theology: A Guide for Artisans of a New Humanity.* New York: Orbis, 2002.

Sheldrake, Philip. *Spaces for the Sacred: Place, Memory, and Identity.* Baltimore: Johns Hopkins University Press, 2001.

Sherman, Amy. *Kingdom Calling: Vocational Stewardship for the Common Good.* Downers Grove: IVP, 2011.

Slade, Giles. *The Big Disconnect: The Story of Technology and Loneliness.* Vancouver: Prometheus, 2012.

Smith, James K.A. *Desiring the Kingdom: Worship, Worldview, and Cultural Formation.* Grand Rapids: Baker Academic, 2009.

Solnit, Rebecca. *Wanderlust: A History of Walking.* New York: Penguin, 2000.

St. John of the Cross. "Spiritual Canticle." Translated by John Frederick Nims, 3-18. Chicago: University of Chicago Press, 1995.

Stevens, R. Paul. *The Other Six Days: Vocation, Work, and Ministry in Biblical Perspective.* Grand Rapids: Eerdmans, 1999.

Stock, Jon R., et al. *Inhabiting the Church: Biblical Wisdom for a New Monasticism.* Eugene: Cascade, 2007.

Swanson, Eric and Sam Williams. *To Transform a City: Whole Church, Whole Gospel, Whole City.* Grand Rapids: Zondervan, 2010.

Taylor, Charles. *A Secular Age.* Cambridge: Harvard University Press, 2007.

Temple, William. *Nature, Man and God.* London: Macmillan, 1934.

Tickle, Phyllis. *Emergence Christianity: What It Is, Where It Is Going, and Why It Matters.* Grand Rapids: Baker, 2012.

Toffler, Alvin. *Future Shock.* Toronto: Batman, 1970.

Tolkien, J.R.R. "On Faery Stories." *Essays Presented to Charles Williams.* Oxford: Oxford University Press, 1947.

_____. *The Silmarillion.* New York: George Allen and Unwin, 1977.

Torrance, Thomas. *Space, Time and Incarnation.* Oxford: Oxford University Press, 1969.

Tuan, Yi-Fu. *Space and Place: The Perspective of Experience.* Minneapolis: University of Minnesota Press, 1977.

Turner, Victor. *Image and Pilgrimage in Christian Culture.* New York: Columbia University Press, 1978.

Van Gelder, Craig and Dwight Zscheile. *The Missional Church in Perspective: Mapping Trends and Shaping the Conversation.* Grand Rapids: Baker Academic, 2011.

Walsh, Brian and Steven Bouman-Prediger. "With and Without Boundaries: Christian homemaking amidst postmodern homelessness." In *The Hermeneutics of Charity: Interpretation, Selfhood, and Postmodern Faith,* edited by James K.A. Smith and Henry I. Venema, 228-250. Grand Rapids: Brazos, 2004.

Walter, Gregory. *Being Promised: Theology, Gift, and Practice.* Grand Rapids: Eerdmans, 2013.

Walton, John H. *The Lost World of Genesis One: Ancient Cosmology and the Origins Debate.* Downers Grove: IVP, 2009.

Weil, Simone. "Love of the Order of the World." In *Waiting for God.* Translated by Emma Crawfurd. New York: Harper & Row, 1951.

Westerhoff, Caroline. *Good Fences: The Boundaries of Hospitality.* Boston: Cowley, 1999.

Wilken, Robert. *The Land Called Holy: Palestine in Christian History and Thought.* New Haven: Yale University Press, 1992.

Williams, Stuart Murray. *Post-Christendom: Church and Mission in a Strange New World.* London: Authentic, 2011.

Wirzba, Norman. *Living the Sabbath: Discovering the Rhythms of Rest and Delight.* Grand Rapids: Brazos, 2006.

Wright, N.T. "Jerusalem in the New Testament." In *Jerusalem Past and Present in the Purposes of God,* edited by P.W.L. Walker, 53-77. Carlisle: Paternoster, 1994.

_____. "Romans and the Theology of Paul." In *Pauline Theology, Volume III,* edited David M. Hay and E. Elizabeth Johnson, 30-67. Minneapolis: Fortress Press, 1995.

_____. *How God Became King: The Forgotten Story of the Gospels.* New York: HarperCollins, 2012.

Yoder, John Howard. *Body Politics: Five Practices of the Christian Community Before the Watching World.* Scottdale: Herald, 1992.

_____ and Michael G. Cartwright. *The Royal Priesthood: Essays Ecclesiological and Ecumenical.* Scottdale: Herald, 1994.

Zscheile, Dwight. *People of the Way: Renewing Episcopal Identity.* New York: Morehouse, 2012.

Zizioulas, John D. *Being as Communion:Studies in Personhood and the Church.* Toronto: Novalis, 2002.

Articles

Aldrich, Brent. "Eric Jacobsen—The Space Between." *The Englewood Review of Books* October (2012).

Bailey, Jeff. "Church of the Savior." *Cutting Edge Magazine* Fall (2001).

Bartholomew, Craig. "Covenant and Creation." *Calvin Theological Journal* 30 (1995) 11-33.

Brueggemann, Walter. "To Whom Does the Land Belong? 2 Samuel 3:12." *Journal for Preachers* Easter (2007).

Cardin, Nina Beth. "The Place of Place in Jewish Tradition." *Crosscurrents* 59:2 (2009) 210-216.

Cavanaugh, William. "The World in a Wafer: A Geography of the Eucharist as Resistance to Globalization." *Modern Theology*, 15:2 (1999) 183.

_____. "The Church as God's Body Language." *Zadok Perspectives* Spring (2006).

Cobb, Jennifer. "A Spiritual Experience of Cyberspace." *Technology in Society* 21 (1999) 393-407.

Crouch, Andy. "Ten Most Significant Cultural Trends of the Last Decade" *Q Ideas,* June, 2012. Online: http://qideas.org/articles/ten-most-significant-cultural-trends-of-the-last-decade/.

Dahal, Ganga Ram. "Bridging, Linking and Bonding Social Capital in Collective Action." *CAPRi Working Paper No. 79*, May 2008. Online: http://www.capri.cgiar.org/pdf/capriwp79.pdf.

Deresiewicz, William. "Solitude and Leadership." *UTNE Reader* September-October (2010).

Dyrness, William. "Poetic Theology and the Everyday Presence of God." *Zadok Perspectives* 20: 118 (2013) 16-20.

Grenz, Stanley. "Jesus as the Imago Dei: Image of God Christology and the Non-Linear Linearity of Theology." *Journal of the Evangelical Theological Society* 47:4 (2004) 617-28.

Hastings, Ross. "Identity in a Missional God." *The Online Pulpit*, Nov. 6, 2012. Online: http://onlinepulpit.ivpress.com/2012/11/.

Jacobsen, Eric. "Redeeming Civic Life in the Commons." *Civitate* Winter (2009) 28-42.

Keyes, Mina. "How Walking and Biking Add Value to Your Community and Change the System." *Project for Public Spaces*, July 10, 2012. Online: http://www.pps.org/blog/how-walking-and-biking-add-value-to-your-community-and-change-the-system-an-interview-with-john-norquist/.

Kilby, Karen. "Perichoresis and Projection: Problems with Social Doctrines of the Trinity." *New Blackfriars* 81 (2000) 432-445.

Kline, Naomi and Simpson, Leanne. "Dancing the World Into Being." *Common Dreams*, March 6, 2013. Online: http://www.commondreams.org/view/2013/03/06.

König, Johann B. 1738. "Blest are the Pure in Heart." *The Episcopal Hymnbook, #274.* 1916.

Lacey, George. "Eucharist as the Intersection Between Memory and Forgetfulness." *Worship* 77:1 (2003) 52-56.

Lane, Belden. "Fierce Landscapes and the Indifference of God." *The Christian Century* October 11 (1998).

Lewis, C.S. "The Weight of Glory." A sermon in the Church of St. Mary the Virgin, Oxford, June 8, 1942.

Luter, A. Boyd. "The Land as Covenant Backdrop: A Modest Response to Burge and Waltke." *Criswell Theological Review* 9:1 (2011) 59-74.

Merrifield, A. "Place and space: a Lefebvrian reconciliation." *Transactions of the Institute of British Geographers* 18 (1993) 516–31.

Middleton, Richard J. "A New Heaven and A New Earth." *Journal for Christian Theological Research* 11 (2006) 73-97.

Mulder, Mark T. "Mobility and the (In)Significance of Place in an Evangelical Church." *Geographies of Religions and Belief Systems* 3:1 (2009) 16-43.

Northcott, Michael. "From Environmental U-topianism to Parochial Ecology: Communities of Place and the Politics of Sustainability." *Ecotheology* 8 (2000) 71-85.

O'Donovan, O. "The Loss of a Sense of Place," *Irish Theological Quarterly* 55 (1989) 39-58.

Panth, Sabina. "Bonding vs. Bridging." *People, Spaces, Deliberation*, June, 3, 2010. Online: https://blogs.worldbank.org/publicsphere/bonding-and-bridging.

Pierce, Martin and Murphy. "Relational Place-Making: the networked politics of place." *Clark University, Graduate School of Geography* (2010) 55-70.

Pinnock, Clark. "Divine Relationality: A Pentecostal Contribution to the Doctrine of God," *Journal of Pentecostal Theology* 16 (2000) 3-26.

Putnam, R. D. "Bowling Alone: America's Declining Social Capital." *Journal of Democracy* 6 (1995) 65-78.

Ramachandra, Vinoth. "Christian Witness in an Age of Globalization." Leonard Buck Memorial Lecture, Melbourne. May, 2006.

Rapoport, Amos. "Sacred Places, Sacred Occasions, and Sacred Environments," *Architectural Design* 52 (1982) 75-82.

Russ, Dan. "Babel: the Fear of Humanity and the Illusion of Divinity." A speech to the Dallas Institute, Spring, 2000.

Sheerin, Martin. "Why I Left World Vision for Finance." *Christianity Today*. Feb. 22, 2013. http://www.christianitytoday.com/thisisourcity/

Shoaf, Robb. "Pedagogy Employs an Old Friend: Beauty and the Quality of Ideas." *The Journal of Aesthetic Education* 46:2 (2012) 36-42.

Stephenson, Bret. "Nature, Technology and Imago Dei: Mediating the Nonhuman through the Practice of Science." *Perspectives on Science and Christian Faith* 57:1 (2005) 6–12.

Swanson, Tod D. "To Prepare a Place: Johannine Christianity and the Collapse of Ethnic Territory." *Journal of the American Academy of Religion* 62:2 (1994).

Sweet, Leonard. "Seven Questions." Interview at www.ginkworld.net, 2003.

Walker, P.W. "Centre Stage: Jerusalem or Jesus." In *Papers Toward a Biblical Mind*, 1996

Walton, John H. "Creation in Genesis 1:1-2:3 and the Ancient Near East." In *Calvin Theological Journal* 43 (2008) 48-63.

Ward, Graham. "Christian Political Practice and the Global City," *Journal of Theology for Southern Africa* 123 (2005) 30.

Weiner, Eric. "Where Heaven and Earth Come Closer" *New York Times*. March 9, 2012

Wiens, Delbert. "Mennonite Brethren: Neither Liberal Nor Evangelical," in *Direction Journal* 20:1 (1991) 38-63.

Wilkinson, Loren. "Imago Mundi." *The Reformed Journal* 37: 4 (1987) 10.

_____. "Saving Celtic Spirituality." *Christianity Today* 44:5 (April 24, 2000.) Online: http://www.christianitytoday.com/ct/2000/april24/2.78.html.

Williams, Rowan. "Faith and History." Lecture, Westminster Abbey, March 19 2008.

Woolcock, M. "The Place of Social Capital in Understanding Social and Economic Outcomes." *Isuma: Canadian Journal of Policy Research* 2:1 (2001) 1-17.

Wright, N.T. "New Law, New Temple, New World." A sermon on the Feast of Pentecost. June 8, 2003.

Audio and Video Sources

Bohannon, John. "Dance vs. Powerpoint, A Modest Proposal." *TED,* November 2011. Online: http://www.ted.com/talks/ john_bohannon_dance_vs_powerpoint_a_modest_proposal.

Bozzo, Sam. "Blue Gold: World Water Wars." Purple Turtle Films, 2008. Online: http://www.bluegold-worldwaterwars.com/.

Cockburn, Bruce. "Thoughts on a Rainy Afternoon." On *Bruce Cockburn.* Toronto: True North Records, 1970.

————. "In the Falling Dark." On *In the Falling Dark.* Toronto: True North Records, 1976.

————. "Lovers in a Dangerous Time." On *Stealing Fire.* Toronto: True North Records, 1984.

————. "The Gift." On *Big Circumstance.* Toronto: True North Records, 1987.

————. "Child of the Wind." On *Nothing But a Burning Light.* Toronto: True North Records, 1991.

————. Cockburn, Bruce. "Life Short, Call Now." On *Life Short, Call Now.* Toronto: Golden Mountain Music, 2006.

————. "Mystery." On *Life Short, Call Now.* Toronto: Golden Mountain Music, 2006.

Cohen, Leonard. "Everybody Knows." On *In The Know.* New York: Columbia Records, 1988.

————. "Anthem." On *The Future.* New York: Columbia Records, 1992.

————. *Stranger Music.* Toronto: McClelland & Steward, 1993.

Croegaert, James. "Here By the Water." From *Heaven Knows.* Evanston: Rough Stones Music, 1993.

————. "Why Do We Hunger for Beauty?" From *Heaven Knows.* Evanston:Rough Stones Music, 1993.

Fathy, Safaa. *Derrida's Elsewhere.* New York: Icarus Films, 2001.

Greenpeace Canada. "Petropolis." *Greenpeace,* February 5, 2014. Online: http://www.petropolis-film.com/.

Mair, Leslea. "Shattered Ground." *CBC*. Winnipeg: Zoot Pictures, 2013. Online: http://www.cbc.ca/natureofthings/episodes/shattered-ground.

Mayer, Peter. "Holy Now." *Million Year Mind*. Blue Boat Records, 1999.

Newcomer, Carrie. "As Holy as a Day is Spent." On *The Gathering of Spirits*. Philo Records, 2002.

Scarry, Elaine. "On Beauty and Being Just." The Tanner Lectures on Human Values. Delivered at Yale University, March 25-26, 1998.

Sweet, Leonard. "Seven Questions." *Ginkworld*, 2003.

Tippett, Krista. "Land, Life and the Poetry of Creatures." *Speaking of Faith*. American Public Media, 2010.

Twiss, Richard. "A Theology of Place." *:redux*. Online: https://vimeo.com/44319803.

About the Author

Len Hjalmarson lives with his wife Betty on the shores of Lake Superior in Thunder Bay, Ontario where they help to lead a faith community on a journey in mission.

Len is the co-author of *Missional Spirituality* (IVP, 2011), the author of *The Missional Church Fieldbook* (Urban Loft, 2012) and editor of *Text & Context* (Urban Loft, 2014).

Len is a member of the Parish Collective and of the Missio Alliance. He is an adjunct professor at Northern Baptist Seminary in Chicago, and at Tyndale Seminary, Toronto. He is also a mentor and expert advisor in the Leadership in Global Perspectives program at George Fox Evangelical Seminary in Portland. He loves walking, good music, good books, and good cooking.

About ULP

Urban Loft Publishers focuses on ideas, topics, themes, and conversations about all things urban. Renewing the city is the central theme and focus of what we publish. It is our intention to blend urban ministry, theology, urban planning, architecture, urbanism, stories, and the social sciences, as ways to drive the conversation. While we lean towards scholarly and academic works, we explore the fun and lighter sides of cities as well. We publish a wide variety of urban perspectives, from books by the experts about the city to personal stories and personal accounts of urbanites who live in the city.

www.urbanloftpublishers.com
@the_urban_loft

15006695R00143

Printed in Great Britain
by Amazon.co.uk, Ltd.,
Marston Gate.